The Cold
War Legacy

THE COLD WAR LEGACY

THOMAS H. NAYLOR

Lexington Books

D.C. Heath and Company · Lexington, Massachusetts · Toronto

Library of Congress Cataloging-in-Publication Data

Naylor, Thomas H.
  The Cold War legacy / by Thomas H. Naylor.
    p.   cm.
  Includes index.
  ISBN 0-669-24984-X (alk. paper)
  1. World politics—1985-1995.   2. Cold War.   I. Title.
D849.N39   1991
327'.09'048—dc20   90-21842
                                                                        CIP

Published simultaneously in Canada
Printed in the United States of America
International Standard Book Number: 0-669-24984-X
Library of Congress Catalog Card Number: 90-21842

The paper used in this publication meets
the minimum requirements of American National Standard
for Information Sciences—Permanence of Paper
for Printed Library Materials, ANSI Z39.48-1984.

Year and number of this printing:

91 92 93 94 8 7 6 5 4 3 2 1

Contents

Introduction   ix

1. The Story of Johnny and Sasha   1

2. The Pot Can't Call the Kettle Black   13

     Moral Indignation   13
     Political Injustice   15
     Crime   20
     Economic Inequality   22
     Inadequate Health Care   26
     Social Ills   30
     Education Problems   32
     National Public Service   34
     Shared Hypocrisy   36

3. The Temple of Doom   39

     Fearless Cold Warriors   39
     The Emigrés   45
     The Military-Industrial Complex   54
     Right-Wing Think Tanks   56
     The High Priests of the Temple of Doom   65
     The Death of Sovietology   67

4. Military Overkill   73

     The Technocrats   77
     The Soviet Threat   92
     Tension Reduction   98
     Nonviolence   99

5. Economic Uncertainty   105

    A Preview of *Perestroika*   105
    Economic Reform   112
    Common Problems   114
    Power Sharing   119
    Democratic Socialism   122
    Economic Conversion   125

6. Lack of Competitiveness   129

    U.S.–Soviet Trade   129
    Unreliable Trading Partners   133
    High-Tech Paranoia   135
    The Jackson–Vanik Amendment   138

7. Declining International Influence   151

    Shattered Illusions   151
    Global Interdependence   157
    Downsizing   165

8. Global Development   171

    War and Terrorism   171
    Poverty, Hunger, and Disease   175
    Drug Abuse   177
    Environmental Pollution   178
    Global Development Strategies   180
    The Eastern European Wringer   186

9. The Leadership Challenge   187

    Our Leadership Gap   187
    Gorbachev's Management Philosophy   188
    Our Denial of *Perestroika*   190
    The United States Needs *Glasnost* Too   196
    A Kinder America and a Gentler World   198
    A Vision of the Future   205
    Real Political Pluralism   207
    Participatory Democracy   209
    We Need More Public Men and Women   214

    Postscript   217

Notes 221

Index 227

About the Author 239

Introduction

N OTHING better illustrates the fact that the cold war is truly over than the response of the United States and the Soviet Union to Saddam Hussein's 2 August 1990 invasion of Kuwait. Not only did President George Bush and Soviet leader Mikhail S. Gorbachev both condemn Iraq for its actions, but they both supported a United Nations–sponsored embargo of Iraq. The Soviets even went along with a UN Security Council resolution calling for military enforcement of the embargo. As further evidence of the new post–cold war superpower cooperation, the Soviet Union supported the U.S.-led 16 January 1991 invasion of Iraq.

The real message coming from Berlin, Prague, Warsaw, Managua, Moscow, the Persian Gulf, and Washington is that the cold war doesn't pay anymore. Just as Stalinism has taken its toll on the Soviet Union and Eastern Europe, so too has Reagan-style anticommunism inflicted enormous costs on the United States. We have spent so much time, energy, and other valuable resources fighting the threat of communism that we have diverted our attention, our energy, and our resources from improving the working of our own capitalist system.

Neither we nor the Soviets can afford a continuation of the military madness. It is no longer in the self-interest of either superpower to continue perpetrating the myths, half-truths, and outright lies that have fueled the cold war since the late 1940s.

For years Americans have condescendingly criticized virtually every aspect of Soviet life. Yet today when we look into the tired eyes of our foremost adversary, we see a reflection of ourselves. American capitalism and Soviet communism share far more problems than most Americans care to admit.

1. *Alienation.* Large American and Soviet companies are among the least democratic institutions in the world. Organized

around poor, ignorant blue-collar workers of the 1940s, who respected military organization, these authoritarian, hierarchical companies are encountering increasing difficulty in motivating the well-educated, affluent Soviet and American workers of the present, who resent authority. With today's workers these industrial giants produce feelings of alienation, powerlessness, ambivalence, and complete disaffection giving rise to absenteeism, low productivity, alcoholism, drug abuse, divorce, and crime. Alienation is one of the principal targets of *perestroika*. Although American companies are suffering from many of the same problems, our managers and politicians are far too arrogant to admit that we need *perestroika* too.

2. *Injustice.* The Reagan administration had a great deal to say about Soviet human-rights violations in the areas of political prisoners, Jewish emigration, repression of religion, and treatment of mental patients. Little or nothing was said about high rates of unemployment, homelessness, violent crime, and drug abuse in the United States, or how we treat African-Americans, Native Americans, Hispanics, and other minorities.

3. *Cold War Paranoia.* Until recently both the United States and the Soviet Union suffered from three common neuroses—an exaggerated fear of each other, "macho pride," and a complete inability to admit error. Although the Soviets now openly admit many of their sins of the past, the U.S. government still has great difficulty ever admitting that it was wrong about anything.

4. *Excessive Militarization.* While accusing the Soviet Union of excessive military aggression, the Reagan administration was participating in nine known wars—in Afghanistan, Angola, Cambodia, Chad, El Salvador, Ethiopia, Lebanon, Morocco, and Nicaragua—not to mention our bombing of Libya, invasion of Grenada, and repeated attempts to bring down Panamanian dictator Manuel Antonio Noriega. Without any sense of irony whatsoever President Bush condemned Saddam Hussein for replicating in Kuwait precisely what he had done in Panama a few months earlier, namely, invading a tiny country with a huge military force and setting up a puppet government. Bush then sent over 400,000 American troops to occupy the Persian Gulf at the "invitation" of the governments of Saudi Arabia and the United Arab Emirates. Just as President Gorbachev found that he could not fix the Soviet economy while spending 15 percent of the Soviet gross national

product (GNP) on military defense; President Bush discovered that he could not balance the U.S. budget without raising taxes while spending $300 billion annually on defense.

5. *Economic Uncertainty.* The Soviet Union suffers from a plethora of well-known economic problems, including economic stagnation, low productivity, shortages of food and consumer goods, and a serious technological gap with the West. Although the standard of living is substantially higher in the United States than in the Soviet Union, the rate of growth of productivity has been declining for the past three decades. Real wages have declined as well. Both the United States and the Soviet Union face an uncertain economic future in which further improvements in the standard of living are by no means assured.

6. *Lack of Competitiveness.* Our nation's huge trade deficits, the demise of many so-called smokestack industries, and the incredible successes of Japan and West Germany in penetrating one important American market after another provide substantial evidence of a decline in the competitiveness of U.S. industry. Soviet industry, on the other hand, has never competed very effectively in the international marketplace.

7. *Declining International Influence.* Both the United States and the Soviet Union are beginning to learn from the Japanese and the Germans that the number of nuclear warheads in a nation's arsenal is not nearly such an important measure of international political power as it once was. Economic clout has become a much more important measure of real political influence than military might. Japan has become a global economic superpower, though it spends only 1 percent of its GNP on defense, in contrast to 5 percent for the United States. Neither Japan nor Germany manufactures nuclear weapons.

8. *Global Development.* Regional wars, terrorism, poverty, hunger, disease, AIDS, drug abuse, and environmental pollution are global problems that will never be solved as long as the United States and the Soviet Union are spending $1.5 billion a day defending themselves from each other. Competitive, zero-sum approaches to these problems have consistently failed and are likely to continue to do so.

9. *Leadership Gap.* Since Winston Churchill, Franklin D. Roosevelt, and Joseph V. Stalin met at Yalta in February 1945 to carve up Europe, relations between the United States and the

Soviet Union have been based on competition, fear, and distrust. Every American president from Harry Truman through Ronald Reagan and every Soviet leader from Joseph V. Stalin through Konstantin V. Chernenko relied almost exclusively on confrontation as the principal means for relating to the other superpower.

In our futile attempts to convince each other and the rest of the world of our superiority, the United States and the Soviet Union have managed to become more nearly alike. That's what the cold war end game is all about. In spite of the unprecedented changes that have taken place in the Soviet Union and Eastern Europe, the lack of trust between the two superpowers will never be fully dissipated until both sides agree that human concerns are far more important than narrowly defined national-security issues.

In his televised 1990 New Year's greeting to the American people, Mr. Gorbachev suggested making the 1990s "a decade of drawing the United States and the Soviet Union closer together on the basis of universal human values and a balance of interests."

Since the beginning of World War II, national security has been the driving force of the domestic and foreign policies of the United States and the Soviet Union. It was as though little else mattered. In the name of national security, foreign trade, improved health care, economic security, and education and the struggles against drug abuse, environmental pollution, poverty, and hunger were all given short shrift. In the absence of a strong consensus in either country supporting alternative national objectives, the Soviet and American superhawks have controlled the foreign-policy agendas in our respective countries for fifty years. In our country, to advocate that the defense budget be cut so that more money might be spent on better health care for the poor, public housing, or cleaning up the environment was to risk being labeled "soft on defense." Soviet military leaders have employed a similar strategy to deny the Soviet people better consumer goods and an improved quality of life.

But so long as our respective end-game strategies are expressed only in terms of conventional forces, intermediate-range missiles, and strategic nuclear weapons, then we shall surely fail in our efforts to end the cold war. Too much attention has been devoted to arms control and not enough attention to our common objectives as human beings. What is needed is not just another agreement on reductions in conventional and strategic forces in

Europe but rather an agreement on fundamental human concerns such as:

1. *Good Health*—affordable health care to enable us to function as responsible human beings.
2. *Economic Security*—the opportunity to earn sufficient income to pay for our food, clothing, shelter, and health care.
3. *Meaning*—an environment that encourages the search for meaning in our individual lives.
4. *Knowledge*—access to information, education, training, and experience required to be a responsible and productive citizen.
5. *Freedom*—the right to express our feelings and opinions through art, literature, religion, the press, and public debate without fear of political or economic reprisal.
6. *Empowerment*—the ability to influence the decision-making processes that affect our lives.

Some may question why peace and equality were excluded from our list of human concerns. Peace and equality are residual concerns based on the degree to which the other six have been satisfied. If one has good health, economic security, a sense of meaning, access to adequate education and training, freedom, and empowerment, then one is likely to be at peace with one's self, one's family, one's employer, and one's nation, as well as other nations. Inequalities in income, wealth, and education are much more important when basic human needs have not been satisfied. What is important is equal access to health-care services, employment, education, et cetera, rather than across-the-board egalitarianism.

The real Bush–Gorbachev challenge is how to formulate a cold war end-game strategy based more on human concerns than on military might. If we don't redefine the cold war end game in more human terms, then Saddam Hussein will be but the first of many post–cold war demons to emerge. Countless American political demagogues are waiting for just the right opportunity to elevate either Japan, Germany, or Columbian drug lords to the status of the next "evil empire."

In each of the following chapters I define one of our nine common problems from both the American and the Soviet perspectives.

For each problem I describe Soviet strategies for dealing with it and propose possible American approaches as well. In both cases I evaluate the impact of alternative U.S. and Soviet strategies on the six fundamental human concerns.

1

The Story of Johnny and Sasha

J OHNNY and Sasha are two fictitious blue-collar workers in their early twenties.[1] Johnny works in a General Motors plant near Detroit, and Sasha works for the Leningrad Shipyard.

Johnny's grandfather also worked for GM and recently retired after forty years on the assembly line. Having grown up in the rural South during the depression, he and his family experienced real poverty during the 1930s. He quit school when he was sixteen to help support the family, but later volunteered for the infantry in World War II.

After the war, Johnny's grandfather moved to Detroit where GM was hiring thousands of unskilled workers to meet the post-war demand for automobiles. His primary aim was to find a stable, secure job to support his family. He remembered the tough times of the 1930s all too well. For forty years he worked at one repetitive, dehumanizing job after another—always doing what he had been told to do and never questioning the authority of his managers.

Sasha's grandfather barely survived the siege of Leningrad while serving in the Red Army during the Great Patriotic War. Not only did he almost starve to death during the war, but he and his family experienced Stalin's reign of terror in the 1930s at very close range. Sasha's grandfather was not a risk taker and had a healthy respect for military authority. After the war he was assigned a job at the shipyard where he worked until 1987.

Throughout the 1950s and 1960s, the hierarchical, authoritarian style of management of GM and the Leningrad Shipyard worked very well. The GM plant where Johnny's grandfather worked was one of the most efficient in the United States. The Leningrad Shipyard produced large tankers and cargo ships for the Soviet commercial fleet. In each case the workers and managers alike were poorly educated, had grown up in poverty, and had no problem whatsoever working under military-style conditions.

When Johnny and Sasha were born, the standard of living in their respective families had improved appreciably since the end of the war. Although Johnny's family was better off than Sasha's, materially speaking, they both enjoyed a relatively comfortable standard of living.

Neither Johnny nor Sasha has ever experienced poverty. They both graduated from high school, took some additional college-level courses, grew up in a middle-class environment, and watched too much television. Johnny has never been exposed to military service. Although Sasha fulfilled his two-year Soviet military obligation, he hated every minute of it and strongly opposed the war in Afghanistan.

Johnny and Sasha are paid quite well, but their work is monotonous and unchallenging. They often wonder why high school degrees were required for such mindless jobs. Both Johnny and Sasha are grossly overqualified for their jobs.

Johnny is not interested in politics and has never registered to vote. Sasha is also apolitical and, unlike his father and his grandfather, is not a member of the Communist party.

Neither Johnny nor Sasha likes to work very hard. Given a choice between more work for more pay and a day off from work, they will always opt for the latter. Both Johnny and Sasha resent the heavy-handed, top-down, authoritarian style of management practiced by their respective employers. They are often late to work and frequently do not show up for work at all. Johnny smokes pot on the job, and Sasha has a drinking problem.

A study by Mercer Meidinger, an insurance consulting firm, has shown that the effects of drug and alcohol abuse are costing American businesses over $100 billion a year. In 1987 alone, substance abuse among GM's 472,000 workers and their dependents cost the automotive giant $600 million.

The story of Johnny and Sasha is a story about the dehumanizing aspects of large industrial companies in the United States and the Soviet Union. Both Johnny's grandfather and Sasha's endured boring, repetitive, and sometimes dangerous jobs for four decades due to ignorance and fear. But the same working conditions in the 1990s produce feelings of alienation, ambivalence, and complete disaffection—feelings which are widespread throughout the industrial world.

Johnny and Sasha are alienated from their work, their supervisors, their fellow workers, their families, their government, and ultimately themselves. Alienation stems from a lack of meaning in one's life. It can precipitate feelings of powerlessness that may lead to a number of different forms of destructive behavior, including alcoholism, drug abuse, divorce, crime, and suicide.

But alienation is by no means limited to blue collar workers either in the United States or the Soviet Union. Consider the forty-five-year-old accountant who has been director of accounting for a large defense contractor for the past five years. His job is also extremely boring, and he is only rarely consulted by senior management on matters of importance. One day while driving to work, he realizes that not only is his secret ambition to become the company president a fantasy, but that he will never move any higher up the corporate ladder. The sheer horror of remaining in the same boring job for another twenty years precipitates a severe anxiety attack followed by months of debilitating depression.

Hardly a month goes by in which there is not at least one article in the business press about some well-known corporate executive who has opted out of corporate life to pursue a quieter, more reflective existence far removed from the executive suite. Often referred to as a mid-life identity crisis, this phenomenon may also be caused by the absence of a sense of purpose or meaning in the lives of these high-level executives. In all too many firms, senior executives are forced to subscribe to the values of the company in order to advance up the corporate ladder. The values they must embrace place too much emphasis on greed, the acquisition of power, and the desire to dominate and manipulate others. For such executives, motivation comes not from internal personal goals but from recognition and approval by others. Eventually, this type of behavior results in anxiety, depression, feelings of emptiness, and burnout. Some executives turn to drugs and alcohol to combat their loneliness and emptiness. Indeed, it is not surprising that there are over three hundred stress-management programs in the United States today.

Most American and Soviet companies employ the same management philosophy and organizational structures today that worked so well for them in the 1950s and 1960s. However, the typical worker in the 1950s was a child of poverty, uneducated, and comfortable with military authority. Today's workers in both countries are well-educated, affluent, and resentful of any kind of authority. Organizational development strategies predicated on yesterday's realities stand little chance of success in tomorrow's world.

In the 1970s American managers often blamed organized labor for our productivity problems. But high unemployment rates and the Reagan administration's anti-labor policies rendered organized labor impotent in the 1980s. Among the more destructive results of increasingly egocentric and autocratic management policies are poor morale, disloyalty, declining productivity, and an inability to compete effectively in the international marketplace.

The rules of the game have changed both in the United States and in the Soviet Union. The old ways of coercing and intimidating employees don't work anymore. If the senior management of a company is serious about wanting to improve its productivity and competitive position abroad, it may have to pay a high price in terms of sharing power with its employees.

As evidence of the undemocratic nature of American companies, union membership has declined from 30 percent in the 1970s to only 16 percent of the work force in contrast to 60 percent in Austria and 85 percent in Sweden. Furthermore, there is little evidence to suggest that our military-industrial complex is any more democratic or uses tactics that are any different from its Soviet counterpart.

Graduate schools of business have done little to reduce the level of alienation among blue-collar workers. If anything, they may have actually exacerbated the problem.

For six years, I taught all of the courses on corporate strategy at Duke University's Fuqua School of Business. Each semester I asked my students to write a personal strategic plan for the ten-year period after their graduation from Duke. The question I posed was "What do you want to be when you grow up?" With few exceptions, they had three desires—money, power, and things—very big things, including vacation homes, expensive foreign automobiles, yachts, and even airplanes. They were primarily concerned with their careers and the growth of their financial portfolios. Their personal plans contained little room for family, intellectual development, spiritual growth, or social responsibility.

Their mandate to the faculty was "Teach me how to be a money-making machine. Give me only the facts, tools, and techniques required to ensure my instantaneous financial success." Everything else was fundamentally irrelevant. Their attitude toward blue-collar workers was arrogant and condescending. They had no interest in the problems of Johnny and Sasha.

Business schools do little to discourage the "anything goes" attitude that prevails in the corporate executive suite. The new breed of me-first managers trained in graduate schools of business is not uncomfortable with insider trading, hostile takeovers, bribery of foreign officials, and heavy-handed anti-union tactics.

The god of today's MBA graduates is technology—particularly the computer. Technology represents the ultimate solution to all of their problems—professional, financial, technical, social, political, and even geopolitical. Only through technology can they deny their finiteness and guarantee their own immortality. They had much rather automate a factory than negotiate with a difficult labor union. Star Wars is preferable to negotiating with the Russians. Courses on business ethics and corporate responsibility are viewed as a frivolous waste of time, if they exist in the first place.

Economist Milton Friedman continues to serve as the unchallenged patron saint of Corporate America and graduate schools of business. His irresponsible cliche that "the only social responsibility of business is to make as much money as possible for the stockholders" is viewed by many businessmen with religious fervor. Is it really surprising that such a morally repugnant statement has such widespread appeal to the me-generation? It represents an ideology to beat all ideologies that resolves any problems of moral or social responsibility. A businessman can do anything he wants so long as it is legal—and he is making as much money as possible for the shareholders.

While real wages were declining in the 1980s, the salaries of corporate executives were soaring. Although corporate profits in the United States increased by only 5 percent between 1977 and 1987, the salaries and bonuses of CEOs rose by 220 percent. The average total compensation of the seven hundred highest-paid executives in 1988 was a little over $2 million—ninety-three times the average pay of a factory worker and seventy-two times that of a school teacher.

A lack of meaning or connectedness to anything no doubt contributed to the greed and narcissism of the 1980s. Americans have no incentive to delay gratification because they place so little faith in a future that has no meaning for them. Instead, they pursue the illusive dream that it is possible "to have it all"— a dream which has turned out to be a lie. They seem to think they can consume their way into a state of never-ending self-enrichment without paying any psychological dues for their lives of unrestrained pleasure.

The search for meaning is a common problem in socialist countries as well as in capitalist countries. The pursuit of meaning in one's life may either be a source of great frustration and anxiety or a source of boundless energy and creativity. Austrian psychiatrist Viktor E. Frankl has suggested three principal ways in which individuals can find meaning in life: (1) by what one accomplishes or gives to the world in terms of one's own creations; (2) by what one takes from the world in terms of encounters, experiences, and personal relationships; and (3) by one's stand toward suffering generated by a fate that one cannot change. Others have tried, often in vain, to find meaning through their children, their job, religion, the approval of parents, power and influence, and the accumulation of wealth and material goods.

A strong sense of meaning is what motivates a person to get out of bed each morning and confront life and all of its uncertainty. Responsibility and engagement are critical to a well-defined sense of meaning. The absence of meaning leads to a sense of alienation from oneself, from one's fellow man, and from one's basic beliefs.

There is little evidence to suggest that either Marxist-Leninist ideology or capitalist dogmas have provided effective shields against alienation and meaninglessness in either the Soviet Union or the United States respectively. The problems of Johnny and Sasha are independent of political ideology.

Problems of meaninglessness in the Soviet Union are further confounded by the fact that until recently the Soviet people lived in a society that was free of economic risk. The absence of risk and the heretofore limited possibilities for significant improvements in the quality of their lives have taken their toll on the Soviet people.

Until very recently, neither Soviet enterprise managers nor employees had much decision-making power. All major decisions were made in Moscow. Central planners decided what should be produced, how it should be produced, how it should be distributed, and what price should be charged. Decisions on wages, employment, training, safety, and local working conditions were also made in Moscow. Not unlike the United States, Soviet workers were not encouraged to participate in important decisions affecting the enterprise where they worked or their individual lives. Is it any wonder that Johnny and Sasha are alienated?

Conspicuously absent in both American and Soviet industrial companies is a high degree of trust between employees and managers. Yet without two-way trust it is impossible to sustain high levels of productivity. But empowerment is the linchpin of trusting relationships in the workplace. Without empowerment there can be no trust. Employees who do not feel empowered by the organization will not internalize the goals, objectives, and values of the company. To feel empowered, the employees must believe that the managers respect and appreciate their contributions.

Until recently managers of large, hierarchical American and Soviet firms showed little interest in sharing power with their employees. But this is about to change in the Soviet Union. Soviet managers not only have been given a great deal more decision-making freedom than was the case in the past, but they must now stand for election by their employees.

The story of Johnny and Sasha gets right to the heart of what *perestroika* is really all about. It is aimed directly at Sasha and millions of other alienated Soviet workers and managers. The old ways don't work, have never worked very well, and are not likely to work in the future. And no one understands this better than Mikhail S. Gorbachev. Alienation and risk aversion are the principal targets of *perestroika*.

Gorbachev is confronting alienation by offering Soviet managers and employees alike a greater psychological and financial stake in the economic activities in which they are involved. He has introduced decentralized decision making, financial incentives, and employee ownership of private cooperatives and shares of state-owned enterprises. General managers of large Soviet firms are no longer appointed by the Communist party but are elected by the employees.

Sweden is one of several countries to whom the Soviets are looking as a role model for breaking away from the shackles of

Stalinism. It consistently achieves high levels of economic efficiency as well as social justice.

The Swedes enjoy one of the highest standards of living in the
world, have one of the lowest rates of unemployment, and have
virtually no poverty. Sweden has often had the lowest *misery index*
(inflation plus unemployment) in the industrialized world. Because Sweden has the highest taxes, one of the largest public
sectors in the West, the narrowest wage differentials, the most
highly unionized work force, and not particularly well paid corporate executives, some Americans consider it to be a socialist country.

Although the Social Democratic party is the most important political party in Sweden, Sweden is certainly not a socialist
country. Ninety-two percent of its industrial sector is privately
owned, and it has an abnormally large number of successful
multinational corporations such as Volvo, Electrolux, Asea,
Saab–Scania, Ericsson, SKF, and Sandvik—all of whom derive 75
percent of their respective revenues from abroad.

Notwithstanding some recent problems with the Swedish
economy, the Soviets are attracted by the Swedish "third way"
strategy to revitalize a sluggish economy and restore international
competitiveness. To improve productivity, quality, and the efficiency of capital utilization, Swedish industry pursued a strategy
based on innovation and investment in research and development,
training, union participation, and organizational development
rather than more traditional investments in plant and equipment. A shift in official economic policy and a system of government incentives for job retraining and mobility also contributed
to the rapid recovery of Swedish industry from the cost inflation,
industrial crises, and anti-business attitudes that were prevalent in
the 1970s.

The Soviets are interested in Sweden's experience with participatory management, employee training, and the cooperative
movement. This interest stems from the fact that since 1988—at
least in theory—Soviet enterprises have been required to be
financially self-sufficient. Soviet managers now have more freedom
and are experimenting with workplace democracy.

Referring to Sweden's experience with participatory management, Bo Ekman, chairman of the Swedish Institute for Opinion
Research, has said that "the real transition has taken place on the
shop floors and in offices, in laboratories and design studios, at

dealerships and in warehouses. Without the involvement and support of the individual employee, no real change in competitiveness could have taken place." In the new Volvo plant in Uddevala, a work team builds an entire car in a product workshop and also has direct contact with customers.

Gorbachev also appears to be attracted to Sweden's nonconfrontational style of management. For example, rather than criticizing striking Siberian coal miners, he acknowledged their dangerous and unhealthy working conditions and thanked them for their support of *perestroika*.

When the bells of St. Basil's Cathedral rang out over Red Square on New Year's Day 1990 for the first time since 1922, when the government began clamping down on the Russian Orthodox church, it was a clear signal that religious repression was on the wane. The construction of new churches and synagogues, the lifting of bans on religious education and the publication of Bibles and religious literature, the establishment of diplomatic ties with the Vatican and the encouragement of religious-based charitable activities all suggested an atmosphere of increased religious freedom.

If Gorbachev is serious about coming to grips with the problem of alienation and rebuilding the Soviet economy—and I believe that he is—then the repression of religion makes no sense whatsoever. To put it cynically, it's much better for the Soviet economy for people to practice the religion of their choice than to either drink or smoke themselves to death. The Soviet Parliament recently enacted legislation guaranteeing freedom of religion.

But what about Johnny back in the United States? His problems of alienation and lack of motivation are very similar to those of Sasha. Unfortunately for Johnny and the U.S. economy, many American managers and politicians are oblivious to the fact that a lot of American companies are suffering from precisely the same kinds of problems as the Soviets. America also needs *perestroika*, but until recently we were too arrogant to admit it.

Only a handful of American companies have experimented with the participatory management practices now widely used in Japan and Western Europe. Historically, our managers have been accustomed to imposing their ideas on company employees rather than drawing on the combined experience of managers and employees. But there are signs that this is beginning to change.

There is an increasing awareness on the part of labor and management that adversarial labor–management relations don't pay anymore. As evidenced by the recent strikes at Eastern Air Lines, Pittston Coal, and Greyhound, neither side wins in the long run. The only real winners from our confrontational labor–management practices are our foreign competitors. Neither unreasonable anti-labor policies nor irresponsible labor demands for shorter hours, narrow job classifications, and artificial workload limits do much to strengthen America's competitive position in the international marketplace.

Having lost more than one-third of the U.S. market to foreign competition, it is not surprising that the Big Three automakers have begun to emulate the participatory management practices of their competitors. At the Reatta Craft Center in Lansing, Michigan, teams of five to eleven people build entire sections of the new General Motors Buick Reatta sports car, rather than thousands of workers performing the same repetitive task on the assembly line. Ford and Chrysler have also introduced the team approach to automobile production.

Raritan River, Nucor, and Florida Steel have achieved efficiency increases and cost reductions by turning to smaller, mini–steel mills. The mini-mills reduce costs through participatory management, reduced capital costs, lean corporate staffs, new technologies, location near markets, and concentration on one or two products.

To help its employees balance the pressures of work and family life, IBM offered them several new options, including leaves of absence of up to three years, greater flexibility in work hours, and a chance for some employees to work at their homes. Chrysler, Pan Am, Kaiser Aluminum, and Weirton Steel now have employee-selected members of their boards of directors.

The ultimate form of participatory management is the employee-owned company. There are now over eight thousand employee-owned companies in the United States, including United Parcel Service (UPS), Chicago-Northwestern Railroad, Northwestern Steel and Wire, South Bend Lathe, and Vermont Asbestos. With annual sales of over $12 billion, UPS is the best known and also the most successful of the employee-owned companies. Known for the reliability of its service and its low rates, UPS is owned by eighteen thousand of its managers and supervisors. It is by far the most profitable transportation company in the United States. Its founder, James E. Casey, declared that the company must be "owned by its managers and managed by its owners." Through a generous annual-bonus plan and an employee stock-option plan, employees who began their careers at UPS as clerks and drivers retire as multimillionaires. The employee-turnover rate is only 4 percent.

What seems to be missing in many companies is a sense of direction for senior management other than narrowly defined financial targets. Are there reasons other than maximizing shareholders' wealth why an enterprise should exist?

The success of some large multinational corporations such as IBM, Federal Express, McDonald's, Sony, SAS, and Volvo is based in part on the fact that they each have a well-defined management philosophy that expresses the fundamental principles on which the business is based. Its aim is to communicate senior management's sense of purpose, values, and ethical principles to employees, customers, suppliers, shareholders, and the public.

A well-thought-out management philosophy should capture the sense of meaning and direction of senior management and have significant impact on the company's objectives, strategies, and policies as well as the corporate culture and style of management. It represents a mirror image of the heart and soul of management and should convey to employees what the business is really all about.

A meaningful management philosophy should provide answers to the questions: What does the company do for people? What does it do to people? How do people participate in the company's business activities?

The rationale underlying the need for a management philosophy was cogently captured by Tennessee Williams in his play *The Glass Menagerie* — "Man is by instinct a lover, a hunter, and a fighter and none of these instincts are given much play at the warehouse." Because these instincts have been given so little attention by senior management, it is not surprising to find so many large companies in the United States and the Soviet Union floundering aimlessly in a sea of economic chaos. Companies whose leaders have no sense of meaning or vision in their personal lives will have great difficulty motivating Johnny and Sasha and millions of others just like them.

2

The Pot Can't Call
the Kettle Black

Moral Indignation

In no area have the judgmental criticisms hurled at each other by
the two superpowers been more vitriolic than in the field of
human-rights abuses. Each side had a long list of deeply resented
grievances against the other, which took the form of political,
economic, and social injustices. Every time there was an alleged
abuse by one side, the other side responded with a compensatory
charge of its own. Both nations were full of self-righteous indigna-
tion and wounded pride. Each country could cite the most minor
malefactions of the other in excruciating detail, but never accepted
responsibility for or acknowledged the pain and suffering inflicted
by its own policies.

Most Americans find it difficult to fathom the tyranny perpetrated by Stalin in the 1930s and 1940s. But Ivan the Terrible in
the sixteenth century, Peter the Great in the eighteenth century,
and Nicholas I in the nineteenth century were all precursors of
Stalin, and each exhibited behavioral patterns all too similar to
Stalin's in the bloody purges of the 1930s. Although Peter the
Great is best known for opening Russia (now part of the Soviet
Union) to the West and introducing a modern army and state
administration, he also introduced measures to improve the
efficiency of authoritarian controls, some of which are still in place.
He established the first police administration, instituted censor-
ship, and introduced the practice of issuing internal passports to
prevent Russians from traveling without special approval.

Mass terror has not been used by Soviet leaders since the days of Stalin as a means of manipulating, controlling, or changing society. However, the treatment of political dissidents under Leonid I. Brezhnev was not fundamentally different from that of the czars. The Soviets have only recently abandoned the practice of putting dissidents in mental hospitals—a practice which can be traced back to the nineteenth century when an eminent scientist was branded as insane for an essay he had written condemning Russia as backward and advocating Westernization and Catholicism.

One of the fundamental differences between Soviets and Americans is in their attitudes towards power and authority. Americans have an aversion to authority and distrust Big Business, Big Labor, and Big Government. The Soviets respect bigness and power. The massive Kremlin walls and the huge buildings built during the Stalin era all connote power and authority. Although the Soviet people feared Stalin, they nevertheless respected him for his power and his authority. Long before the Bolshevik Revolution, the Russians had been subjected to four centuries of authoritarian rule from Ivan the Terrible and Peter the Great to the present.

Another persistent theme of Soviet culture is a strong aversion to risk. To minimize their personal economic risk as well as the risk of outside military invasion, the Soviets have paid dearly in terms of personal freedom and liberty. Until very recently, it was very difficult to become wealthy—legally, that is. But since everyone was guaranteed a job, free medical care, a free education, and low-cost housing, there was very limited personal financial risk. In the United States it is possible to make a lot of money, and many people manage to do so. But it is also possible to go bankrupt in the United States and end up homeless with no income and no health insurance.

A long history of invasions by everyone from the Mongols and Napoleon to Adolf Hitler has made the Soviets particularly paranoid about the possibility of foreign invasion. To ensure political stability, they have been willing to put up with what Americans consider to be a broad range of human-rights violations, including arbitrary arrests, police controls, censorship, labor camps, and enforced intellectual conformity. While most Americans abhor these practices, the Soviets reply that they are no worse than what they consider to be American-style human-rights violations—

unemployment, homelessness, drug addiction, violent crime, political assassinations, and racial discrimination.

The Soviet responses to the destruction of Korean Air Line Flight 007 in 1983 and the Chernobyl nuclear accident in 1986 reflected the influence of Soviet culture. In both incidents order and security took precedence over more human concerns such as health, safety, and compassion. On the other hand, the Soviet response to the 1988 Armenian earthquake was both timely and humane.

Political Injustice

At the heart of American criticisms of the Soviet political system is the fact that until recently the Communist party—representing only 7 percent of the population—claimed to speak for all 285 million people of the Soviet Union. The Party previously maintained a monopolistic stranglehold on political opinion with little tolerance for dissent.

In spite of the sweeping political changes made by Mr. Gorbachev, many Americans still view the Soviet Union as fundamentally undemocratic. They feel that the United States has a much more democratic political system by virtue of our two-party system; the separation of powers among the executive, legislative, and judicial branches of government; our decentralized state and local governments; and our free and open elections. But is the American political system really as democratic as we say it is? Are the differences between the American and Soviet political systems as great as our political leaders would have us believe?

The 1988 presidential election is a case in point. Fewer than half of the eligible American voters actually went to the polls—the lowest voter turnout in sixty-four years. Who actually votes in American elections? Essentially the answer is well-educated, affluent whites. People who have a college education and earn more than $50,000 per year are twice as likely to vote as those who only went to grade school and earn less than $5,000 annually. Voter turnout among African-Americans, Hispanics, Native Americans, and the poor is abysmal.

Even though our voter-registration procedures were simplified during the 1960s, they are still among the most difficult in the

West. President George Bush was actually elected by a plurality of white, affluent men, most of whom live either on farms or in the exclusive suburbs of large cities.

Both presidential and congressional races in the United States are won or lost on the basis of television coverage. Television advertising is very expensive. In one way or another—campaign contribution laws notwithstanding—television advertising is paid for by special-interest groups—particularly big business. With few exceptions, he or she who raises the most money for television advertising gets elected. Obviously, those who finance successful political campaigns expect something in return for their money in the way of favorable treatment from the candidate once he or she is in office. But more often than not, it is accumulated wealth and financial power that drives our political system—not participatory democracy. We have a two-party system, but it functions more like a single party. As Governor George Wallace used to say, "There is not a dime's worth of difference between the Democratic and Republican parties."

A number of political injustices persisted in the Soviet Union even up to the time of Gorbachev, including the repression of political dissent and religion and the abuse of mental patients as well as restrictions on emigration from the Soviet Union. There was a complete absence of basic human rights—freedom of speech, freedom of the press, freedom of assembly, freedom of religion, and freedom of movement in and out of the Soviet Union.

One hundred years after slavery was abolished in the United States, there were still laws on the books in the South and other parts of the nation condoning racial discrimination. Even though segregation has been outlawed in voter registration, education, housing, public accommodations, and employment, racial discrimination is still widespread in the United States.

Stalin's atrocities lasted for a little over twenty years. Our barbaric conquest of the Native Americans continued for several hundred years and involved many of our most cherished national heroes, including George Washington, Thomas Jefferson, James Monroe, and Andrew Jackson, to mention only a few. The story of how Native Americans were relentlessly forced to abandon their homes and lands and move into Indian territories is a story of arrogance, greed, and raw military power. Even today, thousands of Indians live in ignorance, poverty, and squalor on scruffy

invasion and almost total destruction of Lebanon, not to mention its forty-year history of espionage against the United States, cast further doubts on Israel's commitment to human rights. And in 1988 Israel sentenced nuclear technician Mordechai Vanunu to eighteen years in prison for telling the *Sunday Times* of London that Israel was secretly manufacturing atomic bombs in the Negev Desert in violation of international nonproliferation statutes and under false assurances to the United States and Norway. In addition, the Israeli court that convicted Vanunu chose to ignore the fact that he had been brought under the court's jurisdiction by illegal kidnap in Rome by the Mossad.

In the fall of 1989, U.S. intelligence reports revealed that Israel was involved in providing South Africa with medium-range missiles and nuclear-weapons technology. There were also reports that Colombian drug bosses were being trained by Israeli mercenaries.

Until recently, most Soviet Jews entered the West through Vienna. Once they were in Vienna, they were free to immigrate to any country that would accept them. Most chose to go to the United States. However, if they came out through Bucharest, Romania, then they were required to go directly to Tel Aviv, which was what the Israeli government wanted them to do.

In 1988 the Israeli government took steps to force Soviet Jews emigrating with Israeli visas to travel directly to Israel instead of settling elsewhere. By forcing Soviet Jews to pick up their visas at the Israeli embassy in Bucharest rather than at the Dutch embassy in Moscow, which had been the practice, the Israelis could control the final destination of the emigrants. In return for this favor, Israel lobbied the U.S. government to grant most-favored-nation status to the Ceausescu government of Romania—the most repressive government in Eastern Europe until it was brought down in 1989.

In the fall of 1989, the people of Eastern Europe rose up against their self-appointed communist dictators and demanded and got a greater role in the political process. What would happen in this country if millions of Americans began to make similar demands on the C..A, the Pentagon, and the Congress? What if they said to the Congress, "Enough is enough. We want to have more input into our foreign policy, our defense policy, and our domestic policies."

At least for the moment, the American electorate appears to be so complacent, so docile, and so easily manipulated that participatory democracy remains an elusive dream. However, if some of our domestic problems were to worsen significantly, the public might be jarred into action. A further deepening of the health-care crisis, increased alienation, the failure to curb drug abuse, increased environmental concerns, and a widening of the income distribution gap each have the potential of destabilizing our placid political system. Only then will real political pluralism be a possibility.

Crime

In many sections of New York, Chicago, Los Angeles, and other major American cities, one cannot walk the streets at night without the real possibility of being mugged, raped, or even murdered. In Moscow and other Soviet cities the incidence of such crimes is far lower than in the United States but is increasing rapidly.[1] Nearly eight times as many crimes are committed in the United States each day as there are in the Soviet Union. However, during the first half of 1989, the number of crimes committed in the Soviet Union increased by 32 percent while the number of serious crimes increased by 40 percent. During this same period first-degree murders increased by 130 percent, rapes by 120 percent, and crimes involving serious bodily injury by 150 percent.[2]

American politicians respond to our high crime rates with a combination of tough talk and heavy expenditures for law enforcement and prisons, neither of which seem to have much impact in reducing the incidence of crime. The percentage of Americans in prison has more than doubled since 1980. One in every 450 adults in the United States is in prison—the highest rate in the West. By 1989 there were 710,000 inmates in state and federal prisons, over 2,200 of whom were awaiting execution. We spend $20 billion annually on prisons.

Not unlike their response to our drug problem, American politicians seem unwilling to dig into the complex causes underlying our high crime rates—alienation, extreme inequities in the distribution of income, television violence, the breakup of the family, and poor education. It is much easier for a politician to get elected by talking tough on crime rather than proposing substantive solutions to a very serious problem.

Although the typical American stereotype of the Soviet Union portrays it as an aggressive, heavily armed military state, it is the United States, not the Soviet Union, that has the highest homicide rate and is the most heavily armed nation in the world. Due in no small part to the effective lobbying effort of the all-powerful National Rifle Association (NRA), there are sixty million handguns in the United States.

Over 22,000 people are killed each year (including 12,000 suicides) from handguns. In addition, 300,000 crimes are committed annually with handguns. More Americans have been killed by handguns during the twentieth century than were killed in all of the wars during this period. In 1987, of the 943 homicides committed in New York City, 536 involved handguns.

The Federal Bureau of Alcohol, Tobacco, and Firearms estimates that there are over a half-million semiautomatic versions of military machine guns in civilian hands. Among the more exotic paramilitary weapons available to ordinary citizens are the Uzi, MAC-10, TEK-9, Colt AR-15A2, and AK-47. In January 1989 a gunman in Stockton, California, used an AK-47 to kill five schoolchildren and wound thirty others. Nine more people were killed in Jacksonville, Florida, by a lone assassin with an AK-47 in June 1990. Florida has the most lax gun-control laws and the highest crime rate in America.

From a very early age Americans are bombarded with television violence beginning with the Saturday morning cartoons. Is it any wonder that President John F. Kennedy, Senator Robert F. Kennedy, and Dr. Martin Luther King, Jr., were gunned down at the hands of assassins, or that Presidents Gerald Ford and Ronald Reagan as well as Governor George Wallace were also the targets of assassination attempts? Hardly a month goes by in which we don't read about a multiple homicide somewhere in the United States. We don't imprison people for their political beliefs or block them from leaving the country, but we are nevertheless one of the most violent nations in the world.

Although President Ronald Reagan always projected a strong "law and order" image throughout his political career, over one hundred officials in his administration were either accused or convicted of unethical or illegal conduct. So-called white-collar crime, financial manipulation, and insider trading took on a whole new meaning during the "anything goes" Reagan years. Ivan F. Boesky was sent to prison for insider trading and the prestigious Wall Street firm of Drexel Burnham Lambert was charged with violation of security laws, fraud, insider trading, and stock price manipulation. Even President Bush's son Neil has been implicated for his involvement in the savings and loan scandal.

The Reagan administration also tried to defang the 1977 Foreign Corrupt Practices Act. This act was passed in the aftermath of the Watergate affair when an investigation revealed that at least 450 American companies had paid hundreds of millions of dollars in bribes abroad in the 1960s and early 1970s.

The White House was not the only branch of the U.S. government that chose to look the other way when confronted by illegal or unethical behavior. The Congress was actively involved in its own, more-subtle form of bribery and corruption known as the speaker's honorarium. Although one could be sent to prison if convicted of bribing a senator or a representative, there was nothing illegal about paying a congressman a $2,000 honorarium for each time he was invited to speak. Not surprisingly, particularly influential members of Congress were very popular on the speakers' circuit.

As for the Soviet Union, bribery and corruption of public officials were a way of life during the Brezhnev era. As a result of a five-year investigation, Soviet officials uncovered a $6.5 billion bribery and corruption case in the republic of Uzbekistan which involved Brezhnev's son-in-law Yuri M. Churbanov. In February 1988, a 40 percent reduction in the government's fleet of automobiles was announced. These cars and 700,000 chauffeurs had heretofore been assigned to Communist-party elites and senior government officials.

Economic Inequality

Although the U.S. economy is over three times the size of the Soviet economy, it too has some very serious problems. After reaching a peak of over 10 percent in 1982, U.S. unemployment never dropped below 5 percent during the Reagan years, in sharp contrast to Sweden's 2 percent unemployment rate. For the first time since the 1930s, the Soviets are facing unemployment problems of their own.

In 1949, 30 percent of the U.S. population was earning an annual income below the poverty level. By 1963 that figure had decreased to 21 percent, and by 1979, it had dropped to only 11 percent. However, by 1988, approximately 32.5 million Americans or 13.5 percent of the population were living in poverty.

One-third of the African-Americans, 28.2 percent of the Hispanic Americans, and one-fifth of the newborn children in America live in poverty. According to a 1988 Economic Policy Institute study, the number of full-time workers who earned less than the poverty level increased by more than 600,000 between 1979 and 1987.[3] The average family headed by a person between the ages of twenty-five and thirty-four had 12 percent less real income in 1987 than was the case in 1973.

Ten percent of the Soviet population cannot get from one payday to the next without having to borrow money. Twenty-five percent live on or below the poverty level.

There is a growing African-American underclass in the United States—estimated to number more than 1.5 million—which is increasingly isolated from the nation's economic and social mainstream. This underclass of chronically unemployed males and welfare mothers is concentrated in extremely poor, crime-infested inner-city neighborhoods.

Of every 1,000 American babies, 10.8 will die before their first birthday, giving the United States the dubious distinction of having the highest infant-mortality rate in the industrial world. Furthermore, poor children are three to four times more likely to drop out of school than others, thus dooming themselves to lives of lower expected earnings.

In 1987 the Physicians Task Force on Hunger concluded that as many as 20 million Americans do not get enough to eat every day. Of the 32.5 million people living below the poverty level, 18.6 million receive food stamps that provide 51 cents a meal for each person, or about $2 a meal for a family of four.

Ronald Reagan once told the American people that "what I want to see above all is that this country remains a country where someone can always get rich." This is one promise that President Reagan most assuredly kept.

Between 1977 and 1988 only those American families in the highest 20 percent of the income distribution actually increased their average incomes. The middle 40 percent experienced a $1,500 decrease in their average income. The average income increase ($134,513) for those families in the highest one percent of the income distribution was nearly six times the average family income for a family in the middle 40 percent of the income distribution. Furthermore, the richest 10 percent of the population owns 65 percent of all the net worth, and the bottom half only 4 percent.

Between 1980 and 1989, average hourly wages adjusted for inflation declined from $9.84 to $9.66. Employment in relatively high-paying manufacturing declined by 1.9 million jobs over the period from 1979 to 1987 while the service sector added 13.9 million new jobs. During this period 84 percent of the job growth was in the two lowest-paying industries—retail trade and business, personal, and health services.[4]

Although the Soviet Union is known to have an acute shortage of housing, one does not find people sleeping on the streets of Moscow, Leningrad, or Kiev as is the case in New York, Washington, Chicago, Miami, and Los Angeles. On any given night, according to a study cited by the National Academy of Sciences, over 735,000 Americans are homeless. Over 100,000 of these are children. Between 1.3 million and 2 million Americans are homeless for at least one night each year.

Free labor unions are a new phenomenon in the Soviet Union, and only recently have they been allowed to strike. In the United States labor unions are heavily regulated by the federal and state governments. As a result of President Reagan's dismissal of 11,500 striking members of the Professional Air Traffic Controllers Organization in 1981 and other anti-labor practices of his administration, organized labor's membership and influence declined precipitously during the Reagan years. President Reagan's opposition to a congressional bill requiring a company to give its employees sixty-days notice before closing a plant was but one of many examples of his hostility toward organized labor. Many other American companies followed Reagan's lead and intimidated their unions into granting major concessions in the form of reductions in wages and benefits.

Texas Air chairman Frank Lorenzo pursued one of the most aggressive anti-union strategies of any American company in the

1980s. He set up New York Air so that it could be operated without a union contract. Then he took Continental Airlines into bankruptcy to circumvent its unions. At Eastern Air Lines he transferred routes to Continental, sold off the Eastern Shuttle, and eventually drove the airline into bankruptcy. Anti-unionism was the driving force underlying his entire management strategy.

As we have previously noted, the salaries of senior U.S. corporate executives skyrocketed during the 1980s while real wages declined. Junk-bond king Michael R. Milken established a new high-water mark in corporate pay when he received $550 million from Drexel Burnham Lambert in a single year. As we can see in table 2–1, the compensation of the ten highest-paid American chief executives reached zenith levels in 1989.

Nothing better illustrates the powerlessness of American workers in dealing with large corporations than the series of mega-mergers of the 1980s capped off by the hostile, $25 billion, 1988 leveraged buyout of RJR Nabisco by Kohlberg Kravis Roberts & Company. Rarely are the employees of a company consulted prior to a takeover attempt. Nor is their input sought when the management of the acquiring company plans to dispose of its newly acquired assets.

Although American-style capitalism is long on efficiency and output, it has only limited concern for equality and social justice.

Table 2–1
Total Compensation of the Ten Highest-Paid American Chief Executives in 1989

Executive	Company	Total Pay
1. Craig O. McCaw	McCaw Cellular	$53,944,000
2. Steven J. Ross	Time Warner	34,200,000
3. Donald A. Pels	Lin Broadcasting	22,791,000
4. Jim P. Manzi	Lotus Development	16,363,000
5. Paul Fireman	Reebok International	14,606,000
6. Ronald K. Richey	Torchmark	12,666,000
7. Martin S. Davis	Paramount	11,635,000
8. Roberto C. Goizueta	Coca-Cola	10,715,000
9. Michael D. Eisner	Walt Disney	9,589,000
10. August A. Busch III	Anheuser-Busch	8,861,000

Source: John A. Byrne, "Pay Stubs of the Rich and Corporate," *Business Week,* 7 May 1990, p. 57.

This phenomenon is influenced in no small part by the fact that only 36 million Americans own shares in American companies. This means that less than 15 percent of the population has an ownership stake in our economic system. According to a study by Louis and Patricia Kelso, 5 percent of American families own nearly all of the nation's nonresidential productive assets and most of the ownership is concentrated in the hands of the top 2 percent.[5]

Inadequate Health Care

Long before the days of *glasnost* the Soviets used to boast of their free medical and dental care, claiming that they had the largest number of physicians and dentists in the world and the highest ratio of hospital beds to people. While it is true that they do practice state-of-the-art medicine in some fields such as eye surgery, recent revelations by Soviet Minister of Health Yevgeny Chazov indicate that the Soviet health-care system is in dire straits.

Rising alcoholism, poor food quality, environmental pollution, heavy smoking, and declining hygienic and medical standards have all taken their toll on the Soviet people. Increased infant-mortality rates and declining life expectancy serve to dramatize the life-threatening consequences of the sorry state of the Soviet health-care system. The Soviets' infant-mortality rate is comparable to that of a Third World country—2.5 times the U.S. rate.

The spread of infectious diseases and the high incidence of lung cancer and heart disease provide further evidence of the decline in the health of the Soviet people. The latter two problems are directly attributable to their excessive consumption of alcohol and tobacco.

Dr. Chazov has also acknowledged that over a third of the district hospitals in the Soviet Union have no hot water, and that 27 percent have no sewerage facilities. In addition, there are chronic shortages of medicines, bandages, disposable hypodermic syringes, surgical clothing, and basic medical equipment.

The Soviets are finally backing away from their repressive system of psychiatric and mental hospitals, which were often used to incarcerate political prisoners on the grounds that they must be mentally ill or they would not advocate political views in opposition to the party line. As evidence that the Soviets have begun to clean up their act in this field, they were recently readmitted to the World Psychiatric Association, from which they withdrew in 1983 just prior to expulsion for confining political prisoners in mental hospitals.

If one can afford to pay for it or if one has adequate health insurance, then most Americans have access to a quality of health care that is far superior to that of the Soviet Union. In general, U.S. medical technology is years ahead of Soviet. Although the United States spends more on health care—in total dollars and as a percentage of the gross national product—than other industrialized nations, 37 million Americans (18 percent of the population) have no health insurance whatsoever and another 50 million are underinsured. The uninsured are completely at the mercy of local hospitals as to whether or not they will be provided any medical care whatsoever, if they are not able to pay for it.

According to some measures, Canadians are healthier than Americans, they live longer on the average, and their infant-mortality rate is 25 percent lower than that of the United States. Yet they spend less than 9 percent of their GNP on health care, in contrast to nearly 12 percent for the United States. But more importantly, all Canadians are guaranteed medical care at no charge.

Not only is health care very expensive in the United States, but it is becoming even more expensive all the time. Some employers are experiencing health-care cost increases of 20 to 30 percent per year. According to Milt Freudenheim in *The New York Times,* the Ford Motor Company spends the equivalent of $311 a vehicle for health care for its employees in the United States. In Toronto the cost is only $50 per vehicle.[6]

The question is who is going to pick up the tab for health care costs in the future? Who is going to cover the cost of the uninsured? Will it be employers? Employees? Or will the federal and state governments have to intervene?

Some, including Senator Edward Kennedy, have suggested that the U.S. health-care system is on the verge of collapse.

Unlike Western Europe where the practice of medicine grew out of a tradition of public service, American medical care is driven by professional entrepreneurs whose primary aim is to make as much money as possible. It is not uncommon to find private physicians who make over $250,000 per year. For-profit hospitals and pharmaceuticals are also very lucrative businesses in which to be in the United States. Even some physicians were shocked when Burroughs Wellcome initially announced that an annual dosage of AZT for an AIDS patient would cost $10,000. The original research that led to the discovery of AZT was financed by the U.S. government. Burroughs Wellcome reaped huge windfall profits from AZT. Even though Burroughs Wellcome subsequently reduced the price of AZT to $2,500 per annual dosage, the long-run impact of its pricing policy on the American health-care industry remains to be seen.

Intensive-care medicine is by far the most expensive form of medical care money can buy in the United States. We have 87,000 intensive-care beds—more than any other country in the world.[7]

For those who can afford insurance, we seem to have unlimited health-care resources. For those who have no health insurance, our resources are severely limited, and only limited attention is devoted to preventive medicine.

The sky is the limit when it comes to financing exotic multi-organ transplants, high-tech tests and equipment, and emergency helicopter service— all of which are covered by health insurance. But in 1988 alone, 600,000 women in the United States gave birth with little or no prenatal care. Although Boston has the best medical facilities in the nation, Massachusetts has the third-highest infant mortality rate in the country, and it is increasing. The infant mortality rate of our nation's capital exceeds that of most Third World countries. For the nation as a whole, the infant-mortality rate for blacks is twice that of whites.

The first question that a physician should ask a patient is "What can I do to help you?" not "What kind of insurance do you have?" Without good health it is impossible to have a meaningful and productive life.

With regard to long-term health care for the elderly we appear to be approaching a financial crisis. Inadequate insurance and the rising cost of long-term care in nursing homes and elsewhere are the causes of the problem. A study by the U.S. Department of Health and Human Services indicates that over 4,000 of the country's fifteen thousand nursing homes administer drugs to patients without regard to a physician's written orders. Nearly three thousand nursing homes fail to provide rehabilitative nursing care and sixty-five hundred serve food under unsanitary conditions.

Although we have no problem whatsoever coming up with billions of dollars for Stealth bombers and Trident II submarines, we find it virtually impossible to fund rural health clinics, prenatal care for the poor, and routine preventive care for all of our citizens. What possible justification can there be for spending hundreds of billions of dollars on national security, but in so doing putting millions of Americans at risk because of inadequate health care? To function as a responsible human being affordable health care is a fundamental human concern and should be given the priority it deserves by our government.

As the national health-care crisis worsens, proposals that might once have been dismissed as socialized medicine or simply ignored because they were too costly are now getting serious attention in Washington. Not only is opposition to universal health insurance diminishing, but some large corporate employers see national health insurance as the only viable option for curbing spiraling employee health-care costs. Some politically conservative corporate executives are openly advocating national health insurance.

The Canadian national health-insurance plan has been getting much more favorable press in the United States recently than it did ten years ago. The same is true of the Swedish, Finnish, and Austrian health-insurance programs.

A number of national health-insurance proposals are now being considered by the Congress. One such proposal was developed by the Bipartisan Commission on Comprehensive Health Care headed up by Senator John D. Rockefeller IV. The Rockefeller proposal would require employers either to provide their employees with adequate health insurance or to pay a tax to help finance such coverage through a public fund. The proposed insurance would cover hospital treatment, doctors' fees, and preventive services.

Americans severely criticized Soviet leaders in 1986 for their forty-eight-hour delay in informing the rest of the world about the Chernobyl nuclear accident. But in October 1988, the U.S. Energy Department finally got around to telling the American people about the forty-year history of safety violations, nuclear accidents, radioactive contamination, and environmental pollution associated with our country's nuclear-arms industry. For four decades our government simply opted to remain silent about these problems so as to avoid the risk of political backlash from the public. The Pentagon waited twenty-four years to tell the Japanese that in December 1965 a hydrogen bomb fell overboard from an American aircraft carrier located eighty miles from a Japanese island. In a 1989 report acknowledging the nuclear accident for the first time, the Pentagon indicated that the bomb almost certainly burst under intense water pressure and spread radioactive plutonium on the ocean floor.

Social Ills

Although the Soviet Union has come down hard on the United States for its discriminatory practices against African-Americans, Hispanics, Jews, and Native Americans, the Soviets have their own problems with the 130 different ethnic groups that live in the Soviet Union.

Fifty-one percent of the population of the Soviet Union is Russian, and for the most part resides in the Russian republic. The remaining 49 percent of the population lives in the other fourteen Soviet republics. However, the fastest-growing republics are the six Moslem republics—Azerbaijan, Turkmenistan, Kazakhstan, Uzbekistan, Kirghizia, and Tadzhikistan. Today there are forty-five million Moslems in the Soviet Union—16 percent of the total population. As a result of the higher rates of population growth in the Moslem republics, by the year 2000, only 48 percent of the population will be Russian.

In the pre-Gorbachev era, there was considerable evidence to suggest that the Communist party in Moscow was biased in favor of Russians. The most important government positions and privileges usually went to Russians and not to people living in other republics. (Joseph Stalin, a native of the republic of Georgia, was an obvious exception to this rule.)

Recently there has been a great deal of unrest among the non-Russian republics. Lithuania, Latvia, Estonia, Moldavia, Georgia, and Azerbaijan are demanding their independence from Moscow. The Armenians have been demanding that the Nagorno–Karabakh autonomous region of Azerbaijan be merged into Armenia. More will be said about this complex subject in chapter 7.

Another major social problem of the Soviet Union is alcoholism—one of the few Soviet problems that has actually been understated by the American press. Until Gorbachev clamped down on the consumption of alcohol in June 1985, the Soviets were well on their way to drinking themselves to death. With his dramatic campaign against drunkenness, Gorbachev closed most of the country's hard-liquor stores, raised vodka prices, slashed production, and prohibited the sale of alcoholic beverages in restaurants before 2:00 P.M. each day. Furthermore, Soviet workers found drunk at the workplace can be fined as much as one-fourth of their monthly income.

Unfortunately, Gorbachev was forced to temper his alcohol-reform campaign as a result of the public outrage against it, declining state liquor revenues, and shortages of sugar, which are the result of increased moonshining activities.

Although alcoholism is also a serious problem in the United States, drug abuse is a far worse problem. According to former HEW Secretary Joseph A. Califano, Jr., eighteen million Americans either abuse alcohol or are addicted to it, twenty-one million have used cocaine, over one million are addicted to crack, seven million smoke marijuana at least once a week, and nearly a million are addicted to heroin. In addition, millions of others abuse tranquilizers and other psychoactive drugs as well as hallucinogens such as LSD and PCP.[8] In spite of increases in drug-law enforcement expenditures by the Reagan administration from $800 million in 1981 to $2.5 billion in 1988, there are six million drug addicts in the United States and facilities to treat only 250,000. Only recently have the Soviets admitted that they too have drug-related problems.

A commission established by the American Medical Association and the National Association of State Boards of Education concluded in July 1990 that American teenagers have profound behavioral problems including drug and alcohol abuse, sexually transmitted diseases, and violence. According to the commission, "Never before has one generation of American teenagers been less healthy, less cared-for, or less prepared for life than their parents were at the same age." In today's younger generation, the rich are afflicted with many of the same problems as the poor. They too seek instant gratification through the abuse of drugs, alcohol, and sex. In addition, the U.S. Advisory Board on Child Abuse and

Neglect reported that 900,000 American children were physically or sexually abused in 1989.

Education Problems

A certain minimum level of information, education, training, and experience is required to be a responsible and productive citizen capable of earning sufficient income to pay for one's own food, clothing, shelter, and health care.

Although education at all levels is free in the Soviet Union, only primary and secondary education are free in the United States. American colleges and universities—particularly private ones—have priced themselves out of the market for students from lower-middle-income and poor families. The percentage of low- and middle-income African-American and Hispanic youths entering college from high school declined significantly during the 1980s. There is a serious problem of access to higher education for the less fortunate.

As we noted in the story of Johnny and Sasha, neither the United States nor the Soviet Union is doing a particularly good job of preparing its young people to work in existing American companies and Soviet enterprises. In many cases blue-collar workers and white-collar workers alike are actually overeducated for their industrial jobs.

On the other hand, American public schools continue to graduate many students who are barely able to read. Over twenty-three million adult Americans are actually functionally illiterate. Millions of workers are not adequately trained for high-tech jobs.

It is much easier to raise money for high school football teams in America than it is to raise taxes to pay higher teachers' salaries. And it's no different at the college level. In all too many American universities, the athletic tail wags the academic dog. Throughout the 1980s, the University of North Carolina lost a lot of good faculty members because it could not afford to pay competitive academic salaries. But its alumni association had little difficulty in raising $33.8 million to finance its new indoor basketball stadium known as the Dean Dome—named after its highly successful basketball coach Dean Smith. In 1987, UNC's administration came up with one million dollars to buy out the football coach's contract ahead of schedule. Winning national football and basketball championships is far more important to most American universities than training young people to help solve some of our very real economic, political, and social problems.

It is impossible to have a real democracy in either the United States or the Soviet Union without a strong commitment to high-quality public education. But it is equally difficult to obtain strong public support for education if there is no strong democratic tradition. Which comes first, real democracy or high-quality public education? This is one of the toughest challenges facing the United States and the Soviet Union.

Although President Bush has proclaimed himself the "education President", organized an education summit, and generated a lot of pro-education hype, he has raised no new money to support either public education or higher education and does not appear to possess the political will to do so. In the meantime the United States spends relatively less on elementary and secondary education than do thirteen other industrial nations.

The problems of public education in this country are very complex and do not lend themselves to quick-fix solutions. They range from underpaid teachers, insufficient parental commitment and participation, the breakup of the family, and too much television to unimaginative and incompetent management. We will never solve our public education problem without broad-based participation from all of the relevant stakeholders. There has been far too much public-education rhetoric and too little analysis of the problem.

We expect our inner-city public schools to solve all of our social, economic, and political problems, and then are disappointed when they don't meet our expectations. Children who grow up in impoverished, broken homes where there are no successful role models have their work cut out for them, even if they are bused to shiny, new upscale schools in the more-affluent suburbs. As Hodding Carter III has suggested, there will be no solution to the public-education problem in America, until the children of the rich return to the public schools.

Excessive academic professionalism, research grantsmanship, and functional isolationism have not only driven up the cost of higher education but have reduced the quality of teaching as well. Degree requirements were significantly reduced by most colleges and universities in the early 1970s. It's much easier to get a college degree today than it was twenty years ago. Students expect to be entertained by professors, and hard work is to be avoided at all cost. There is intense competition for grades. Teacher–course evaluations—a product of the early 1970s—are used to coerce professors into giving unjustifiably high grades. Higher education in this country is in a state of disarray. Conspicuously absent in most colleges and universities are well-defined goals, objectives, and strategies for coping with a rapidly changing world.

National Public Service

The closest I ever came to military service was three years of high-school ROTC, where I was a senior officer. I still vividly recall almost shooting the sergeant one day during target practice. During the 1950s and 1960s it was possible—quite unfairly—to avoid the draft through college deferments, marriage, or parenthood. Since I was married, had a child, stayed in college for ten years, and had a lenient draft board I had little difficulty in beating the system.

Although I am not in favor of compulsory military service, I now appreciate the fact that it did perhaps offer our nation some social and political benefits that are not currently provided by any other institution. With today's predominantly white private schools and suburban public schools, it is quite possible for upper- and middle-class white Americans to avoid any significant social contact with the poor, the homeless, and the economically underprivileged. For many Americans the poor are completely invisible. It is almost as though they do not exist.

Required military service did provide a kind of melting pot in which people of all socioeconomic backgrounds were at least temporarily thrown together with a common purpose—the defense of our nation. It meant that the son of a wealthy New York banker might have a glimpse of what life was like for poor blacks in the Mississippi Delta. A pre-medical student might gain some insight into the quality of medical care in Harlem. Is it really very surprising that American yuppies have so little empathy with the poor? They have virtually no contact with people outside of their protected socioeconomic sphere.

Most Western European countries have required military service but with a nonmilitary option for those who prefer to contribute their time to hospitals, homes for the elderly, or other public institutions.

Some Democrats have proposed a Citizenship and National Service Act (CNSA), which ties federal college student aid to prior national service either in the military or in civilian community service. I believe that the CNSA has the potential to exacerbate the significant class differences that already exist in our country. Only the poor would be required to pay for their college education through public service. In most Western European universities tuition is either free or very nominal.

I believe that the United States should seriously consider establishing a National Public Service Corps (NPSC) in which everyone—not just the poor—is expected to devote twelve to eighteen months to public service after graduation from high school. A broad range of public-service options should be offered to the participants, including the opportunity to work in rural health clinics, drug-rehabilitation centers, mental hospitals, Indian reservations, and urban ghettos. Others might elect to work on more-traditional public-works projects, such as cleaning up our environment, rebuilding our highways and bridges, and upgrading our parks and recreational areas. Every effort should be made to assign participants to jobs that reflect their preferences.

The benefits of a National Public Service Corps are threefold. First, every American—male or female—would be given the opportunity to make a tangible contribution to the welfare of our nation. Second, before entering college or the work force, everyone would have a chance to experience the real world and to have contact with people from different socioeconomic backgrounds. Third, a number of worthwhile public-works and social-welfare projects could be implemented that might not otherwise have been given serious consideration.

Participants in the National Public Service Corps should be paid wages comparable to those of recruits in the armed services. Obviously, anyone who elects to serve in the military would automatically meet his or her public-service obligation.

As a positive incentive for those who provide loyal and effective service, there should be a relatively liberal college-tuition voucher program available. Participants who do good work would be eligible

ble for tuition vouchers that could be used to help pay their college tuition after service in the NPSC.

Obviously, a National Public Service Corps will not be an inexpensive undertaking. The real question is, how many Stealth bombers would we be prepared to give up in order to afford the benefits of such a program?

Shared Hypocrisy

One need not search very far for a long list of reasons why the Russians should not be trusted beginning with the millions of Soviet citizens who were killed in the 1930s as a result of Stalin's policy of forced collectivization; the mass deportation of peasants; the 1932–33 famine; and the inhuman political purges, arrests, and executions. These atrocities were followed by Stalin's 1939 nonaggression pact with Hitler and his delayed response to the Nazi invasion of Russia, which resulted in the deaths of millions of Soviet citizens who might otherwise have survived. In addition, the forced Soviet annexation of Latvia, Lithuania, and Estonia and parts of Finland, Poland, and Romania did little to raise the level of trust of Americans in Stalin's style of communism. The coercive measures used by the Soviets to bring Bulgaria, Czechoslovakia, East Germany, Hungary, Poland, and Romania under their control were viewed by Americans as more of the same. And, until very recently, there were widespread restrictions imposed by the Soviets on many basic human rights.

But before we are so quick to judge the Soviets, we need to take a long hard look at ourselves. Although our nation was founded on the principles of life, liberty, and the pursuit of happiness, the United States was the last major country to abolish slavery. Many of our most-famous founding fathers, including George Washington and Thomas Jefferson, were slave owners. One hundred years after the American slaves were freed, racial segregation was still being legally protected. De facto segregation still exists in many parts of America today.

Although we have never been attacked by the Soviets, we did invade the Soviet Union and unsuccessfully attempted to turn back the clock on the Bolshevik Revolution. Not only did we invent nuclear weapons, but we were the first nation to use them—killing hundreds of thousands of men, women, and children. Long before the Soviets developed their first nuclear weapon, we already had military plans to annihilate them. And contrary to what we are often told by American politicians, we are the driving force behind the nuclear arms race—not the Soviets.

In a little-noticed piece, which appeared on page 3 of the *The New York Times*, it was reported that on 25 October 1989 the United States had sold South Korea 120 jet fighters.[9] If the Soviet Union had sold 120 MIGs to one of its allies, the story would have been the front-page headline of every major newspaper in the United States. Indeed, if the Soviets had sold only a half-dozen MIGs to a country such as Libya or Syria, the story would have also made the front page.

During our two-hundred-year history, we have been involved in the invasion of other countries on over 130 separate occasions. There was certainly nothing new about President Reagan's attempt to overthrow the Sandinista government of Nicaragua or President Bush's invasion of Panama. We began intervening in the internal affairs of our Latin American neighbors long before the Bolshevik Revolution. When we invaded Vietnam—a nation which had never harmed us or even threatened us—fifty-eight thousand Americans and over a million Asians were killed.[10] Finally, unemployment, poverty, homelessness, violent crime, and serious drug abuse are an integral part of the American way of life.

No matter how you slice it, both the Soviet Union and the United States have inflicted a great deal of pain and suffering and bloodshed on a lot of people over the past hundred years or so. Neither side is clean. Maybe on balance the Soviet Union is a more evil country than the United States? Maybe not. Does it really matter? There is plenty of evil to go around.

3

The Temple of Doom

Fearless Cold Warriors
COLD WAR PARANOIA

Although right-wing politicians, religious fundamentalists, and American Sovietologists have been telling us since the late 1940s that "You can't trust the Russians," former President Ronald Reagan was without equal in terms of his ability to stir up anti-Soviet feelings among Americans. His entire career was based on unabashed anticommunism. From the first day he came into office, Mr. Reagan and his defense secretary, Caspar W. Weinberger, acted on the belief that the only way to deal with the Soviet Union was through the use of intimidation, insult, and humiliation. Tough talk and military overkill were viewed as necessary and sufficient to bring the Soviets to their knees.

My first personal encounter with the Reagan administration's intense hatred of the Soviets was in Boston in June 1984 at a meeting of the Edison Electric Institute where Caspar Weinberger was speaking. In a forty-five-minute speech, Mr. Weinberger never acknowledged the fact that he was addressing an electric-utility convention. He led off with two vehemently anti-Soviet jokes and then spent the remainder of his time engaged in a hard-line sales pitch for the Strategic Defense Initiative. During all of the years in which I lived in Mississippi, I never saw a white racist display such rage as that which consumed Secretary Weinberger as he cast one insult after another at the Soviet Union.

Every president since Harry Truman has engaged in red-baiting. The fact of the matter is that in the United States nothing sells like anticommunism. To label one's opponent "soft on communism" is a sure-fire way to turn around a floundering political campaign in any part of the United States. Politicians like North Carolina Senator Jesse Helms would be virtually unknown, if it were not for their anticommunism.

President Reagan was driven to show that literally everything the Soviets did was suspect and that no part of the Soviet arms buildup in the 1970s and 1980s was in response to American arms building or to the Soviets' perceptions of U.S. motives. According to this view, the only way to end the arms race was for the United States to press the Soviets to the wall and force them to back down. Diplomatic negotiations have little value with this type of zero-sum mind-set. Everything that is true and good is on our side, and the Soviets are to blame for everything that goes wrong in the world. Simplistic though it may be, the American people were mesmerized by this view of the Soviet Union during the 1980s.

Psychologists use the term *character disorder* to describe the neurotic behavior of people who blame all of their problems on someone else. Psychologist Ralph K. White analyzed the United States and the Soviet Union as suffering from three common neuroses—an exaggerated fear of each other, "macho pride," and a complete inability to ever admit error.[1] Most Americans have a paranoid fear of Soviet-style communism—particularly the repressive form that it took under Stalin. Although the Soviet Union has changed a great deal since Stalin's death, many Americans still firmly believe that it is incapable of significant change.

Since the Bolshevik Revolution in 1917, our politicians, our press, and our academic experts have viewed the Soviet Union as anathema. Not only is the Soviet Union constantly denigrated by the United States, but it is most often portrayed as evil, inhuman, and imperialistic.

What is particularly remarkable is our complete lack of trust of the Soviets, who were our allies in World War II, in contrast to our attitude towards the Japanese, West Germans, and Italians, who were our enemies. Because few Americans have ever visited the Soviet Union or ever known any Soviet people, they rely entirely on the American press for information about the Soviets. But with few exceptions, the editorial policy of even the most liberal American newspapers is decidedly anti-Soviet.

The Soviets' paranoia towards the United States stems from a fear of foreign invasion. For over a thousand years the Soviet

Union has been the object of countless foreign invasions, of which the most disastrous was the invasion by the Germans in World War II, which resulted in twenty million Soviet casualties—in contrast to the U.S. war losses of only 300,000. Although the Germans occupied the Soviet Union, our homeland remained untouched during World War II. Few Americans know that between 1918 and 1920 we actually sent troops to the Soviet Union to fight against the Revolution. Thus, when President Reagan spoke of "containing" Soviet aggression, the Kremlin was contemplating the risks of "encirclement."

Both sides have viewed each other as diabolical enemies. Before Gorbachev, Soviet leaders portrayed Americans as "imperialist warmongers," and President Reagan depicted the Soviets as the source of all evil. While these epithets had popular appeal on the home front, they hardened bellicose attitudes on the other side far more than American and Soviet politicians realized.

As Soviet dissident Boris Kagarlitsky has pointed out in *The Thinking Reed,* the way of thinking of Stalinists is very similar to that of Reaganite neoconservatives both psychologically and ideologically. "They're always talking about national pride, traditional values, moral climate, while at the same time urging struggle against subversive external influences, liberal tendencies of an allegedly counterproductive nature."[2]

Exaggerated fear of an opponent is one of the two forms of delusion often associated with paranoid personalities. The other form of paranoia shared by U.S. and Soviet leaders is macho pride and narcissism. Macho pride is a form of delusion of grandeur that first blinds a leader, then his followers, and thus paves the way for aggression. It often accompanies an overstated fear of an opponent's strength and hostility. In a psychotic person, delusions of persecution stem from a projection of one's inner conflicts, which are too painful to acknowledge, onto other people. On the other hand, delusions of grandeur are also based on dissatisfaction with oneself. They are derived in part from delusions of persecution ("They must think I am important since they persecute me") and in part from a cover-up of the individual's basic sense of weakness and unworthiness. These personality descriptions fit Hitler and Stalin, not to mention Ronald Reagan and Leonid Brezhnev, like a glove.[3]

Both the United States and the Soviet Union have an excessively high moral self-image. We Americans believe we can do no wrong. Although the Vietnam War caused some American leaders to be hesitant about intervening in foreign conflicts, it did not deter President Reagan in Grenada, Beirut, Libya, Nicaragua, or the Persian Gulf. Soviet leaders justified their 1979 intervention in Afghanistan as a necessary defensive action to prevent the United States from destabilizing its socialist neighbor.

THE EVIL EMPIRE

Nothing more accurately portrayed the heart and soul of the Reagan administration's eight-year anticommunist crusade than the President's 1983 "evil empire" slur. It characterized what came to be the most vitriolic attack ever waged by an American president against a foreign nation since the end of World War II. There appeared to be no limitations on the amount of anti-Soviet venom Reagan was prepared to spread in the name of "freedom." Just prior to his 1984 landslide reelection, while preparing for one of his weekly Saturday-afternoon radio broadcasts, he said, "My fellow Americans, I am pleased to tell you I just signed legislation which outlaws Russia forever. The bombing begins in five minutes." And the American people loved every minute of it.

To support its claim that the Soviet Union is an evil empire, the Reagan administration embarked on a broad-based campaign of accusations of Soviet adventurism, Soviet arms-treaty violations, Soviet nuclear war plans, Soviet use of chemical warfare, Soviet human-rights violations, and Soviet support of international terrorism.[4]

According to Seymour Hersh in his book, *The Target Is Destroyed,* within a few hours after the Soviets shot down Korean Air Lines Flight 007 on 31 August 1983, killing 269 people, American intelligence agencies had concluded that the commercial airliner had been attacked in error. The Soviet pilots believed that Flight 007 was an American RC-135 reconnaissance plane that had been in the area that night.

With full knowledge of the actual circumstances surrounding the KAL tragedy, the Reagan administration did everything in its power to suggest to the media that the Soviets had knowingly shot down the Korean airliner. In one speech Reagan said, "Make no mistake about it, this attack was not just against ourselves or the Republic of Korea. This was the Soviet Union against the world and the moral precepts which guide human relations among people everywhere." Continuing, he asserted, "It was an act of barbarism born of a society which wantonly disregards individual rights and the value of human life and seeks constantly to expand and dominate other nations."

But on 3 July 1988, when the crew of the guided-missile cruiser USS Vincennes mistook Iran Air Flight 655 for an Iranian F-14 fighter and shot down the airliner killing 290 people, the Reagan administration attempted to blame Iran. A few weeks later, Admiral William J. Crowe, Jr., Chairman of the Joint Chiefs of Staff, said, "I believe the actions of Iran were the proximate cause of this accident and would argue that Iran must bear the principal responsibility for the tragedy." Soviet leader Gorbachev said nothing about American involvement in downing Iran Air Flight 655.

STALIN'S REIGN OF TERROR

The forced collectivization of agriculture, the centralization of the economy, the political purges, the secret police, and the gulag penal-labor camps are all an integral part of the American perception of the atrocities imposed on the Soviet people by Stalin. Although historians disagree widely on the number of deaths caused by Stalin, millions of Soviet people were either murdered or executed for their political views or died from torture, starvation, or disease.

This grim period in Soviet history was made even more real through the novels of Aleksandr Solzhenitsyn. *The Gulag Archipelago* and other Solzhenitsyn novels graphically portray the pain and suffering endured by the Soviet people under Stalin. In *The Gulag Archipelago*, Solzhenitsyn asserts without any evidence whatsoever that there were twelve million people in Soviet labor camps at the end of the 1930s of whom six million were political prisoners. Even though Solzhenitsyn's figures were sheer invention, they were often used by Sovietologists as indisputable facts.[5]

Sovietologists have conveniently fitted the events of the 1930s to match the American stereotype of the Soviet Union—a totalitarian dictatorship with no concern for human rights. V. L. Allen has suggested that Sovietologists have typically made three common assumptions about this period in Soviet history. First, they have lumped everything that happened during this period into a single totality, which they call the "Great Purge" or the "Great Terror." Second, they assume that this totality had a single common cause, namely Stalin. Third, they assume that the "Great Purge" took place on a mammoth scale, indeed that it pervaded the entire country.[6]

Allen shows convincingly that there was no single cause of the purges in the 1930s, but rather there were at least three distinctly different phenomena taking place simultaneously in the Soviet Union during this period. First, there were indeed purges of members of the Communist party, including public trials of well-known politicians and military officers accused of treason. Second, there was also an antibureaucratic campaign waged against middle-level party officials and government bureaucrats—not unlike the Cultural Revolution in China under Mao Zedong. Third, there was a paranoia surrounding attempts by alleged fascists to destabilize the Soviet government and stage a coup d'etat in collaboration with either Nazi Germany or Japan. Although these events overlapped in time, they each had an independent life of their own—a fact which was fully understood by the Soviet people.[7]

When the United States and the Soviet Union were allies during World War II, we were willing to overlook Stalin's atrocities, just as we were willing to forgive Germany and Japan after World War II.

MARXIST-LENINIST IDEOLOGY

In his early speeches Mr. Gorbachev occasionally lapsed into anticapitalistic, Marxist-Leninist rhetoric. Although these speeches were laced with quotations from Lenin, they were much less strident than those of Stalin, Khrushchev, and Brezhnev. Gone was the Leninist doctrine of an inevitable, final, physical battle between capitalism and communism in which communism would ultimately prevail. Instead, there were frequent references to Lenin's New Economic Policy (NEP) of the 1920s and how it was used to overcome some of the disastrous results of War Communism between 1918 and 1921. Not only is Lenin now virtually ignored by Gorbachev, but the Soviet press began openly criticizing him in 1988.

Most of what is happening in the Soviet Union today has little or nothing to do with Marxist-Leninist ideology. It has much more to do with political pragmatism. The Soviet Union is moving towards the type of democratic socialism found in Sweden, Finland, Austria, and Canada. In Eastern Europe, the old communist parties are now either completely defunct or in the process of being reconstituted as democratic socialist parties.

NAYSAYERS

I am convinced that the political will existed in Moscow in the mid-1970s not only to sustain détente, but to extend it beyond the initial boundaries defined by Richard Nixon and Leonid Brezhnev. The intellectual foundation was in place on which to begin introducing Gorbachev-style reforms ten years earlier than was actually the case. Although the CIA and many Sovietologists were aware of these possibilities, they were never shared with the American public nor the Congress. If Presidents Jimmy Carter and Ronald Reagan had given the Soviets just a modicum of positive encouragement, détente might have survived, and the cold war could have ended at least ten years earlier. But that was not to be.

Instead, throughout the late 1970s and early 1980s, self-serving American Sovietologists—who live in the temple of doom—convinced the American public that the Soviet Union single-handedly killed détente through its military buildup, its aggressive behavior in the Third World, its 1979 invasion of Afghanistan, and its implicit support of martial law in Poland in 1981. I believe that it was not the Soviet Union who killed détente but rather a coalition of right-wing American anticommunists consisting of anti-Soviet emigres from the Soviet Union, Eastern Europe, and Cuba; the Israel lobby; ultraconservative political foundations and think tanks; a group of scientific technocrats; and a number of high priests of the military-industrial complex. I will show how this group deliberately set out to end détente, kill the SALT II treaty, elect Ronald Reagan president, and prolong the cold war unnecessarily for over a decade.

The Emigrés

Since the end of World War II American foreign policy toward the Soviet Union has been unduly influenced by a small band of extremely powerful anti-Soviet emigrés, including former-Nazi war criminals, Eastern Europeans, Soviets, and Cubans. These highly vocal emigrés have played a major role in shaping our cold war foreign policy beginning with the Truman Doctrine in 1947 and continuing with the Berlin airlift, the Korean War, the Bay of Pigs invasion, the Vietnam War, the Jackson–Vanik amendment, U.S. aid to the Nicaraguan contras, and President Reagan's massive military buildup.

Although most Nazi war criminals are now dead, other emigrés such as Zbigniew Brzezinski, Richard Pipes, Aleksandr I. Solzhenitsyn, and Edward Teller exerted enormous influence over our foreign policy during the late 1970s and early 1980s.

Having suffered personally at the hands of the Soviets, embittered emigrés have helped energize a substantial network of right-wing think tanks, institutes, and political organizations whose aim is to make the American people more aware of the perceived threat to the United States.

In the case of the Eastern Europeans and the Soviets, their hostility towards the Soviet Union is further accentuated by the guilt they feel for having left their respective countries in the first place. Polish emigrés, for example, have a deeply felt psychological need to justify their decision to leave Poland. By expressing their strong negative feelings against Soviet communism, they can at least partially assuage the pain associated with their guilt.

Emigrés are certainly entitled to their opinions, but all too often theirs have been the only views heard by our government.

Nazi War Criminals

When Nazi Germany surrendered on 7 May 1945, Nazi fascism—an ideology held by millions of Germans and Eastern Europeans—did not suddenly die. Rather fascism soon began to spread to the United States.

In his highly provocative book entitled *Blowback*, Washington journalist Christopher Simpson has exposed a little-known dark side of the United States government.[8] Simpson documents the sordid story of the role that our government—particularly the CIA—played in creating a network of former-Nazi war criminals to spy on the Soviets and to influence American foreign policy towards the Soviet Union.

The CIA, Radio Liberty, Radio Free Europe, the Voice of America, and other U.S. government agencies employed hundreds of Russians, Ukrainians, Latvians, and other Eastern Europeans who had collaborated with the Nazis during the occupation of their homelands. Former Schutzstaffel (SS) officers were hired for their expertise in anticommunist propaganda, psychological warfare, and even guerrilla warfare. Nazi war criminals were among the primary beneficiaries of the cold war. American anticommunist hysteria provided a convenient cover-up for thousands of them to escape prosecution for the murders and other crimes they committed during World War II. Since it was clearly in their self-interest to do so, these Nazi veterans consistently exaggerated the threat the Soviet Union posed to the United States. Their influence in shaping our attitudes and foreign policy towards the Soviet Union has been enormous.

Essentially the quid pro quo between our government and the Nazis brought to this country was very straightforward—"You tell us what we want to hear about the Russians, and we will grant you immunity from prosecution for your war crimes." Since the Nazis already hated the Russians, they had little difficulty in living up to their end of the bargain.

Simpson has carefully documented the roles played by former Secretary of State John Foster Dulles, former CIA Director Allen Dulles, and noted diplomat George F. Kennan in helping organize clandestine programs that brought high-ranking Nazi war criminals to America, including former SS officers Klaus Barbie, Otto von Bolschwing, and General Walter Dornberger; former honorary SS officer Wernher von Braun; and members of Adolf Eichmann's personal staff—to mention only a few.

Fledgling Russian-studies programs provided an attractive haven for displaced Nazis looking for a respectable identity in academia. Is it any wonder that most Russian-studies programs in the United States have maintained a strong anti-Soviet bias all of these years?

These Nazi emigrés managed to convince our government that, although we had won the war with Germany, Soviet communism was a far greater threat to our national security. American diplomats and politicians were looking for answers to explain Stalin's takeover of Eastern Europe. Nazi war criminals posing as experts on the Soviet Union were able to provide quick and simple answers to what in reality was a very complex problem.

By equating Soviet communism with Nazi fascism, these Nazi sympathizers in effect helped prolong World War II unnecessarily for another forty-five years — only now it was known as the cold war.

Although communism has many well-known flaws, fascism it is not. Fascism of the brand practiced by Benito Mussolini and Adolf Hitler was an ideology based on militarism, exaggerated nationalism, and extreme racism. Communism, on the other hand, rests on egalitarianism, class struggle, and the dictatorship of the proletariat. Stalin—like Mussolini and Hitler—was a ruthless military dictator who was responsible directly or indirectly for the deaths of millions of Soviets in the 1930s and 1940s. Stalin died in 1953 (as did many of his policies shortly thereafter), but anti-Sovietism in the United States continued unabated through the 1980s.

Mussolini said, in *The Doctrine of Fascism*, "War alone keys up all human energies to their maximum tension, and sets the seal of nobility on . . . peoples." "Mankind has grown strong in eternal struggles, and it will only perish through eternal peace," and " . . . might alone makes right," said Adolf Hitler in *Mein Kampf*. There are no comparable statements attributed to either Karl Marx, Vladimir Lenin, or any twentieth-century Soviet leader.

Although there is anti-Semitism in the Soviet Union, it can hardly be compared to the Holocaust. Likewise, Brezhnev was responsible for the deaths of tens of thousands of Afghans, but millions lost their lives when Hitler invaded the Soviet Union.

EASTERN EUROPEANS

Although few former-Nazi war criminals are still alive, our foreign policy continues to be influenced by a small number of highly opinionated Eastern European emigrés. While these emigrés share a strong hostility towards the Soviet Union, they do not speak for all of the people in their respective home countries. Most of them immigrated to the United States because they were very unhappy with life at home. Since most emigrés are so vocal about their anti-Soviet feelings, Americans conclude that everyone in Eastern Europe is equally unhappy with life there. Even totally unknown emigrés soon learn that they can attract large audiences on the Rotary Club circuit by telling conservative Americans what they want to hear; namely, how awful the Soviet Union is. One of our most destructive forms of tension-increasing activity has been the practice of making national heroes out of Soviet defectors— particularly celebrities from the arts, well-known sports figures, refuseniks, and former KGB officers. Even though some of these emigrés have turned out to be charlatans and outright thugs, they are the people to whom the CIA, the Pentagon, and the Congress turn for advice on our foreign policy.

Two Polish emigrés, Zbigniew Brzezinski and Richard Pipes, played a major role in prolonging the cold war during the late 1970s and early 1980s. As President Jimmy Carter's National Security Advisor, Brzezinski provided the intellectual basis for Ronald Reagan's "evil empire" policy. Harvard professor Richard Pipes, Reagan's National Security Council "expert" on Soviet affairs, greatly enhanced the pattern of anti-Soviet rhetoric initiated by Brzezinski after the Soviets invaded Afghanistan in 1979.

I first met Zbigniew Brzezinski—the son of a Polish diplomat—at Duke University in December 1987. Although charming, witty, and very aristocratic, Brzezinski's intense hatred of the Soviet Union is diabolic. His anti-Soviet lecture to a standing-room-only audience of cheering Duke students was so full of hate that it embarrassed my wife Magdalena—herself a Polish emigŕe not noted for her sanguine views on the Soviet Union.

Brzezinski cynically transformed Carter's human-rights policy into a mechanism for destabilizing U.S.–Soviet relations. He used the Soviet invasion of Afghanistan to consolidate his position in the White House, drive Secretary of State Cyrus Vance out of office, and gain control of U.S. foreign policy.

Nowhere are Brzezinski's anti-Soviet biases more blatant than in his 1986 book *Game Plan*. A year after Gorbachev had come to power Brzezinski was still predicting that the U.S.–Soviet conflict would go on endlessly. He not only accused the Soviets of aspiring to be the "Third Rome" in their efforts to achieve global supremacy,[9] but he suggested that the "predatory character of Great Russian imperialism is undeniable."[10] His lukewarm support for President Carter's SALT II Treaty was fully understandable in light of his view that arms control was promoted by the Soviets as a "political tool to promote U.S. strategic impotence."[11] Brzezinski enthusiastically embraced President Reagan's Strategic Defense Initiative and called for tripling the funding of Radio Liberty and Radio Free Europe.

Brzezinski's harsh anti-Soviet views were always welcomed at the Reagan White House. In 1988 he revealed his true colors by endorsing George Bush. Among the organizations used by Brzezinski to disseminate his anticommunist venom in the 1980s were the conservative Washington-based Center for Strategic and International Studies, the President's Foreign Intelligence Advisory Board, the National Endowment for Democracy, Freedom House, and the Trilateral Commission.

In his latest book, *The Grand Failure*, Brzezinski gloats over the demise of Soviet communism, equates Stalinism with communism, ridicules *glasnost* and *perestroika,* and suggests that, "Hitler was as much a Leninist as Stalin was a Nazi."[12]

Second only to Brzezinski among Eastern European emigrés who have helped prolong the cold war is Harvard historian Richard Pipes. Pipes gained national attention in January 1976 as the chairman of the so-called Team B authorized by then CIA Director George Bush to produce a "competitive analysis" of CIA data. The CIA was accused by Team B members of having an "arms-control bias." The final Team B report portrayed the Soviet Union in extremely gloomy, threatening terms.[13]

Under the leadership of Professor Pipes, Team B was redesignated the Committee on the Present Danger (CPD) on 11 November 1976—two days after Jimmy Carter was elected president. The stated purpose of the CPD was "to alert American policymakers and opinion leaders and the public at large to the ominous Soviet military buildup and its implications, and to the unfavorable trends in the U.S.–Soviet military balance." The CPD became the driving force underlying American foreign policy toward the Soviet Union during the late 1970s and early 1980s.

Pipes was one of sixty CPD members who found their way into high-ranking positions in the Reagan administration by 1984. He was Director of East European and Soviet Affairs for the National Security Council under President Reagan. In his 1984 book, *Survival Is Not Enough,*[14] Pipes laid out his own anti-Soviet agenda as well as that of the CPD, which provided the rationale underlying the Reagan military buildup.

Since the 1950s, Sovietologists such as Brzezinski and Pipes have blamed all of Eastern Europe's woes on Soviet-style communism. In a recent collection of essays entitled *The Origins of Backwardness in Eastern Europe*, editor Daniel Chirot has effectively dispelled this myth.[15] These essayists demonstrate that most of the political and economic problems found in Poland, Hungary, Czechoslovakia, Bulgaria, and Romania have historical origins that predate the Soviet takeover of Eastern Europe by several centuries.

Without exception these countries were isolated, undemocratic, heavily dependent on a relatively weak agricultural sector, and lacking political freedom. Also there has always been basic lack of respect for the individual in most of these countries. Feudalism lasted well into the nineteenth century and vestiges of serfdom persisted right up to the time of the communist takeover in the late 1940s.

Professors Brzezinski and Pipes have also contributed to the divisive role that Poland has played in East–West relations since the 1950s. Egged on by more than eight million Polish-Americans, Radio Free Europe, the CIA, and such politicians as Ronald Reagan, Senator Jesse Helms, Zbigniew Brzezinski, and Richard Pipes, Poland has never accepted the fact that not only was it defeated by Germany in World War II but that it did not get to choose who would occupy it after the war.

Hungarian-born Edward Teller is another Eastern European emigré who suffers from extreme anti-Soviet paranoia. Teller was the father of the hydrogen bomb and is credited with having sold President Reagan on the Strategic Defense Initiative.

Not all Eastern European emigrés are cold warriors. One notable exception is Hungarian-American financier George Soros. Soros has done more to improve East–West relations than industrialist Armand Hammer, but since he operates in a much less ostentatious mode than Hammer, few Americans are familiar with his work.

Since the early 1980s, Soros has contributed millions of dollars to the education of Hungarian managers in market-oriented management practices. He was one of the catalysts and financial backers of the International Management Center in Budapest—the first Western-style business school in the Eastern bloc. He is also involved in supporting Soviet–American exchange initiatives—particularly bringing Soviet academics to the United States.

SOVIETS

Most Soviet-born experts on the Soviet Union tend to be extremely anti-Soviet in what they write and say. For example, even though

Duke University economist Vladimir Treml left the Soviet Union
in 1950, his research always has a decidedly negative twist to it.
Considered to be the foremost American expert on Soviet economic data, Treml concentrates his energy on the Soviet alcohol
problem, the "second economy" (black market), inadequacies of
Soviet economic data, and the vulnerability of the Soviets to trade
sanctions.

Once President Reagan invited Treml to the Oval Office after
the price of crude oil had taken a precipitous downward plunge.
Reagan hoped Treml would tell him that the sharp oil-price
decline would push the Soviet economy over the brink just as his
cold war advisors had promised. To Treml's credit, he could not
bring himself to tell the president what he wanted to hear.

Treml is currently engaged in a major study of the Soviet
second economy in collaboration with another emigré, Professor
Gregory Grossman of the University of California at Berkeley. The
study is based on Radio Liberty interviews of Soviet emigrés.
Treml is but one of many Soviet and Eastern European emigrés
with very close ties to Radio Liberty and Radio Free Europe.

The shrill anti-Soviet views of emigré Dimitri Simes are well
known to Americans, since he is a popular television spokesman
on Soviet affairs. When former Soviet diplomat Arkady N.
Shevchenko was granted political asylum by the United States in
1978, he was given a hero's welcome. His American political stock
rose even higher during the Reagan years. But of all the Soviet
emigrés Nobel laureate Aleksandr I. Solzhenitsyn has had by far
the most negative influence on our foreign policy toward the Soviet
Union.

With the publications of his devastating indictments of the
Soviet Union—*The Gulag Archipelago, Cancer Ward,* and *The First
Circle* —Solzhenitsyn became the instantaneous hero of the anticommunist right wing of American politics. He told them exactly
what they had always wanted to believe about the Soviet Union. It
was truly the source of all that is evil in this world. The fact that
Solzhenitsyn had chosen fiction as the literary form through which
to express his contempt for the Soviet system was unimportant to
his anticommunist admirers.

His 1976 arrival in the United States proved to be a windfall for the CPD and other kindred souls bent on bringing an
end to détente. A kind of symbiotic relationship evolved between

Solzhenitsyn and the far right, which demanded no documentation for his eloquent attacks on the Soviet Union. This was convenient, for he had none.

CUBAN AMERICANS

For over thirty years the aim of our foreign policy towards Cuba has been to try to get Fidel Castro to "cry uncle." Not only have we been unable to force the collapse of Castro's regime, but rather we have increased his economic dependence on the Soviet Union and hardened his bellicose Marxist-Leninist revolutionary spirit. Our Third World foreign policy has been unduly influenced by our paranoid fear of avoiding at any price a "second Cuba."

Castro's nationalization of American-owned property, the abortive 1961 Bay of Pigs invasion, the 1962 Cuban missile crisis, Cuba's military involvement in Africa, the 1980 Mariel sealift, Moscow's Cuban-based electronic eavesdropping network, and President Reagan's decision to put Radio Marti on the air have all contributed to three decades of mutual distrust between the United States and Cuba.

Even with the Soviet Union's $14 million-a-day subsidy, Cuba's economy is hardly thriving. But it certainly is not the failure that President Reagan would have had us believe. As Jay Berman has reported in *The Christian Science Monitor,* old neighborhoods in Havana are being restored, roads are in good repair throughout the island, telephones actually work, it is safe to drink the water, and there are no beggars on the streets. Furthermore, independent health-care agencies have confirmed that Cuba has the best medical care in Latin America.[16]

According to former diplomat Wayne S. Smith in his book *The Closest of Enemies,* our government has finessed numerous opportunities for improved relations with Cuba since 1959.[17] In spite of increasing evidence that Castro is indeed interested in improving ties with the United States, our government has thus far refused to budge one inch. The future of Cuba's $5 billion annual subsidy from the Soviet Union is uncertain, and it must now pay for its imports from Eastern Europe in hard currency. The first Cuban troops began leaving Angola in 1989 and all fifty thousand are scheduled to be out by 1991. Castro has released additional political prisoners and has indicated increased flexibility towards religion—particularly Roman Catholicism.

Over 110 countries maintain diplomatic relations with Cuba, including all of out NATO allies and most Latin American nations. Our government not only refuses to recognize Cuba diplomatically, but continues to treat it as a political pariah. Even though Gorbachev has distanced himself from Castro's revolutionary brand of communism, American politicians continue to vilify Cuba. Castro-bashing has always played well.

As John Spicer Nichols has reported in *The Nation*, the underlying force behind the strong anti-Cuban bias that pervades the U.S. Congress is the fanatical anticommunist organization known as the Cuban American National Foundation (CANF).[18] The CANF has an extraordinary track record of success in persuading the Congress to engage in Castro-bashing activities. CANF members not only reject any form of rapprochement with Cuba but effectively brand anyone who disagrees with their right-wing policies as a communist sympathizer.

These rabid anticommunists not only have contaminated our foreign policy for three decades, but they have an unruly habit of showing up anywhere there is anticommunist covert activity involving our government, including presidential assassination plots, the Watergate break-in, and the CIA operations in Vietnam, Nicaragua, and Honduras.

Through the efforts of the Cuban-American lobby, a tiny island of only ten million inhabitants has effectively paralyzed U.S. foreign policy in Latin America for over thirty years. Any U.S. policy action anywhere in Latin American must be able to pass muster with the anti-Castro crowd on Capitol Hill—and that is a very tough test to pass.

Recognizing the power that the Cuban Americans have exercised to block U.S. economic aid to the Soviet Union, in May 1990 Gorbachev sent a Soviet delegation to Miami to meet with Cuban exiles, including Jorge Mas Canosa, chairman of CANF. He hoped to soften their opposition to expanded U.S.–Soviet economic relations.

The Military-Industrial Complex

In 1982, President Reagan became the first U.S. president to tell his people that the United States no longer held the lead in the arms race with the Soviet Union. He repeatedly traded on the paranoid fear of communism to gain public and congressional support for his staggering military program. He not only convinced Congress that the weapons he wanted were urgently needed to redress what he called an "adverse imbalance" of military power, but that the Soviets held a definite margin of "strategic superiority" over the United States.

In his 1986 book, *The Myth of Soviet Military Supremacy*, Tom Gervasi showed that not only had the Soviet Union never had a margin of strategic superiority over the United States, but it probably never would.[19] Instead it was the United States that held the lead in strategic power by virtually every significant measure. In most categories of military hardware, the United States and NATO allies actually held a numerical lead over the Soviet bloc. In a few categories such as tanks where the Soviets held the numerical edge, the Soviet lead was more than offset by NATO's advantage in terms of quality.[20]

President Reagan's $2.2 trillion military buildup was based on the lie of the century—a lie which our Congress, our press, and the American public were eager to buy into. The Committee on the Present Danger, the Pentagon, and the CIA did a masterful job of convincing the American people that we were in imminent danger.

Why does the Pentagon continue to prepare for a Soviet threat, if there is more than sufficient military force in place to meet any conceivable Soviet challenge that might arise? Why did the Reagan administration deceive and manipulate the American people into supporting what was essentially a wholly gratuitous effort? Why does President George Bush resist declaring a "peace dividend"? The answer is that there is no other way to meet the never-ending demands of what President Dwight D. Eisenhower called the military-industrial complex. In his farewell address to the American people on 17 January 1961, President Eisenhower defined the problem we face today all too well:

> In the councils of government, we must guard against the acquisition of unwarranted influence, whether sought or unsought, by the military-industrial complex. The potential for disastrous rise of misplaced power exists and will persist.
>
> We must never let the weight of this combination endanger our liberties or democratic processes. We should take nothing for granted. Only an alert and knowledgeable citizenry can

compel the proper meshing of the huge industrial and military machinery of defense with our peaceful methods and goals so that security and liberty may prosper together.[21]

The military-industrial complex has become the most powerful and the least democratic institution in the United States today. It is powerful not only because it appeals to our patriotism and exploits our need for security, but also because it distributes income and wealth. The more wealth the military establishment can control, the more dependent on it do business, labor, and government become. The more dependent they become on the military, the more actively they will support its goals and objectives.[22]

For years the political left in our country has portrayed the military-industrial complex—particularly defense contractors—as the real villains of the cold war. To be sure the defense industry bears its share of the blame for prolonging the hostilities between the United States and the Soviet Union. But on another level, defense contractors are simply patriotic Americans who are out to make a fast buck and respond to the grim accounts of Soviet aggression reported by Sovietologists like Zbigniew Brzezinski, Richard Pipes, and Edward Teller. Which comes first, the Sovietologists who provide the rationale justifying the defense buildup, or the military-industrial complex, which directly or indirectly keeps the Sovietologists in business?

Right-Wing Think Tanks

COMMITTEE ON THE PRESENT DANGER

Our demoralizing defeat in Vietnam, the Nixon–Brezhnev era of détente, the Watergate affair, and the 1976 election of Jimmy Carter created a temporary right-wing political vacuum from which the Committee on the Present Danger emerged. The CPD became the political catalyst behind a plethora of right-wing philanthropic foundations, think tanks, and lobbying groups whose objectives included putting an end to détente, electing Ronald Reagan president, and bringing the Soviet Union to its knees. It successfully achieved most of its objectives, but in so doing prolonged the cold war for at least another fifteen years at enormous cost to the American taxpayers and the rest of the world.

The primary objectives of the CPD were to frighten the American people into believing the Soviet threat was imminent and to persuade our Congress to foot the bill for the largest peacetime military buildup in history. This objective was made crystal clear in the CPD's 11 November 1976 policy statement:

Our country is in a period of danger, and the danger is increasing. Unless decisive steps are taken to alert the nation, and to change the course of its policy, our economic and military capacity will become inadequate to assure peace and security.

The principal threat to our nation, to world peace, and to the cause of human freedom is the Soviet drive for dominance based upon an unparalleled military buildup.

The Soviet Union has not altered its long-held goal of a world dominated from a single center—Moscow.

For more than a decade, the Soviet Union has been enlarging and improving both its strategic and its conventional military forces far more rapidly than the United States and its allies. Soviet military power and its rate of growth cannot be explained or justified by considerations of self-defense.

The process of Soviet expansion and the worldwide deployment of its military power threaten our interest in the political independence of our friends and allies, their and our fair access to raw materials,the freedom of the seas, and in avoiding a preponderance of adversary power.

This ominous language found a receptive audience among Americans eager to find a scapegoat for declining U.S. influence abroad. It was far easier to blame our foreign policy failures on the Soviets than to endure the painful process of self-examination. Table 3–1 contains a partial list of CPD directors who held important positions in the Reagan administration.

The CPD, under the leadership of former Deputy Secretary of Defense Paul H. Nitze, played a major role in blocking Senate ratification of the SALT II treaty. The Soviet Union's invasion of Afghanistan made the CPD's SALT II blitz a lot easier than might otherwise have been the case. After the invasion, no one in the Senate wanted to risk appearing "soft on communism."

The CPD provided the anti-Soviet script that helped persuade the Congress to spend hundreds of billions of dollars in unnecessary

Table 3–1
Reagan Administration Appointees from the Board of
Directors of the Committee on the Present Danger

Name	Title
Ronald Reagan	President of the United States
Kenneth L. Adelman	Director, Arms Control and Disarmament Agency
Richard V. Allen	Assistant to the President for National Security Affairs
James L. Buckley	President, Radio Free Europe/Radio Liberty
William J. Casey	Director, CIA
Fred Charles Iklé	Under Secretary of Defense for Policy
Max M. Kampelman	Chairman, U.S. Delegation to Conference on Security and Cooperation in Europe
Jeane J. Kirkpatrick	United Nations Ambassador
John F. Lehman, Jr.	Secretary of the Navy
Paul H. Nitze	Chief Negotiator to Intermediate Range Nuclear Forces Talks
	Special Representative for Arms Control and Disarmament Negotiations
Richard N. Perle	Assistant Secretary of Defense for International Security Policy
Eugene V. Rostow	Director, Arms Control and Disarmament Agency
Richard M. Scaife	Member, President's Commission on Broadcasting to Cuba
George P. Schultz	Secretary of State
Edward Teller	Member, White House Science Council

Source: Charles Tyroler II (editor), *Alerting America.* Washington: Pergamon-Brassey's International Defense Publishers, 1984, pp. ix–xi.

military outlays. Among the major new warfighting systems supported by the CPD were the MX missile, the Trident II missile, the Stealth bomber, and the Strategic Defense Initiative.

PHILANTHROPIC FOUNDATIONS

Although the CPD was the most important political catalyst for the right wing's frontal assault on détente, several policy-analysis groups provided additional leverage and intellectual energy to convince the American people that it was in their self-interest to rekindle the cold war flame in the late 1970s and early 1980s. The Hoover Institution, the Rand Corporation, the Center for Strategic and International Studies, the American Enterprise Institute, the Heritage Foundation, and a dozen or so other right-wing think tanks produced endless tomes justifying the need to rebuild America's military might. Financial support for the CPD and these anticommunist institutes was provided by a network of interlocking conservative foundations such as the Carthage Foundation, the Sarah Scaife Foundation, the John M. Olin Foundation, the Fannie and John Hertz Foundation, the Pew Charitable Trusts, and the National Endowment for Democracy. CPD members were well represented as either consultants to these think tanks and foundations or as members of their boards of directors.

The CPD had access to the financial resources, the contacts, and the political power to implement a full-court press on the U.S. Congress between 1976 and 1990. Just as the ancient Egyptians built pyramids to deny their mortality; the CPD built its own pyramids—MX missiles, Stealth bombers, space-based laser weapons, and the like.

To illustrate how the CPD works, consider the case of one of its founding members, Richard M. Scaife, publisher of the Tribune-Review Publishing Company. Scaife was the chairman of two Pittsburgh-based foundations—the Carthage Foundation and the Sarah Scaife Foundation—both of which were largely endowed by Gulf Oil. Both of Scaife's foundations were major supporters of the CPD.[23] They also supported several of the major conservative think tanks including the Cato Institute, the Center for Strategic and International Studies (CSIS), the Heritage Foundation, and the Hoover Institution, as well as a number of the smaller anticommunist policy-analysis groups such as Freedom House, chaired by CPD member Max M. Kampelman, and the National Strategy Information Center, whose president was CPD member Frank R. Barnett. Table 3–2 contains a partial list of anticommunist think tanks supported by the Scaife Foundation in 1988.

Unique among the anti-Soviet philanthropic foundations is the Fannie and John Hertz Foundation located in Livermore, California, near the Lawrence Livermore National Laboratory.[24] John D. Hertz of Yellow Cab and Hertz rental car fame created the foundation

Table 3–2
Anticommunist Think Tanks Supported by the
Sarah Scaife Foundation in 1988

Institute	Amount of Support
Cato Institute	$ 75,000
Committee for the Free World	$ 35,000
Committee on the Present Danger	$ 75,000
Foreign Policy Research Institute	$ 50,000
Freedom House	$ 50,000
Heritage Foundation	$850,000
National Endowment for Democracy	$ 10,000
National Strategy Information Center	$206,000
Hoover Institution	$365,000

Source: *Annual Report 1988,* Sarah Scaife Foundation, Pittsburgh, Pennsylvania, 1988, pp. 13–20.

to help bright young American scientists cope with what he perceived to be the serious technological threat posed by the Soviet Union. The foundation grants $12,500 annual fellowships to support the Ph.D. training of exceptionally bright graduate students in the applied physical sciences.

In the 1950s, CPD member and father of the hydrogen bomb Edward Teller became a director of the Hertz Foundation as well as an interviewer for the fellowship program. Since that time the foundation moved from Chicago to Livermore where Teller was located, and the Livermore nuclear-weapons lab became the largest employer of Hertz Fellows and alumni.

According to *New York Times* writer Philip M. Boffey and his coauthors of *Claiming the Heavens,* many of the scientific concepts on which Star Wars is based originated with Hertz Fellows working at Livermore lab. In 1979 in a scientific breakthrough heralded as "the most innovative idea in nuclear weaponry since the hydrogen bomb," Peter Hagelstein, a twenty-four-year-old physicist, became the first person to create a nuclear x-ray laser.[25] Much of the scientific basis for believing Star Wars might just be possible stems from Hagelstein's invention.

POLICY ANALYSIS GROUPS

Most of the "research and analysis" used by the CPD to sabotage SALT II, kill détente, and justify the Reagan–Weinberger defense buildup was done by a group of conservative, anticommunist think tanks. Former high-ranking Reagan administration officials and emigres from the Soviet Union and Eastern Europe were well represented on the boards of directors and professional staffs of these right-wing think tanks. Old cold warriors never die. They simply take refuge in one of the prestigious anticommunist think tanks after they take leave of their positions of power.

The oldest and most prestigious right-wing think tank—because of its Stanford University connection—is the Hoover Institution on War, Revolution, and Peace, founded by Herbert Hoover in 1919. Hoover's Board of Overseers includes CPD members Jeane J. Kirkpatrick, Hewlett–Packard chairman David Packard, Donald H. Rumsfeld, and Richard M. Scaife. Among the Hoover Institution's fellows and visiting scholars are several former–Reagan-administration officials, NSC adviser Richard V. Allen, Attorney General Edwin Meese, and President Reagan himself. Other Hoover fellows are Aleksandr I. Solzhenitsyn and Edward Teller, as well as CPD members Seymour M. Lipset and William R. Van Cleave.

Created in 1948 to do sophisticated contract research for the U.S. Air Force, the RAND Corporation (RAND) with its $85 million annual budget has had enormous influence on U.S. foreign policy and defense policy. Its research staff includes many world-class scientists. RAND combines the knowledge of experts in the physical, social, and biological sciences with that of specialists in mathematics, engineering, and computer science. Today, besides the Air Force, the Army, and the Office of the Secretary of Defense, RAND has over seventy other sponsors. Although most of the conservative think tanks have close ties to the CIA, RAND is one of the few that openly acknowledges its CIA support.

The Washington-based Center for Strategic and International Studies claims to be "an independent institution for public policy research in the field of foreign and national security affairs." Yet when one examines the list of right-wing foundations and major defense contractors who support CSIS, it is hard to imagine how it could conceivably be "independent." Its major supporters include Boeing, General Dynamics, IBM, LTV, Rockwell International, General Electric, Grumman, Lockheed, and McDonnell Douglas.

The cold war is the economic lifeblood of these companies. Without the Soviet threat, some of them would either cease to exist or operate on a much smaller scale than is the case today. Former National Security Council Advisors Zbigniew Brzezinski and Robert McFarlane, who are CSIS counselors, as well as many other CSIS advisers over the years, have done everything possible to prolong the cold war. The defense industry supported CSIS because CSIS told the American people what the military industrial complex wanted them to believe—the only way to protect ourselves from the Soviet Union was to spend ever-increasing amounts on military defense.

Another highly visible Washington-based think tank during the Reagan years was the American Enterprise Institute for Public Policy Research (AEI). Its prestigious board of trustees is made up primarily of the CEOs of blue-chip banks and corporations. Neoconservative anticommunist Irving Kristol is John M. Olin Distinguished Fellow at AEI. Other AEI fellows include CPD members Jeane J. Kirkpatrick, Richard N. Perle, and Herbert Stein. Mr. Perle, known best for the vehemence of his anti-Soviet views, organizes monthly luncheons for senior editors and columnists of the nation's leading newspapers, magazines, and networks to explore such issues as U.S.–Soviet relations, arms-control agreements, the Strategic Defense Initiative, and the continued Soviet threat. AEI scholars are often cited in newspapers, magazines, and broadcast-news reports and they appear frequently on all of the major television news programs including *Nightline,* the *Today Show, Good Morning America, Meet the Press,* and *Face the Nation.*

Established in 1973, the Heritage Foundation was one of the most important script writers for Ronald Reagan. It opposed the SALT II and INF treaties as well as trade and joint ventures with the Soviet Union. It strongly supported all of Reagan's military programs, but particularly the militarization of space and the Strategic Defense Initiative.

One month after President Reagan met General Secretary Gorbachev in Moscow in the summer of 1988, yet another anti-Soviet think tank opened its doors in Washington—the Center for Security Policy (CSP). Headed up by Frank J. Gaffney, Jr., the CSP is one of the most militantly anti-Soviet policy groups to appear on the Washington scene. Gaffney was Deputy Assistant Secretary of Defense for Nuclear Forces and Arms Control Policy under Assistant Secretary Richard Perle. The board of advisers of the CSP contains no less than eleven CPD members plus spy novelist Tom Clancy. According to Mr. Gaffney, the CSP "deals exclusively with current defense and foreign policy issues." Star Wars, technology transfer, and U.S.–Soviet trade are among the issues about which the CSP is concerned. The essence of the CSP's distrustful view of the Soviet Union is contained in one of its working papers dated 25 January 1989:

> . . . Gorbachev's use of *perestroika* and *glasnost* to advance Soviet foreign policy constitutes a sophisticated form of Lenin's classic adversarial strategy of "peaceful coexistence" to woo the democracies while rebuilding strength.

These are but a few of the most important right wing policy analysis groups. Others include the Hudson Institute, the Cato Institute, Freedom House, the Committee for the Free World, the Institute for Democracy in Eastern Europe, the International Security Council, and the American Security Council.

COLD WAR PUNDITS

To leverage their anti-Soviet gloom and doom the CPD and the right-wing think tanks relied on a tight network of highly opinionated, anti-Soviet intellectual hardhats—including editors and journalists such as Jeane J. Kirkpatrick, Richard N. Perle, Irving Kristol, A. M. Rosenthal, William Safire, George Will, Norman Podhoretz, Ben J. Wattenberg, William F. Buckley, Jr., Patrick Buchanan, Rowland Evans, and Robert Novak. These pundits helped convince many Americans of the irreversibility and malignant nature of Soviet foreign policy, and that communism was a euphemism for organized savagery and lust.

In response to Gorbachev's sweeping reforms, these diehard cold warriors claimed that *glasnost* and *perestroika* were a Soviet sham—a smokescreen—and that the real Gorbachev would soon emerge and lead the Soviet Union on a path back to Stalinism and repression. With each dramatic change in the Soviet Union, these pundits raised the ante higher for Gorbachev to prove that he was real. Unable to break away from the old rhetoric, their stale anti-Soviet message become even less credible with each new Gorbachev reform.

Radio USA

The Chinese students in Tiananmen Square were unrealistically and irresponsibly egged on by the Voice of America (VOA) in May 1989, just as Radio Free Europe (RFE) raised the expectations of Hungarian dissidents in 1956, Czechoslovaks in 1968, and Poles in 1981. In each case the change agents were led to believe that if they made the first move, U.S. support would be forthcoming. The only support provided by our government to any of these dissident groups was more anticommunist rhetoric beamed into the respective countries by VOA and RFE. In each case the expectations of the would-be revolutionaries were violently crushed and a period of even greater political repression ensued.

For forty years Radio USA—the Voice of America, Radio Free Europe, and its sister station Radio Liberty—has broadcast anticommunist propaganda aimed primarily at socialist countries. Although VOA first went on the air on 24 February 1942, during World War II, it did not become a cold war policy instrument until the late 1940s under President Harry Truman. Operated by the United States Information Agency (USIA), VOA broadcasts in English and forty-two other languages to an estimated weekly worldwide audience of 129 million listeners. The programming consists of news, editorials reflecting official U.S. government policies, and programs that VOA claimed "portray various aspects of American society and culture and which reflect the variety of American opinion on major issues."

As a result of an intense lobbying effort by the Cuban American National Foundation, radio broadcasts to Cuba on the Voice of America's Radio Marti began 20 May 1985. Named for Cuban patriot José Marti, Radio Marti provides "news, commentary, and other information about events in Cuba and elsewhere to promote the cause of freedom in Cuba." TV Marti began broadcasting in early 1990.

The rationale underlying Radio USA was that millions of people in communist countries could be turned against communism if they were promised increased political, economic, and religious freedom and the end of police-state rule. Radio Free Europe began broadcasting in Eastern Europe in 1950 and Radio Liberation from Bolshevism (renamed Radio Liberty in 1963) began service to the Soviet Union in 1953.

Many of VOA's original employees entered the United States under the auspices of the State Department's Operation Bloodstone which brought the leaders of Nazi collaborationist organizations into this country in the late 1940s.[26] The same was also true of Radio Free Europe and Radio Liberty. These anti-Soviet broadcasting stations have always provided havens for Soviet and Eastern European emigres—many of whom go back and forth between one or more of the right-wing think tanks and Radio USA.

RFE/RL programs were directly sponsored by the CIA until 1973 when a new, so-called public Board for International Broadcasting was established to fund and administer the radio propaganda. Board members include CPD members Lane Kirkland and Michael Novak as well as CPD sympathizer Ben J. Wattenberg.

Even though the radio broadcasts of Radio USA are no longer jammed in either the Soviet Union or Eastern Europe, it continues to broadcast its message of gloom and doom. Despite the major political changes that have taken place in the Soviet Union and Eastern Europe, Congress is unlikely to touch the sacrosanct budget of Radio USA. Indeed, a new $290 million relay station is in the works for Israel.

The High Priests of the Temple of Doom

Since 1974, a tightly knit group of ten very powerful and very conservative professional naysayers has had a profound influence on our foreign policy towards the Soviet Union. I call this group the "high priests of the temple of doom" (table 3–3). The patriarch and spiritual leader of the high priests—but *not* their intellectual leader—was Ronald Reagan. There was a kind of symbiotic relationship between Reagan and the high priests—each using the other to achieve their common objectives.

Of particular interest are the activities of the high priests between 1974 and 1984—the period over which détente was laid to rest and before the first Reagan–Gorbachev summit in Geneva in 1985.

Two of the high priests are no longer living. Although Senator Henry M. Jackson died in 1983 and former CIA Director William J. Casey died in 1987, their influence on our foreign policy lives on. Four of Jackson's proteges were among the most outspoken

Table 3–3
The High Priests of the Temple of Doom

Name	Title
Zbigniew Brzezinski	National Security Advisor to President Carter
William J. Casey (deceased)	Director, Central Intelligence Agency under President Reagan
Henry M. Jackson (deceased)	U.S. Senator and Co-Sponsor of the Jackson–Vanik Amendment
Max M. Kampelman	Chairman, U.S. Delegation to Conference on Security and Cooperation Europe and Head of U.S. Delegation to Negotiations on Nuclear and Space Arms under President Reagan
Richard N. Perle	Assistant Secretary of Defense for International Policy under President Reagan
Richard Pipes	Director of Soviet Affairs, National Security Council under President Reagan
Eugene V. Rostow	Director, Arms Control and Disarmament Agency under President Reagan
Aleksandr I. Solzhenitsyn	Russian Novelist and Noble Laureate
Edward Teller	Scientific Advisor to President Reagan
Caspar Weinberger	Secretary of Defense under President Reagan

anti-Soviet members of Reagan's team. They include former Assistant Secretary of Defense Richard N. Perle, Perle's own protege Frank J. Gaffney, Jr., former Assistant Secretary of State Elliot Abrams, and *Public Opinion* magazine editor Ben J. Wattenberg.

The role of Perle and Gaffney was to make the Soviet Union appear as dangerous and as threatening as possible so as to justify the Reagan military buildup. They achieved unequivocal success in selling their military agenda to the Congress. Of the ten high priests, Perle is by far the most active today in continuing to play out all of the old prejudices. He is one of the principals of the pro-Israel, anti-Soviet lobby, which uses the human-rights issue to destabilize the Soviet Union and make the case for increased U.S. military aid to Israel. Perle once described the Soviet Union as "a place where everyone lies all the time."[27]

Abrams was the point man for U.S. aid to the contras in Nicaragua. His role was to convince the Congress that unless the Sandinistas were driven from power by the CIA that the communists would soon enter the United States through our unprotected Mexican back door. He came very close to succeeding with his Congressional hard sell. Abrams is presently cooling his heels at the Heritage Foundation where he writes op-ed pieces criticizing the Bush administration for being too lenient on Nicaragua and the Soviet Union.

Without exception, all of the high priests were strongly anticommunist and strongly anti-Soviet during this period. Their links to the military-industrial complex were without equal. Seven of the ten were high-ranking officials in the Reagan administration; four were academics; four were Eastern European emigres; four were actively involved in the Jewish-American pro-Israel lobby; and six were members of the Committee on the Present Danger.

The Death of Sovietology

To be a card-carrying Sovietologist one need not speak Russian, have ever traveled to the Soviet Union, nor have taken a single course in Russian Studies. It is so easy to attract a following by expressing anti-Soviet views that academic training is not a prerequisite. Ronald Reagan had been condemning the Soviet Union for over thirty years before his first trip to Moscow. Richard Perle did not visit the Soviet Union for the first time until shortly before he left the Reagan administration in 1987.

Since the late 1940s the American public has been the victim of faulty scholarship, unrestrained prejudice, and unbalanced financial support only for right-wing, anti-Soviet views. Ironically, the closed-minded way of thinking and the deceptive tactics employed by Sovietologists are no different from those which they claim are used exclusively by their archenemy—the Soviet Union. While Gorbachev opens the Soviet Union to new ideas and new practices, it's business as usual with Sovietologists.

With few exceptions, Sovietologists failed to predict the timing and the nature of virtually every major political change that has taken place in the Soviet Union and Eastern Europe since 1985. In no other field in recent history have so many "experts" disseminated so much misinformation at such an enormous cost to our nation and the rest of the world. Not since Copernicus, perhaps, "have so many been so wrong so frequently with so little humility," said Eric Alterman in *The New York Times*.[28]

Shortly after Gorbachev came to power, Dimitri Simes assured us that Gorbachev "has no new ideas," and Zbigniew Brzezinski warned that Gorbachev was even "more dangerous" than other Soviet leaders because he was attempting to blind-side us with *perestroika*. Henry Kissinger's advice was "watch and wait," and former President Richard Nixon accused Gorbachev of being "more aggressive"—not less.[29]

Just before the Malta summit Caspar W. Weinberger and Richard Perle blazed a trail through major newspaper op-ed pages and national television news interview shows warning Americans of the continued Soviet threat. Weinberger told *New York Times* reporter Eric Pace, "The Soviet military threat remains just as great despite a great deal of soothing rhetoric."[30]

As Eastern Europe opened its doors to increased freedom and democracy, the American national security establishment remained a bulwark of cold war stability. So powerful was the U.S. Navy that at the Malta summit President Bush refused to even discuss the possibility of cuts in our naval nuclear arsenal. While Sovietologists condemn the Soviet *nomenklatura* for its self-serving rigidity, our own equivalent—the military-industrial complex—goes virtually unnoticed.

While Gorbachev attempts to diffuse military tensions on a global scale, the Pentagon has not yet abandoned its plans to build seventy-five Stealth B-2 bombers at a cost of $815 million per plane. Pentagon cold warriors want hundreds of billions of extra dollars to build more cruise missiles, Trident II missiles, and Midgetman missiles to haul even more nuclear weapons to the Soviet Union.

The Reagan military buildup was justified by Central Intelligence Agency (CIA) and Defense Intelligence Agency (DIA) claims of an alleged acceleration in the growth of Soviet defense outlays during the late 1970s and early 1980s. Since 1983 the CIA has acknowledged that Soviet weapons-procurement growth has, in fact, been flat since 1975. The CIA has also acknowledged that the rate of growth in overall Soviet defense spending since that time actually decreased between 4 and 5 percent to 2 percent per year. But Tufts University economist Franklyn D. Holzman has shown that the CIA has failed to make the necessary adjustments in its figures in recent years to reflect this reduction in the Soviet military-spending growth rate. Using the unadjusted Soviet military-expenditure growth rates, the CIA and DIA claimed that the Soviets were spending between 15 to 20 percent of their GNP on military defense. Holzman's analysis suggests that the actual figure for Soviet defense spending is approximately 8 to 10 percent.[31]

The inescapable conclusion from Holzman's research is that CIA and DIA Sovietologists deliberately misled the Congress during the 1980s so as to exaggerate the extent of the Soviet threat. For all too long, Sovietologists within the government as well as academics have been telling the Pentagon exactly what it wants to hear about the Soviet Union.

Fearing congressional pressure to reduce the CIA's bloated budget in response to improved U.S.–Soviet relations, CIA Director William Webster warned in late 1989 that the world had become even more dangerous as a result of terrorism, drug trade, Third World instability, and increased economic and technological cooperation.[32]

Some of the most vocal critics of *perestroika* are economists. Many who advise the CIA, the Pentagon, the Congress, and the White House about the Soviet economy not only have never been in a Soviet factory, but some have never even been in an American factory. They have only limited knowledge of practical management practices in the United States or the Soviet Union. Their principal sources of information are Soviet academic economists, technical statistical data, and public decrees that appear in the Soviet press. They approach the Soviet economy from a legalistic, technocratic perspective and completely ignore many of the important political, social, and cultural reforms initiated by Gorbachev, including democratization, increased openness, participatory management practices, increased freedom to travel abroad and emigrate, as well as increased religious freedom.

Until very recently, economists have wielded little influence over the Kremlin's economic policies. Most Soviet economists, not unlike many of their American counterparts, are applied mathematicians with no hands-on experience with the Soviet economy. Even today, one can find few Soviet economists who have firsthand practical experience with Gorbachev's reforms at the factory level. To find out what is going on inside the Soviet economy, one has to talk to factory managers and workers, store managers, and shop foremen and not just to academic theorists and bureaucrats.

The public decrees often lag behind what is actually happening. Only now are we beginning to read decrees supporting reforms initiated months ago. Economists have been particularly critical of the new Soviet joint-venture laws. They point out endless examples of ambiguities and shortcomings of the laws failing to realize that most of the terms of Soviet joint ventures are completely negotiable whether or not they are covered by some decree. The fact that everything is not set in concrete is often an advantage to the Western partner.

The view of economists such as Marshall I. Goldman and Ed A. Hewett is that Gorbachev has only a limited amount of time in which to improve the standard of living of the Soviet people. They define quality of life in very narrow economic terms—income, production, output, and so forth. If precise numerical targets for economic growth are not met according to some preconceived schedule, then they predict a major political upheaval will occur leading to the overthrow of Gorbachev. But where is the precedence for such a myopic view of economic progress? Unlike Americans who believe they can "have it all—now," the Soviet people have demonstrated an historical ability to delay gratification endlessly. Furthermore, this narrow view of economic progress overlooks the fact that Gorbachev has already improved the quality of life of millions of Soviet citizens by providing them with political, economic, and cultural freedoms that they never dreamed possible in the past. Many American economists equate the Soviets' reluctance to decontrol prices and make the ruble convertible with the complete failure of *perestroika*. Gorbachev's economic reforms go far beyond those ever envisaged by previous reformers such as Vladimir I. Lenin and Nikolai Bukharin in the 1920s, Nikita S. Khrushchev in the 1950s, and Alexei Kosygin in the 1960s. American economists seem to be unable to see the forest for the trees.

In early 1990, when Gorbachev temporarily held back on flexible prices, a fully convertible ruble, and a broad sell-off of state-owned enterprises, and retained some elements of state planning, Sovietologists arrogantly responded with a resounding, "We told you so!" In their eyes Gorbachev's go-slow approach to *perestroika* was proof that he was not really committed to serious economic reform. To most American economists, whether they be Soviet experts or not, if the Soviets don't follow all of our rules, then their reforms don't count. It may be one thing for our economists to call for the transformation of the Soviet economy into a market economy all at once, but it may be quite another thing to do so without precipitating political disaster. Whether we like it or not, Gorbachev may attach some importance to his own political survival. By slowing down the pace of reform, he buys himself some additional time to prepare the Soviet people for price reform, a convertible ruble, and private property. Economists such as Leonid Abalkin, who advise Gorbachev, know exactly what is required to fix the Soviet economy, but Gorbachev alone controls the political timetable for implementing these reforms.

Ironically, the track record of American economists who forecast the U.S. economy is not impressive. Why should they be expected to do any better with the Soviet economy about which they know even less?

Economics has long been known as the "dismal science." Economists who are also Sovietologists combine the worst of both worlds. Is it any wonder that Gorbachev has had so much difficulty trying to convince American economists that *perestroika* is here to stay? Gorbachev is attempting to open his closed society—the Soviet Union. The doors to ours—the temple of doom—remain tightly barred against any new ideas.

To sustain the cold war for forty-five years it was necessary to train hundreds of Sovietologists, who would find their way into the Pentagon, the CIA, the DIA, congressional staffs, the National Security Council, the Rand Corporation, and right-wing think tanks. A number of leading American universities responded to this need by establishing Soviet-studies programs right after World War II. The best-known Soviet-studies programs are at Columbia University, Harvard University, Indiana University, Stanford University, the University of California at Berkeley, and the University of Washington at Seattle. A number of former-Nazi war criminals took refuge in some of these institutions. They have provided safe havens for a disproportionately high percentage of disgruntled Soviet and Eastern European emigrés such as Zbigniew Brzezinski and Richard Pipes.

While claiming to be legitimate academic institutions, these Soviets-studies programs have consistently produced one-sided, anti-Soviet rhetoric that has effectively poisoned the minds of two generations of American politicians, diplomats, Pentagon specialists, CIA analysts, journalists, and academics. They not only served as cold war midwives but bear much of the responsibility for the unnecessary prolongation of U.S.–Soviet hostilities. They have consistently provided the intellectual basis for our government's hardline anti-Soviet military and foreign policies since the 1950s.

No self-respecting university would ever support a program dedicated to the spread of racism. Yet these Soviet studies programs have been in the business of disseminating anticommunist, anti-Soviet propaganda for over four decades. Anticommunism is a very profitable business. It not only attracts funding from the CIA and the Pentagon, but it has considerable appeal for wealthy, politically conservative alumni.

No doubt there will always be a legitimate academic need for courses in Soviet history and the Russian language. But as the Soviet Union rejoins the world, why is it any longer important to study every single aspect of life in the Soviet Union? As the Soviet Union becomes more nearly like other nations, why should it continue to receive so much academic attention?

Most Soviet-studies programs have outlived their usefulness. They not only failed to predict the changes taking place in the Soviet Union and Eastern Europe, but they are completely out of touch with reality there. They have been thoroughly discredited by the unfolding of events in the area in which they specialize, and should be disbanded and deprived of further taxpayer support.

4

Military Overkill

W hen Ronald Reagan was elected president in 1980, he called for reduced government regulation, claiming that more often than not such regulations end up causing more harm than good. He was a vigorous advocate of free enterprise, free trade, and privatization of the U.S. economy. But in his effort to regulate, manipulate, and control the Soviet Union, he managed to create in the United States one of the two largest and most unwieldy military bureaucracies in the world as well as the largest budget deficit and the largest foreign-trade deficit in history.

Between 1947 and 1989 the United States spent nearly $11 trillion on the cold war. Since 1985 U.S. military spending has hovered around the $300 billion mark annually. The Reagan administration's defense program cost each American household about $20,000. Between 1981 and 1988 the number of active-duty military men and women and the number of civilians in the Pentagon each increased by over 100,000. At the end of 1989, the size of the U.S. military force stood at 2.1 million troops. According to the Center for Defense Information, over nine million Americans were on the Pentagon's payroll. This figure includes active-duty forces, civilian employees, the National Guard, the Reserves, defense-industry employees, and military retirees.[1]

Although U.S. military spending is estimated to be 5 percent of GNP, Soviet spending remains a matter of considerable debate. In May 1989, for the first time in history, the Soviets began publishing the total amount of their defense budget—a figure which was, of course, disputed by the CIA.

Higher military spending has contributed significantly to the dramatic increase in our national debt, which grew from $1 trillion in 1981 to over $3 trillion in 1990. The Soviets have recently acknowledged that they too have substantial budget deficits related to excessive military spending. We have the capability to explode over sixteen thousand nuclear weapons in the Soviet Union; the Soviets have the capability to explode over eleven thousand nuclear weapons in the United States.

As the Soviet Union and the other Warsaw Pact countries were announcing significant unilateral cuts in troops and conventional weapons in January 1989, President Reagan called for an even larger defense budget. Not satisfied with the congressional support he had received for the B-1 bomber, the Stealth bomber, the MX missile, and the Strategic Defense Initiative, he asked for more— even though the Soviet threat had been significantly reduced. When pressed by the Congress to decide between the MX and the Midgetman mobile missile systems, President George Bush opted for both. His 1991 budget contained only a token reduction in real defense spending.

Worldwide military spending each year is approximately $1 trillion—two-thirds of which is attributable to the two superpowers. In early 1990, the United States had approximately 540,000 troops stationed in thirty-five foreign countries while the Soviets had over 700,000 troops located in twenty-one countries.

In his seminal book *The Rise and Fall of the Great Powers*, Paul Kennedy argued convincingly that nations such as the United States and the Soviet Union that choose military over economic superiority as their modus operandi suffer eventual loss of power, influence, and standard of living. Kennedy claimed that both the United States and the Soviet Union have overextended themselves militarily and are suffering from what he calls "imperial overstretch." According to Kennedy, the sum total of the United States's global interests and military obligations exceeds its capacity to defend them all simultaneously, and that the same thing was true of the Soviet Union prior to the dismantling of its Eastern European empire.[2]

In the name of national security, Congress bought almost every high-tech military project Caspar Weinberger had to sell during the "anything goes" days at the Pentagon. Weinberger's appetite for expensive, sophisticated military gadgetry knew no limits. He spent $30 billion for one hundred B-1 bombers, $14 billion for the Strategic Defense Initiative, and proposed to spend

$75 billion for the Stealth bomber. And with each of these projects, there are very serious doubts as to whether they will ever come close to meeting performance criteria.

To sell his extravagant military program to the Congress, Weinberger began publishing an expensive slick-covered book in 1981 entitled *Soviet Military Power*. Throughout the Reagan years, this annual publication portrayed the Soviets in only the darkest and most threatening terms. However, the Bush administration backed away from this strident approach. The cover of the 1989 issue of *Soviet Military Power* contained a photograph of a smiling Soviet soldier leaving Afghanistan.

In such a permissive environment, it was hardly surprising that within a few months after Weinberger stepped down as secretary of defense there were dozens of revelations of massive fraud in military spending at the Pentagon. The only surprising thing was that the U.S. Senate refused to confirm Senator John G. Tower, President George Bush's nominee for secretary of defense, after learning that Tower had accepted consulting fees in excess of $1 million from major military contractors such as Martin-Marietta, Rockwell International, LTV, Textron, and British Aerospace.

Just as President Bush discovered that he could not balance the federal budget without raising taxes while spending nearly $300 billion annually on military defense, President Gorbachev will never be able to reform the Soviet economy without significant reductions in military spending.

As evidence that the Soviets cannot afford to continue their military lunacy, on 7 December 1988 Mr. Gorbachev began announcing his plans for the unilateral withdrawal of Soviet troops and tanks from Eastern Europe. Czechoslovakia, East Germany, Hungary, and Poland soon followed suit with troop reductions of their own. Terms like "reasonable sufficiency" and "defensive doctrine" began to replace the more bellicose rhetoric of the Brezhnev era.

Not unlike President Lyndon B. Johnson during the Vietnam War in the 1960s, Gorbachev has discovered how difficult it is to support a massive military machine and also maintain a healthy economy. As the competition for resources between the military and civilian sectors intensified in the 1980s, the Soviet economy began slowly grinding to a halt. The old ways of doing things simply were not adequate to meet the needs of the Soviet people as well as the Soviet military-industrial complex. The economy did not possess the resources nor the flexibility to satisfy the economic and military needs of the nation simultaneously.

Some congressmen are finally beginning to take note of the huge burden imposed on the U.S. economy by our continued military support of some of our allies—particularly NATO, Japan, and South Korea. About 60 percent of our entire defense budget goes towards the defense of Western Europe. Our NATO expenditures exceed the amount spent by the other fifteen members of the alliance combined. We spend $1,164 per capita on defense while West Germany and Japan spend $454 and $163 respectively. In terms of percentage of GNP, West Germany and Japan spend 3 percent and 1 percent respectively on defense.

Although we have huge trade deficits with Japan and South Korea, we maintain thousands of military personnel in each country. We have fifty thousand in Japan, which costs us more than $3 billion annually. These troops are of questionable value since there appears to be no imminent external threat to Japan. More than thirty-five years after the Korean War there are still forty-four thousand Americans stationed in South Korea—considered by some to be a country we must defend indefinitely. This costs American taxpayers $3 billion annually. Finally, our fifteen thousand personnel in the Philippines appear to be of only marginal importance to our national defense.

During a trip to the Far East in February 1990, Secretary of Defense Dick Cheney proposed troop withdrawals of five thousand and seven thousand from South Korea and Japan respectively in response to mounting congressional pressure.

When NATO celebrated its fortieth anniversary in 1989, there already was increasing apprehension among some of its members regarding its future role in Europe. Throughout most of its life the sixteen-nation alliance has been completely dominated by the United States—particularly during the Reagan years. Under Reagan our state department would often make unilateral decisions affecting the alliance, then simply inform the other fifteen members of what had already been decided.

However, there were clear signs that this dynamic was starting to change even before the Warsaw Pact unraveled in the fall of 1989. An increasing number of questions are being raised by our

European allies concerning European sovereignty and the future of NATO. Formed in the wake of the Soviet takeover of Eastern Europe after World War II and the Berlin blockade, the entire raison d'être for NATO's existence has been systematically challenged by Gorbachev's troop reductions, the collapse of the Berlin Wall, increased political freedom in Eastern Europe, and German reunification. An alliance based on forty-year-old perceptions is not likely to survive when the realities on which the perceptions were based have so clearly changed.

By early 1990, Poland, Hungary, and Czechoslovakia were pressuring the Soviet Union to withdraw all of its troops from their territory. To make it easier for Gorbachev to respond to these troop-withdrawal demands, President Bush proposed some major troop reductions of his own in his 31 January 1990 State of the Union address.

What is likely to bring NATO down is the very real possibility that Gorbachev will seek membership in NATO to obtain protection for the Soviet Union in "our common European home." It's hard to imagine that American taxpayers would be willing to continue financing NATO when the Soviet Union is asking to be included in an alliance originally conceived to protect its members from the Soviet threat.

It was not until April 1990—responding to increased political pressure—that Secretary of Defense Dick Cheney proposed the first cuts in existing U.S. military programs. He proposed to reduce the number of orders for Stealth bombers, C-17A transport planes, and A-12 advanced tactical aircraft. Three months later Cheney called for the deployment of a $4 billion radar-jamming device that had consistently failed crucial flight tests on the fighter planes it was designed to test. However, Saddam Hussein's foray into Kuwait injected new life into NATO and the U.S. defense budget.

The Technocrats

The intense hatred for the Soviet Union shared by the Nazi, East European, Soviet, and Cuban emigrés was based at least in part on the personal suffering that they or their families had experienced at the hands of the Soviet government. However, for the most part, the scientists, engineers, and technocrats who design, develop and implement sophisticated high-tech weapons systems have had no firsthand contact with the Soviets. Their anticommunism stems more from a psychological need to justify their decision to spend their lives producing instruments of death.

The Pentagon is the only institution in the world that can provide these high-tech enthusiasts with endless resources to do state-of-the-art research and development on the cutting edge of science. For many technocrats, the thrill of overcoming scientific and technological hurdles is the driving force that motivates them to pursue ever-more sophisticated weapons systems. Their spiritual and political guru is Hungarian emigré Edward Teller—father of the hydrogen bomb, scientific confidant of President Reagan, and father of the Strategic Defense Initiative. To rationalize developing weapons capable of producing so much destruction one must have a truly formidable enemy—a role which the Soviet Union was all too willing to play for over forty-five years.

THE NIKE-X PROJECT

During the summer of 1966, Secretary of Defense Robert S. McNamara was under considerable pressure from the Pentagon to deploy the Nike-X antiballistic missile (ABM) designed to intercept offensive missiles launched by China or the Soviet Union. At that time I was invited to become a member of a six-person consulting team organized by the U.S. Army Research Office to review the Nike-X project in White Sands, New Mexico. The team was headed up by the distinguished physicist and Edward Teller protege, Hans Mark of the Lawrence Livermore National Laboratory. Mark later became secretary of the Air Force under President Carter and is now chancellor of the University of Texas system.

Since this was my first—and what turned out to be my last—time to consult with the U.S. military, I found the experience to be somewhat intimidating. All of the other members of our team had been consultants to the military for years and understood very well that, if you wanted to be invited back, you told the military what it wanted to hear. Unfortunately, no one had bothered to explain this to me.

The reason I had been asked to join the team was because of my knowledge of computer-simulation techniques. Most of the arguments in support of deployment of Nike-X were based on computer-simulation studies of the SPRINT and SPARTAN missiles, which were expected to drive the Nike-X system. Both the SPRINT and the SPARTAN had been subjected to extensive simulation analyses based on hundreds of different variables. In trying to make some sense out of the reams of computer printouts, I asked the project's systems analysts what criteria would be used to compare and evaluate the two missiles? They seemed puzzled by this question. There were no criteria for comparing the two systems. Basically, they were spending hundreds of thousands of dollars doing computer simulation experiments for the sake of doing simulation experiments. Without any well-defined evaluation criteria, the results were completely meaningless.

The Nike-X was designed to protect a limited number of major U.S. cities from a relatively small-scale nuclear attack. The cities that were to be afforded such protection were encircled on a large map of the United States. I asked how the project leaders went about deciding which cities should be saved? Who drew the circles? Was the Congress consulted on this matter? The answer was, "No, a mathematician sitting in his cubicle down the hall made the decisions on which cities should be saved."

The state-of-the-art of ABM technology then—as it is now with the Strategic Defense Initiative—was that it was not possible to protect a city like New York or Los Angeles from an attack by Soviet missiles without some prior knowledge of the enemy's deployment strategy. That is, one could not assume an infinite number of Soviet strategies and have any chance of making a city like New York safe from attack. I then asked the obvious question, "Where do you get your information about Soviet and Chinese missile deployment strategies?" I expected a non-answer such as, "We have our sources," or "the CIA." Instead, once again, I was told that the mathematician down the hall provided such information. Since that time my level of confidence in antiballistic missile systems has never been the same.

Throughout the three-day visit to White Sands we were wined and dined and subjected to a very hard sell by the Nike-X project leaders. Finally, one evening at an outdoor barbecue at the home of the project director, he concluded his hard-line pitch by saying, "We need a production decision from McNamara for the sake of the morale of the Nike-X project team." It did not matter how many billions of dollars the Nike-X would cost or its possible destabilizing effect on U.S.–Soviet relations, it was needed to boost the morale of the technicians who wanted to build it. Whether it was good for the United States or not, Nike-X already had a life of its own.

During the drive back to the airport in El Paso, Texas, Hans Mark turned to me and asked, "What are your impressions about consulting with the Army?" After expressing my awe at the science-fiction-like technology of the Nike-X project, I voiced my concern at the way in which the Army was attempting to use us to put pressure on the secretary of defense to deploy the Nike-X. The Army viewed us as sophisticated prostitutes who would give them what they wanted provided the price was right. Dr. Mark and the other members of our team riding in the car all indicated that they agreed with me and encouraged me to express my true feelings about the project in my written report.

A few days before I submitted my written evaluation, I received a telephone call from the Army Research Office to schedule a follow-up visit to White Sands. The contact officer went to some effort to accommodate my schedule. Several weeks after I turned in my very critical report, which not only questioned the Nike-X technology but raised a number of fundamental questions about ABMs, I was given the opportunity to read the reports of the other five members of our consulting team. Without exception they each gave Nike-X a clean bill of health. None of the reservations that we had discussed in the car en route to the El Paso airport appeared in their reports. They gave the Army exactly what it wanted—the justification for a Nike-X production decision.

A few days later I received a call from the Army indicating that it would not be necessary for me to participate in the follow-up visit to White Sands, since I was interested in topics that were beyond the scope of the project. I have never been asked to be a consultant to the military again.

In 1967 McNamara succumbed to the pressure and gave the go-ahead to deploy a sequel to the Nike-X known as the Sentinel, which later evolved into the Safeguard ABM in the early 1970s.

Interestingly enough, the technical limitations of the Nike-X project are identical to some of the major shortcomings of the Strategic Defense Initiative twenty years later. It was technological fantasy in 1966 to believe that one could design a fail-safe ABM system. Even with today's computer technology, such a system remains an illusion.

THE B-1 BOMBER

The Nike-X was but one of a many multibillion-dollar high-tech military projects that emerged during the past twenty years—all aimed at preventing the spread of communism.

In March 1989 the Air Force grounded the entire fleet of ninety-seven B-1 bombers following three crashes and an unexplained malfunction of the "swing-wing" on one of the aircraft leading to the puncture of a fuel tank. The B-1 was one of the most controversial, expensive, and ill-conceived projects ever undertaken by the Pentagon. By the time the first of the one hundred B-1 bombers, which cost $280 million each, went into service in September 1986, the plane was already hopelessly obsolete. The aircraft's radar-jamming devices—designed in the late 1960s and early 1970s—were simply inadequate to fend off attacks from modern Soviet aircraft and missiles.[3]

As envisaged by its principal supporter in the Nixon administration, Deputy Secretary of Defense David Packard, the B-1 was designed to lead any airborne nuclear attack against the Soviet Union. Honoring a 1976 campaign commitment, President Jimmy Carter canceled the B-1 bomber on 30 June 1977. This decision enraged the Committee on the Present Danger—one of whose members was David Packard. Carter's decision was used by the CPD as evidence that he was "soft on defense" and should be defeated.

In 1971 OMB Director Caspar Weinberger led the charge against the B-1 by a group of Nixon administration officials who were skeptical about the cost effectiveness and practicality of the eighteen-hundred-mile-per-hour nuclear bomber. Ten years later, Weinberger convinced the Congress that the B-1 was absolutely essential to our national security. Throughout the 1980s, Congress was so intimidated by Weinberger and Richard N. Perle that it gave them literally everything they asked for—the B-1, the Stealth bomber, the MX missile, the Trident II missile, and the Strategic Defense Initiative. When it came to national security, the sky was the limit.

THE STEALTH BOMBER

After a decade shrouded in nearly total secrecy, the Air Force unveiled the B-2 Stealth bomber in July 1989—eighteen months behind schedule.[4] The most expensive warplane in history, the Stealth bomber is considered by some to be the military boondoggle of the century.

The B-2 was begun during the Carter administration and announced by Secretary of Defense Harold Brown during the summer of 1980 to shore up Carter's failing bid to seek reelection. It represented a last-ditch effort to show that Carter was tough on defense. The prime contract on the Stealth was awarded to Northrop Corporation by the Reagan administration in 1981.

The high-tech bat-wing bomber is designed to avoid radar detection while flying at low altitude over enemy territory. Its supporters claim that "it will be virtually invisible to Soviet air defense." Its primary mission would be to seek and destroy—with nuclear weapons—Soviet nuclear missiles carried on trucks and trains. The B-2 was designed to carry nuclear bombs and, along with the conventional B-1 bomber, replace the aging B-52 fleet.

After its 1989 maiden flight the Stealth bomber continued to be plagued by numerous technical problems. By reducing the number of B-2 bombers planned from 132 to 75, the Pentagon opened the door for congressional debate on whether the project should be scaled back further or abandoned altogether. The debate centers on whether we can afford the extravagant B-2 now estimated to cost $61 billion and whether it is technically capable of carrying out its sophisticated mission. Hard-liners argue that the Stealth is necessary in the event Gorbachev is overthrown and the Soviet Union returns to Stalinism. More recently they have claimed that it could also be used against terrorism. Two Stealth bombers were deployed in the December 1989 invasion of Panama. Much to the embarrassment of the Pentagon, one of the bombers missed its target by hundreds of yards.

Work on the B-2 accounted for half of Northrop's 1988 revenues, which amounted to $5.8 billion. Increasing doubts have been expressed whether Northrop is up to the task of producing the B-2 while simultaneously developing radical, unproven new technologies aimed at making it possible for the aircraft to escape enemy radar detection. Northrop has been the target of three different Federal investigations. One was concerned with the company's billing practices related to the Stealth bomber and its huge cost overruns. Another involved possible violations of the Foreign Corrupt Practices Act in conjunction with the sale of fighter planes to South Korea. Federal prosecutors have also looked into Northrop's work on the MX missile.[5] The ominous-looking Stealth bomber was saved from extinction when Iraq annexed Kuwait.

THE STRATEGIC DEFENSE INITIATIVE

Inspired by physicist Edward Teller and the 1940s film *Murder in the Air,* on 23 March 1983 President Reagan called on scientists to develop the Strategic Defense Initiative (SDI)—a missile defense shield in space that would render nuclear weapons "impotent and obsolete." In *Murder in the Air,* Reagan portrayed an American secret agent who fought communist spies using a sophisticated weapon that blasted planes out of the sky. In their book *Claiming the Heavens,* Philip M. Boffey and his other *New York Times* coauthors argue convincingly that Reagan's "love of cinematic heroes and fascination with technology" can be traced back to the powerful image created by *Murder in the Air.*[6] In proposing SDI, Reagan attacked the traditional theory of nuclear deterrence by retaliation—mutual assured destruction (MAD)—as immoral and unreliable.

As originally envisaged by Teller, SDI would consist of a complex network of systems including x-ray laser beams; particle beams; electromagnetic "sling shots," which would hurl nonexplosive projectiles called "brilliant pebbles" through space at great speed; and sensing, tracking, and aiming devices. All of these systems require the extraordinary coordination of advanced computers and other technologies to detect missiles, compute their trajectories, and direct intercepting weapons over great distances.

The Reagan administration originally proposed a six-year SDI research program. By 1990 SDI had already cost the American taxpayers well over $20 billion. If it could ever be completed at all, scientists estimate that SDI would take between fifteen and twenty years to complete at a cost in excess of $1 trillion.

President Eisenhower not only warned of a military-industrial complex but also of a scientific elite who would exploit global tensions to create and expand their research laboratories as well as their own political power. No one comes closer to the type of scientist Eisenhower had in mind than Edward Teller. All of Teller's research on expensive, high-tech weapons is based on a paranoid view of the Soviet Union shaped by his reaction to Stalin. It is difficult to imagine any changes in the Soviet Union that would ever cause Teller to back away from his harsh anti-Soviet mentality.

SDI is the brainchild of Teller and two of his younger proteges—Dr. Lowell L. Wood, Jr., and Dr. George A. Keyworth II. Wood was an astrophysicist at the Livermore laboratory, and Keyworth, a physicist at the Los Alamos National Laboratory in New Mexico, was named the President's scientific adviser in May 1981. Wood and Teller have been accused by their colleagues at the Livermore laboratory of "overselling" and "potentially misleading" Reagan administration officials about the prospects for a nuclear-driven x-ray laser.[7]

SDI began to take shape during the summer of 1981 in a series of meetings at the Heritage Foundation in Washington. These meetings—organized by Teller, Wood, and Keyworth—included an influential group of scientists, industrialists, military men, defense executives, and close friends of President Reagan. Members of this group first met with Reagan in the White House on 8 January 1982.[8]

That Mr. Reagan was attracted to SDI should have come as no surprise given his penchant for large-scale, high-tech enterprises such as the B-1 bomber, the MX missile, the Stealth bomber, the Trident II, the Clinch River Breeder Reactor, the space shuttle, the space station, and the supercollider. Reagan administration proponents claimed that SDI would spawn valuable nonmilitary technologies for American industry—an argument also advanced by Star Wars enthusiast Zbigniew Brzezinski.[9]

In his 1986 State of the Union address, President Reagan was almost euphoric over SDI:

> Technology transforming our lives can solve the greatest problem of the twentieth century. A security shield can one day render nuclear weapons obsolete and free mankind from the prison of nuclear terror.

But many scientists do not share President Reagan's optimism over SDI. The 1986 explosion of the space shuttle Challenger; the grounding of the B-1 bomber and the Titan and Delta rockets; problems with the Stealth bomber and the Trident II missile; the flawed mirror in the Hubble space telescope; the temporary grounding of the space shuttle program in July 1990; and the Three Mile Island and Chernobyl nuclear accidents have all raised serious doubts whether it is possible to make SDI as invincible as Reagan claimed.

Some scientists believe that it would be much easier to design, build, and deploy countermeasures to defeat SDI than it would be to construct the system itself. They argue that any space-based defense system would be useless against bombers, low-flying cruise missiles, short-range submarine-launched weapons, and concealed nuclear devices. The complexity of the computer software that would be required to manage the large array of computers necessary to support a weapons system, that would work when confronted with a salvo of nuclear missiles, is incomprehensible. It would be virtually impossible to test realistically the huge array of computers that would operate and control a complex system of sensors, antimissile weapons, guidance and aiming devices, and battle management stations.

Star Wars was strongly criticized by two 1988 reports — one by the nonpartisan Office of Technology Assessment (OTA) and the other by the Defense Science Board (DSB), an independent scientific panel convened by Secretary of Defense Frank C. Carlucci. The nine-hundred-page OTA report said that SDI was vulnerable to catastrophic equipment and computer-software failures at the moment it might be needed.[10] The study also concluded that President Reagan's original vision of a space-based shield "seems infeasible." The DSB report recommended scaling back SDI spending and substantially slowing development.[11]

To counteract criticisms of SDI, the Pentagon embarked on a strategy of exaggerated claims, cover-up of scientific failures, hyperbolic tests, and high-priced public-relations razzle-dazzle. The objective was to create the illusion of major technical breakthroughs, no matter how small the actual accomplishments might be. The Pentagon trades heavily on the fact that many SDI skeptics are scientists and engineers with security clearances who are legally barred from revealing classified information about the limitations of SDI. Pentagon advocates of SDI have access to all classified information about SDI and can say whatever they like without the risk of being charged with security violations. The public gets a very one-sided view of SDI.

SDI received an unexpected boost from spy-novelist Tom Clancy in his best seller, *The Cardinal of the Kremlin*. The novel describes an intense competition between Soviet and American SDI scientists to develop a space-based missile-defense system. One side has developed an operational ground-based laser, the other an orbiting mirror, each of which is an incomplete part of an integrated SDI system. Both sides are desperate to learn the other's secrets.

In addition to the Pentagon hype, the most powerful vehicle for attracting SDI support is the lure of fat government contracts. With the likelihood that tens of billions of dollars will be spent on SDI research over the next decade, the Defense Department has had little difficulty in stimulating the interest of American, Western European, Israeli, and Japanese military contractors, not to mention American universities, which have also shared in the financial bonanza.

SDI had just barely gotten off the ground when TRW and Boeing received contracts amounting to $424 million and $217 million respectively. Martin-Marietta received a billion-dollar contract to develop an SDI computer complex to simulate the effects of alternative strategic defense systems and evaluate whether it is technically feasible to repel a nuclear attack. Subcontractors to Martin-Marietta include IBM and Carnegie-Mellon University.[12] The General Electric Company was awarded a $236 million contract to play a leading role in the development and the initial deployment of the first phase of SDI in the late 1990s.[13]

We were repeatedly told by President Reagan that we had Gorbachev on the run and that the only reason he came to the bargaining table was out of fear of SDI. In reality Star Wars made Gorbachev's task of injecting new vitality into the Soviet political system much easier than might otherwise have been the case.

Publicly, Gorbachev denounced SDI, claiming it was a destabilizing threat to world peace that would accelerate the arms race. Not unlike many of their U.S. counterparts, Soviet scientists, including Nobel laureate Andrei Sakharov, also expressed serious doubts about the technical feasibility of SDI. SDI is to Gorbachev what Sputnik was to John F. Kennedy's 1960 presidential campaign. When the Soviets launched Sputnik on 4 October 1957,

American pride was dealt a severe blow. Kennedy very effectively used Sputnik to play on Americans' psychological need to catch up with the Russians. Sputnik played a major role in his defeat of Richard Nixon. Throughout the 1960s the Congress rarely said no to NASA's ever-increasing requests for funding. So too SDI has enabled Gorbachev to play on national pride and to urge the Soviet people to make even greater sacrifices for the Motherland and to close the technological gap with the West.

While publicly condemning SDI, Gorbachev cleverly used it to consolidate his political power within the party, the Politburo, and the military establishment. By promising protection from the alleged Star Wars threat, he soothed Soviet paranoia over an attack by the West.

As Mr. Gorbachev pursued his strategy of globalizing the Soviet economy, SDI may have enhanced his image as a peacemaker opposed to the arms race. It enabled him to project himself as a man of peace in contrast to Reagan, who was portrayed as an inflexible warmonger with an unyielding commitment to SDI at any price.

In January 1989, former Senator John G. Tower, President Bush's unsuccessful nominee for secretary of defense, acknowledged what many people thought to be true about SDI at his Senate hearing. Tower said that the Bush administration did not consider it possible to "devise an umbrella that can protect the entire American population from nuclear incineration." He went on to say, "I think that's unrealistic."[14]

The Bush administration has taken a more cautious approach to SDI than the Reagan administration did. However, it has embraced the concept of a brilliant-pebbles space defense system—another brainchild of Edward Teller and Lowell Wood, Jr., who oversold the Reagan administration on shooting down missiles with x-ray lasers. Brilliant pebbles could also be used as a first-strike weapon by the United States to launch an attack that would wipe out most Soviet nuclear weapons.

The credibility of SDI was dealt another serious blow in July 1989 when a group of ten American physicists, congressmen, and journalists were allowed inside the heretofore highly secret Soviet proving ground located at Sary Shagan in Kazakhstan. Throughout the Reagan years the Pentagon portrayed the huge space laser being developed at Sary Shagan in only the most threatening terms. According to the American team, the Reagan administration's claims about Sary Shagan amounted to "much ado about nothing." Two of the team members, Frank von Hippel and Thomas B. Cochran, reported in *The New York Times* that the lasers at Sary Shagan were "very ordinary" and "1,000 times less powerful" than those of SDI. Thus the Pentagon's so-called "laser gap" proved to be just as big a lie as its previous "bomber gap" and "missile gap." Only this time around, the Pentagon had been caught red-handed in its campaign of deception.[15]

In September 1989, the Soviets backed away from their previous position in which they insisted that the Americans abandon their plans to deploy SDI as a precondition for concluding a strategic arms treaty, providing further evidence that Gorbachev had never been intimidated by Star Wars. By year-end 1990, SDI was facing increasing congressional budgetary pressure.

OUR LOVE AFFAIR WITH NUCLEAR ENERGY

In spite of the enormous death and destruction that resulted from our bombing of Hiroshima and Nagasaki in 1945 and the cloud of uncertainty that has blanketed the nuclear power industry since its inception, both military and civilian technocrats continue to be drawn to nuclear technology.

According to a 1989 report by the Center for Defense Information, the United States has spent almost $1 trillion producing sixty thousand nuclear warheads and bombs and their delivery systems since 1945. The bombs and warheads alone cost over $100 billion.[16] By the end of 1988 the United States had conducted 927 nuclear test explosions since 1945 in contrast to 625 by the Soviets.[17] Although shrouded in a veil of secrecy for more than four decades, spending on nuclear weapons has increased every year for over ten years—all with absolute minimum of congressional oversight.

As a result of recent disclosures about the safety and environmental hazards surrounding the production of nuclear weapons, all U.S. nuclear reactors producing tritium and plutonium for nuclear warheads were shut down. To deal with these safety problems, which were covered up by the nuclear weapons industry for over forty years, the Department of Energy plans to spend about $10 billion for the construction of two new tritium reactors and one new plutonium-processing facility. The DOE also plans to spend $244 billion for new construction, maintenance, operations, and cleanup of nuclear bomb factories over the next twenty years.[18]

According to *The New York Times,* workers in these nuclear-weapons plants who complained about safety and environmental problems were ordered by their superiors to see psychiatrists and psychologists approved by management. Mandatory psychological counseling has been a part of a pattern of harassment and intimidation imposed on workers who criticized working conditions that included threats to have their security clearances revoked.[19]

For years Americans have been told that President Harry Truman's decision to drop two atomic bombs on Japan in 1945 was morally justified because it saved hundreds of thousands of lives by making it unnecessary to invade Japan to bring World War II to an end. However, a top-secret 1946 study found in the War Department's files by Gar Alperovitz suggested that Truman knew before the bombing of Hiroshima and Nagasaki that such action was not required to force Japan's surrender.[20]

The continuation of our nuclear buildup for over four decades has been rationalized in terms of the need to have sufficient nuclear power to dissuade the Soviets from ever considering a first-strike nuclear attack on the United States. The Soviets in turn have used a similar argument to justify the size of their nuclear arsenal.

Prior to the Three Mile Island nuclear accident in 1979 and the Chernobyl disaster in 1986, Americans were also told that further investment in nuclear technology was necessary because of its peacetime application to the electric-utility industry.

President Reagan championed a number of major nuclear-energy projects that failed in the 1980s and cost American tax-payers billions of dollars. These included the Clinch River Breeder Reactor ($1.5 billion), the Hanford Fast Flux Test Facility ($540 million), the Rocky Flats Plutonium Processing Building ($225 million), the Portsmouth Gas Centrifuge Uranium Enrichment Plant ($3.5 billion), the Brookhaven High Energy Physics Atomic Particle Accelerator ($172 million), and the Hanford Nuclear Reactor ($110 million).[21] More recently, the Bush administration abandoned the three-year-old $176 million Savannah River Fuel Materials Facility.

The U.S. government-owned Tennessee Valley Authority originally planned to build seventeen nuclear reactors—the largest commitment to nuclear power of any utility in the country. By 1982, eight of these had been canceled, and for a period of time during the mid-1980s literally all of the completed nuclear plants were forced to shut down for safety reasons.

In January 1984, a week-long chain of disasters put the nuclear power industry through its darkest days since the Three Mile Island (TMI) accident. Within a few days of each other Commonwealth Edison was denied a license by the Nuclear Regulatory Commission to operate its $3.4 billion twin-reactor Bryon plant, the Public Service Company of Indiana canceled work on its $2.5 billion Marble Hill nuclear plant, and Cincinnati Gas and Electric announced that it would convert its $1.6 billion William H. Zimmer nuclear facility, which was 99 percent complete, into a coal-fired plant.[22]

Even with the Reagan administration's nuclear-power hype and the utility industry's claim that TMI was a fluke, no electric power company in the United States has ordered a new reactor since 1979.

Neither the nuclear-weapons industry nor the nuclear-power industry has yet to come up with an effective, safe way to dispose of nuclear waste after forty-five years of experience. Each year the Congress closes its eyes and pretends the problem does not exist.

In spite of the inherent risks associated with nuclear power, there will be increased pressures in the United States to resume construction of nuclear power plants in the 1990s as an alternative to high-polluting fossil-fuel power plants, which have a very adverse effect on the environment. The surge in oil prices caused by the Persian Gulf crisis will no doubt rekindle further interest in nuclear power.

HIGH-TECH EUPHORIA

The $155 billion submarine-launched Trident II missile system is the most expensive weapons program in U.S. history. It includes 899 nuclear missiles and 21 submarines to carry and launch them.[23] Unfortunately, the Trident II is just one more example of the dozens of very expensive high-tech military systems developed for the Defense Department over the past fifty years.

Beginning with the World War II Manhattan Project, and continuing with the Apollo moonwalks, the Space Shuttle, the B-1 bomber, the Stealth bomber, the Trident II, and SDI, our government has spent hundreds of billions of dollars each year on military and space-related high technology. The common and distinguishing characteristic of these high-tech ventures has been managerial indifference to costs backed by the political will to foot the bill.[24]

What drives Americans to continue spending on military technology far beyond what might be reasonably required to guarantee our national security? I believe there are several factors contributing to our mystical obsession with high technology—particularly computer technology.

Today's engineers and managers feel much more comfortable entrusting matters of national security to the sophisticated computers of SDI rather than counting on either the Russians or the U.S. State Department—neither of whom can be trusted. It is far better to deal with the Soviets from a position of technological and military strength rather than counting on arms-control negotiations, which imply weakness.

In addition to the pollyannaish attitude of the new breed of me-first managers towards high technology, there is another factor that enables scientists such as Edward Teller to sell their technological snake oil to the American people. I call this factor the high-tech intimidation factor.

Throughout the 1970s I was the president of a computer-software firm that produced sophisticated decision support systems for use by Fortune 500 companies on large mainframe computers. Although I had a working knowledge of computer programming, I found communicating with programmers to be very stressful. They not only have a unique, serial way of thinking, which makes it difficult for them to deal with multidimensional problems, but they often express themselves in an unintelligible technical jargon. Whenever I discussed matters related to software design with them, I could never be certain whether I was getting a straight technical response or whether they were merely expressing their own personal preferences disguised in technical garb.

Whenever a policymaker has to make a decision based on a technology that he or she does not fully understand, then the policymaker becomes vulnerable to being run over by a high-tech steamroller. But that is precisely the dilemma faced by the Congress in its efforts to deal with Edward Teller, the Pentagon, and greedy defense contractors.

The high-tech military zealots come on so strong with their forecasts of Soviet technological gloom and doom that the Congress is easily intimidated into believing anything the Pentagon high priests have to sell—all in the name of national security. Our Congress neither knows how to ask the right questions, nor how to evaluate the answers. This is one reason why we are still spending almost $300 billion each year on defense.

Unfortunately, the Soviets are no different from the Americans with regard to their obsession with high technology. Most of the Soviet economists, scientists, engineers, and company managers with whom I am acquainted are mesmerized by personal computers. Fortunately, or unfortunately, as the case may be, they don't have nearly as many microcomputers as we do.

The Soviet Threat
RUSSIAN AGGRESSION

Since the late 1940s most American military strategists—professional or otherwise—have assumed that the Soviet Union sought military superiority over the United States and the rest of the world. Once this goal had been achieved, it was further assumed that the Soviets would either attack the United States or blackmail the West into submission to Soviet domination. This widespread view was based on early Leninist declarations of world revolution, Khrushchev's statement that he would "bury" us, the heavy-handed tactics used by the Soviets to gain control of Eastern Europe, the force they used to snuff out economic and political reforms in Budapest in 1956 and Prague in 1968, and their initial support of Mao Zedong in the 1950s—as well as their support of North Korea, Cuba, and North Vietnam. During the Brezhnev era, Soviet support for Third World socialist nations such as Angola, Ethiopia, Mozambique, and Nicaragua did little to change American perceptions of Soviet foreign policy. In the eyes of most Americans, the 1979 Soviet invasion of Afghanistan represented the ultimate example of Soviet military aggression.

Obviously, the Soviets have a somewhat different interpretation of these events—claiming that Lenin and Khrushchev have been misinterpreted, that their behavior in Eastern Europe and Afghanistan was primarily defensive, and that their support of Third World socialist countries was by "invitation only."

But it was the United States, not the Soviet Union, that dropped the first nuclear bomb in 1945. The Soviets did not test their first nuclear weapon until 1949. With the exception of the 1957 launching of Sputnik, the Soviets did not initiate any other nuclear-weapon development. It was the United States that first introduced intercontinental ballistic missiles, submarine-launched missiles, multiple-warhead weapons, laser weapons, kinetic-energy weapons, and space-based weapons.

Very often when we accused the Soviets of developing excessive offensive military capabilities, they were simply trying to reach a state of parity with the United States. This was particularly true of the charges leveled against them in the late 1970s by the Committee on the Present Danger. They were attempting to close the military gap created by our defense buildup in the 1960s and early 1970s. Although the NATO alliance was organized in 1949, the Warsaw Pact did not come into existence until 1955.

Our criticisms of Soviet military aggression often appear to be rather hypocritical in light of the heavy-handed military and political influence that we exercise in Latin America. In his unsuccessful effort to topple the Sandinista government of Nicaragua, President Ronald Reagan tried everything possible short of actual military invasion of Managua. Both Presidents Reagan and Bush invested substantial amounts of energy in their attempts to overthrow the government of Panamanian strong man General Manuel Antonio Noriega. In December 1989, President Bush finally succeeded in deposing Noriega and forcibly bringing him to the United States to face drug-trafficking charges. The U.S. invasion of Panama was in clear violation of the U.S. Constitution, the United Nations Charter, the Organization of American States Charter, and the Panama Canal Treaties. It remains to be seen whether the drug charges leveled against Noriega are real or were trumped up to punish him for his lack of cooperation with our government's unsuccessful attempts to overthrow the Sandinista regime in Nicaragua.

The American military influence in Honduras and El Salvador is substantial. Although we have no troops in Mexico, we have always exerted considerable economic and political influence there. It does not take much imagination to guess what action we would take if a communist government were ever elected in Mexico. When we disapproved of the Marxist government of Chilean President Salvador Allende in 1973, we simply arranged to have him overthrown just as we invaded Cuba in 1961 and the tiny island of Grenada in 1983.

We have recently turned up the political heat on Colombia, Bolivia, and Peru in the "war" on drugs. Colombia is receiving substantial military aid, and the Bush administration has proposed a naval blockade of Colombia as well as military support for Peru. We ridiculed the Soviets when they claimed they were invited by the Hungarians to Budapest in 1956 and by the Czechoslovaks to Prague in 1968. *But our behavior in Latin America and the Persian Gulf is absolutely no different.*[25]

But Soviet foreign policy has produced few benefits for the Soviets since the 1940s to offset the corresponding economic, military, and political costs, which have proven to be enormous. Because of the heavy financial costs of its foreign ventures and the fact that it cannot continue spending over 15 percent of GNP on military defense, the Soviets appear to be operating in a retrenchment mode in terms of foreign policy. The withdrawal of all Soviet troops from Afghanistan, reductions in economic and military aid to Cuba and Nicaragua, and Soviet troop reductions in Eastern Europe all point to a more restrained Soviet foreign policy. A replication of past Soviet military policies is incompatible with Gorbachev's objective of strengthening the Soviet economy by integrating it into the global economy.

TREATY VIOLATIONS

The Reagan administration frequently claimed that the Russians could not be trusted because they did not honor their commitments to international treaties. These arguments were used to justify our own deliberate decision to break the SALT II treaty and to circumvent some of the limitations imposed on space-based research by the ABM treaty. These actions were taken in spite of substantial evidence suggesting that the Soviets had violated neither of these treaties.

Time and time again the Reagan administration failed to prove its contention that the Soviets deliberately and systematically violated their obligations under existing arms-control agreements. According to the Center for Defense Information, the Reagan administration created a myth of Soviet noncompliance by repeatedly representing as established facts allegations about Soviet behavior that represented "worst case" interpretations based on ambiguous evidence.[26]

But in an unexpected act of national contrition in October 1989, Soviet Foreign Minister Eduard A. Shevardnadze told the Supreme Soviet that the 1979 Soviet invasion of Afghanistan violated Soviet law as well as international norms. He then went on to acknowledge that the radar station near Krasnoyarsk in Siberia was indeed "an open violation" of the Anti-Ballistic Missile Treaty—just as the Reagan administration had often charged. One month prior to Shevardnadze's speech, the Soviets agreed to dismantle the radar installation.

But what about our own track record with regard to honoring treaty commitments? Historical records indicate that we have systematically violated more than three hundred treaties we signed protecting the rights of the American Indians. After condemning Iran for mining the Persian Gulf, we then proceeded to mine Nicaraguan harbors in clear violation of international law and then sneered at the World Court, whose jurisdiction we chose to ignore. When Third World countries began voting against us in the 1980s, we simply reduced our financial support to the United Nations. When General Noriega's arrogance became unbearable to President Bush, we retaliated by invading Panama.

HIGH-TECH SPY SCANDALS

On 23 October 1987, Secretary of State George P. Schultz met Mikhail S. Gorbachev in Moscow expecting a Washington summit commitment. Instead, he returned home empty-handed claiming that Gorbachev refused to set a date because of differences over space-based weapons. A week later, Foreign Minister Eduard A. Shevardnadze confirmed a 7 December summit date.

Why did Gorbachev waffle on the summit? The answer may lie in a series of bizarre, high-tech spy scandals precipitated by the Pentagon before each Reagan–Gorbachev meeting.[27]

Before Geneva there was "spy dust"—a powdery chemical that the Soviets were accused of using to track U.S. embassy employees in Moscow. Before Reykjavik, U.S. agents arrested Soviet physicist and UN employee Gennadi F. Zakharov, charging him with espionage. Moscow responded in kind by detaining U.S. journalist Nicholas S. Daniloff.

Prior to the Washington summit, Pentagon superhawks outdid themselves. There was the bugging of our embassy in Moscow, which involved illicit sex between U.S. Marines and attractive female KGB agents. Then came the outcry against Toshiba for selling the Soviets submarine parts. Next was the aborted sale of a large IBM computer to a Soviet-owned West German firm, which resulted in the Japanese getting the business.

On the night before Schultz's 23 October meeting with Gorbachev, NBC television showed the dramatic arrest of alleged KGB agents—one of whom was said to work for the head of the Soviet space program, who reports directly to Gorbachev. They were accused of stealing Star Wars computer-software secrets. Armed with the arrest information and the knowledge of President Reagan's growing list of woes—the Iran–contra affair, the 19 October stock-market crash, and the faltering nomination of Robert Bork to the Supreme Court—is it possible that Gorbachev said to Schultz, "Enough is enough—Reagan needs a deal far more than we do?"

That the United States had four different Soviet foreign policies had not escaped Gorbachev's attention. The State Department, the Pentagon, the CIA, and the National Security Council each conducted its own independent foreign policy towards the Soviet Union.

The 23 October Gorbachev–Schultz showdown in effect gave Schultz—for the first time—absolute control over U.S. foreign policy. Suddenly Schultz was holding all of the trumps in his endless feud with Defense Secretary Caspar W. Weinberger—a rivalry which goes back to their days together at Bechtel. One of them had to go. But without Schultz there would be no summit or INF treaty. Weinberger had finally overplayed his high-tech hand!

Four days after Shevardnadze confirmed the summit, *The New York Times* reported that Weinberger would soon resign—which he did two days later. Frank C. Carlucci was named his successor. Pentagon hard-liners Deputy Secretary Fred C. Iklé, Assistant Secretary Frank J. Gaffney, Jr., and Navy Secretary James Webb also resigned. Carlucci trimmed $33 billion from the 1989 military budget and softened the Pentagon's opposition to U.S.–Soviet trade. Soviet Chief of Staff Sergei Akhromeyev met with his U.S. counterpart Admiral William Crowe. Later, Carlucci sat with Soviet Defense Minister Dmitri T. Yazov in Switzerland. When two U.S. Navy vessels and Soviet warships bumped in the Black Sea ten days before Schultz's next Moscow trip, the incident was played down by Schultz and Soviet Foreign Ministry spokesman Gennadi I. Gerasimov.

Throughout the remainer of 1988, Reagan's anti-Soviet rhetoric became decidedly more subdued than was the case in the past. Since October 1987 our foreign policy toward the Soviets has been much more consistent and appears to be based more on hard work and serious diplomacy and less on ideological zealotry.

Although we will probably never know what really happened between Schultz and Gorbachev on 23 October 1987, or what took place the following week in the White House, we do know that Tom Clancy's high-tech Russian spy novels do not sell as well as they once did. In fact, his latest novel is about drugs, not Russian spies.

Although not nearly as imaginative as the high-tech spy scandals of the Reagan years, there have been a couple of incidents where the Bush administration has attempted to destabilize the Soviet Union with unsupported inferences and accusations of Soviet military activity in Central America. The week before the 1989 Malta summit, twenty-four Soviet-made SAM-7 missiles were found aboard a twin-engine plane that crashed in El Salvador while ferrying arms from Nicaragua. At the Malta summit President Bush hinted that the Soviets had been involved in the shipment of these antiaircraft missiles to Salvadoran guerrillas. Gorbachev flatly denied any Soviet involvement in the incident. Then a week before a February 1990 meeting between Secretary of State James Baker and Soviet Foreign Minister Eduard A. Shevardnadze, the CIA accused the Soviets of shipping military helicopters to Nicaragua. The helicopters turned out to be civilian helicopters. In both of these incidents, the American media was quick to accuse the Soviets of broken promises and irresponsible behavior. Some things never seem to change.

Tension Reduction

Mr. Gorbachev's approach to U.S.–Soviet relations stands in sharp contrast to that of every previous Soviet and American leader. His psychological sophistication in dealing with conflict is virtually without precedent in the Soviet Union—or anywhere else for that matter. Whether dealing with Ronald Reagan, Fidel Castro, angry Baltic republics, Eastern Europe, China, irate Soviet consumers, or Siberian coal miners, Gorbachev's style of conflict management is always the same—nonconfrontational and often very disarming.

Consider his relationship with President Reagan. In October 1987, as we previously indicated, Reagan was confronted with the Iran–contra scandal, the stock-market crash, and the rejection of Supreme Court nominee Robert Bork. If Leonid Brezhnev or Nikita Khrushchev had still been in power, they would have been all over Reagan's case—particularly with regard to the Iran–contra affair.

Instead, Gorbachev said absolutely nothing about the Iran–contra affair. He then gave Reagan a Washington summit, an INF treaty, a Moscow summit, and a New York summit. Gorbachev helped save Reagan's presidency and paved the way for the election of George Bush. President Reagan's anti-Soviet rhetoric decreased significantly in 1988. It's very difficult to pick a fight with yourself.

Gorbachev encouraged the Poles to discuss the 1940 Katyn Woods massacre, the Baltic republics to express their feelings about the long covered-up 1939 Hitler–Stalin agreement, and the coal miners to express their grievances about working conditions in the mines. He invited President Reagan to give a lecture at Moscow State University on freedom and democracy and former National Security Council Advisor Zbigniew Brzezinski to talk about a new political order in Europe. There is even talk of a voluntary Soviet army.

If one wants to energize the Soviet economy, then individual citizens must be allowed to speak their minds. But that is precisely what *glasnost* is all about. Permitting people to blow off steam and criticize the Soviet system is psychologically quite therapeutic. Fundamentally, the heart and soul of *glasnost* is tension reduction.

Nothing illustrates Gorbachev's nonconfrontational style any better than the amazing events which took place in Eastern Europe in 1989. Rather than viewing the disintegration of Eastern Europe as a defeat for communism, he treated it as a victory for democratic socialism.

Striking Siberian coal miners were thanked for their support of *perestroika* in 1989 rather than being criticized for disrupting the Soviet economy. When he visited Vilnius and met with angry Lithuanians, Gorbachev did not rule out the possibility of Baltic secession. However, with the economic sanctions imposed on Lithuania by Moscow, Gorbachev made it quite clear to the Baltic republics that secession talks could only proceed in accordance with Soviet law. Lithuania overplayed its hand both with Gorbachev and the West.

One of the most dramatic and visual examples of Gorbachev's conciliatory management style occurred in July 1990 when he and West German Chancellor Helmut Kohl appeared on international television together to announce the end of Soviet opposition to NATO membership for a unified Germany. The television cameras showed Gorbachev—dressed informally in white sneakers— seated beside Kohl around a makeshift table consisting of three tree trunks near Gorbachev's home in Stavropol. In this relaxed, informal setting an issue which had divided the East and the West for over four decades was quietly laid to rest before the entire world.

Once again Gorbachev had transformed a complex zero-sum conflict into a relatively straightforward win-win situation.

Nonviolence

Although the United States claims to be steeped in Judeo-Christian traditions, we are one of the most heavily armed, violent nations in the world. Whether the issue is foreign affairs, terrorism, crime, or drug abuse, the American way of dealing with conflict is firmly grounded in the principle, "An eye for an eye and a tooth for a tooth." Whenever an injustice has been carried out, there is an immediate call for revenge.

Our response to the Soviet military buildup of the 1970s was to embark on our own massive military-spending venture. If we don't like what's going on in Libya, Grenada, or Panama, we simply bomb them or invade them—always in the name of freedom and democracy.

The United States and the Soviet Union have managed to inflict enormous economic, political, social, and psychological costs on each other. By always assuming the worst about the other side and attempting to put the other country in the worst possible light, we have done irreparable damage to our two great nations.

Just as distrust between two people breeds more distrust, distrust between nations breeds further distrust. In the psychodynamics of people as well as nations, distrust becomes a self-fulfilling prophecy.

The only way to end the cold war between the United States and the Soviet Union is to break the cycle of distrust. We can't change the past, but we can create a different future. Which side is prepared to assume the risk of taking the first step towards reducing the level of distrust? Who can afford the risk of not taking the first step?

Why is it that our government is so willing to spend so much to protect its citizens from attack by the Russians and so little to help these same people defend themselves against the ravages of unemployment, poverty, poor health, homelessness, and ignorance? Implicit in our government's behavior for the past forty-five years is the assumption that the only human concern that really matters in Washington is unlimited protection from military attack by the Soviet Union. All other social, economic, political, and psychological concerns are secondary to this obsession with military security.

Yet the opportunity to earn sufficient income to pay for one's food, clothing, shelter, health care, and education is basic. Military security without economic security is void of substance and meaning.

To combat violent crime and drug abuse, we call for tougher law enforcement, capital punishment, and more prisons—none of which seems to work. Inspired by the overwhelmingly positive public response to its invasion of Panama, the Bush administration proposed an air and sea blockade around Colombia.

Many colleges and universities offer credit for courses in ROTC. But the aim of ROTC is to train young Americans to be efficient killers. Paradoxically, while American medical schools are teaching physicians how to save lives, professors of military science at these same institutions are helping produce more trained killers.

But there are some very impressive recent examples of where nonviolence has proven to be an effective strategy for dealing with conflict. For example, the military dictatorships of Argentina, Brazil, and Chile were all brought to an end by peaceful means with democratic elections following in the wake of years of military rule.

Within a matter of a few weeks, the iron-fisted communist regimes in Bulgaria, Czechoslovakia, East Germany, Hungary, and Poland were replaced by more democratic governments with little or no violence involved in the transition. Romania was a bloody exception to this rule in Eastern Europe.

Gorbachev's radical political and economic reforms have been implemented with a minimum of violence. South African President F. W. de Klerk's 3 February 1990 speech to his country's parliament outlining sweeping changes in his country's apartheid laws and policies represented a significant departure from the violence of the past. A week later, the seventy-one-year-old African National Congress spokesman Nelson R. Mandela, who had been imprisoned for over twenty-seven years, was released from jail. These actions have prompted some to call de Klerk the "Gorbachev of Southern Africa."

Albeit it involved substantial U.S. financial and political influence, the Sandinista regime of Daniel Ortega was finally removed by quasi-democratic elections rather than by the military force of the U.S.-backed contras.

Perhaps it is time for the United States to reconsider its long held tit-for-tat approach to conflict in favor of less-violent options.

If the Soviet Union can restrain itself from intervening in the internal affairs of Eastern Europe no matter how uncertain the outcome may be, can't we do the same in Nicaragua, El Salvador, Panama, and the Persian gulf?

No matter how tempting it may be to bomb the drug lords of Colombia and Peru, there is no military solution to America's drug problem. Thus far, we have devoted virtually all of our resources to the supply side of the drug problem while completely ignoring the demand side. People take drugs because they are alienated and powerless and have no sense of meaning in their lives. All the aircraft carriers and battleships in the world will not make Americans less dependent on drugs.

We need to step back and ask ourselves why people commit violent crimes and take drugs. The boom-boom approach to crime and drugs is not working, has never worked, and never will work. Drugs and violence are very human problems and cry out for human solutions, not simplistic public-relations gimmicks.

Nonviolence is not a passive approach to conflict but rather a proactive approach that goes right to the crux of power relationships. It can undermine power and authority by withdrawing the approval, the support, and the cooperation of those who have been dealt an injustice. It demands strength and courage and not idle pacifism. Nonviolence derives its strength from the energy buildup and very real power of powerlessness.

Violence begets more violence. World War II paved the way for the cold war. Every vengeful act by Israel precipitates a similar Arab response and the Arab–Israeli war goes on and on. The threat of the death penalty does not curb violence but rather makes criminals more desperate. Ronald Reagan claimed that the only way to deal with Arab terrorists was to be tough on them. Maybe the terrorists who bombed Pan Am flight 103 in December 1988 did not get the message from Reagan? Or maybe they did?

The Presidential Commission that investigated the Pan Am tragedy recommended that the United States retaliate with force against countries thought to be supporting or sheltering terrorists. Once again American foreign policy was based on vengeance rather than intelligence.

U.S.–Soviet relations have improved because Mr. Gorbachev chose to ignore Mr. Reagan's hostile anti-Soviet rhetoric—not because Gorbachev was afraid of Reagan. The Soviets have taken some giant steps to reduce global tensions since 1985. The United States has taken much smaller steps.

This is not a pitch for unilateral disarmament on the part of the United States. Rather it is an argument in favor of giving more serious consideration to nonviolent options in dealing with conflicts related to foreign relations, terrorism, crime, and drug abuse. Instead of always being so quick to respond to violence with violence, we should give more attention to nonviolent options such as diplomacy, negotiations, persuasion, education, and rehabilitation.

A less-hysterical American response to Soviet intervention in Eastern Europe, Cuba, Afghanistan, and Nicaragua might have resulted in the cold war ending much sooner and saved American taxpayers several trillion dollars in defense outlays. A more-balanced American foreign policy toward Israel might have led to fewer acts of Arab terrorism in the 1980s; and a less hostile American reaction to Iraq's invasion of Kuwait not only might have reduced the likelihood of further bloodshed, but prevented the global economy from going into a wrenching recession.

5

Economic Uncertainty

A Preview of *Perestroika*

When Ronald Reagan visited Moscow in June 1988, few Americans realized that most of the economic reforms he observed had been the subject of countless computer-simulation experiments for over ten years before Mr. Gorbachev came to power in 1985. Although it was not politically feasible to implement radical reforms in the 1970s, several hundred Soviet economists and management scientists were quietly simulating the effects that such reforms might have on the Soviet economy.[1]

While American Sovietologists were engaged in their never-ending harangues against the Soviet Union, economists like Abel G. Aganbegyan and Leonid I. Abalkin were laying the groundwork for the most radical socioeconomic, political experiment of the twentieth century—the opening of the Soviet Union. Although many high-ranking officials in the Reagan administration were fully aware of these simulation studies as far back as 1982, they simply chose to ignore them. It would not have helped the Pentagon's case for its massive military buildup if the Congress had become aware of the extent to which Soviet economists and intellectuals were committed to radical reform. The Reagan administration's superhawks had their own agenda, and they had no interest in the fact that the Soviet Union was looking toward radical economic, political, and foreign-policy reform long before Caspar Weinberger became secretary of defense.

My contacts with the Soviets go back to 1972 when I visited Dr. Alexander Schmidt, a mathematician at the Central Computer Center of the Soviet Academy of Sciences in Moscow. In my first meeting with Dr. Schmidt, the subject of economic reform surfaced immediately. Dr. Schmidt had obviously given a lot of thought to this topic. We began to speculate on the possible use of computer-simulation models to evaluate the effects on the Soviet economy of alternative economic reforms. As a direct result of this conversation, two years later one of my books on computer-simulation modeling was translated into Russian and Polish. To my surprise, over ten thousand copies of the Russian edition of the book were sold—twice as many as in the United States. Literally all of the examples in the book were based on a free-enterprise, capitalist economy.

Stalin snuffed out economics as a discipline in the 1930s, and it did not begin to reemerge until several years after his death in 1953. Most Soviet and Eastern European economists in the 1960s and 1970s had little or no formal training in economics. Many were warmed-over mathematicians, aerospace engineers, and physicists. Thus it was not surprising that they were quite comfortable with technically sophisticated simulation models.

Shortly after my book was published in Russian, I began receiving numerous visitors from the Soviet Union, Hungary, and Poland, all of whom were interested in computer-based planning models. What was particularly striking about most of my Soviet visitors was their very limited knowledge of the practical, hands-on aspects of the Soviet economy. They could describe very elegant mathematical models of the Soviet economy in very technical terms, but they had considerable difficulty explaining how prices and wages were determined in the Soviet Union. Most of them had never been in a Soviet factory.

Although economists were not taken very seriously by Brezhnev in the 1970s, they did speak often of the use of simulation models to evaluate the effects of "changing the economic mechanism" in the Soviet Union. Their descriptions of these studies were often vague and unclear.

In December 1980 I was visited by Dr. Vassily Presnyakov, a junior-level economist from the Central Mathematical Economics Institute (TsEMI) of the Soviet Academy of Sciences. One night on a Delta Air Lines jet flying from O'Hare Airport in Chicago to Raleigh–Durham, North Carolina, Presnyakov sketched out on a napkin the key elements of the fascinating research he and his colleagues were doing in Moscow. He described a variety of different computer models used to evaluate the effects on the Soviet economy of introducing decentralized, market-oriented planning and management. Having taken note of my interest in his work, Presnyakov invited me to Moscow to observe his research at close range. With the rapidly deteriorating political relationship between the United States and the Soviet Union at that time, I was not able to visit Moscow until May 1982.

Academician Nikolay Fedorenko, director of TsEMI, was my host for the 1982 visit, which included ten major research institutes in the Academy of Sciences, Moscow State University, and the State Planning Agency (Gosplan). Although unknown to me at the time, I was given a personalized preview of most of the economic reforms that Gorbachev has implemented under the umbrella of *perestroika*. I met with over 250 economists, management scientists, and computer scientists who were using state-of-the-art analytical techniques on IBM 360-vintage computers — easily ten years behind the computers in the West. But in every institute the research agenda was always the same — evaluating the effects of introducing decentralized planning and management, flexible prices and wages, profits and incentives, finance and banking, and even a freely convertible ruble. And all of this took place six months before the death of Brezhnev and nearly three years before Gorbachev came to power.

A particularly interesting project was an interactive, computer-simulation game to show the effects of flexible wages, incentives, and participatory management on employee productivity, absenteeism, and turnover. There were also simulation studies to evaluate the possibility of creating a Soviet monetary sector with venture-capital banks and industrial bonds, as well as financial markets and a convertible ruble.

The primary objective of these studies was to convince the successors of Brezhnev that the only way to "fix" the Soviet economy was to introduce radical economic reforms. These economists could show that everything is related to everything else in the Soviet economy and that fixing one part of the system was likely to precipitate problems in other parts of the economy. There were models dealing with such problems as alcoholism, high death rates and infant mortality rates, low birth rates, and alienation. Others dealt with democratization, foreign-trade reform, foreign policy, and arms control. There were studies to evaluate the impact on the Soviet economy of the end of the cold war.

This research went well beyond the Soviet reforms of the 1960s and was being conducted throughout the Soviet Union and Eastern Europe. Most importantly, it was being done with the full knowledge of the Soviet government. Indeed, Gosplan was one of the sponsors.

Upon returning to the United States, I sought the advice of Sydney Gruson, who was then vice-chairman of *The New York Times,* as to what I should do with the information that I had uncovered in Moscow. Sydney told me, "You have a moral obligation to get this information into the hands of the people at the highest levels of the U.S. government." With Sydney's help I tried unsuccessfully to convince the U.S. State Department, the Pentagon, the National Security Council, and the CIA that what I had seen in Moscow was serious business.

Unfortunately, when I visited the State Department, we were without the services of a secretary of state. Alexander Haig had just resigned, and George Schultz had not yet come on board. As a result of the transition, the highest-ranking official who agreed to see me was Mark Palmer, the head of the Soviet desk at the State Department. However, Palmer was not without some clout in the Reagan administration. He managed Reagan's game plan for the Geneva summit in 1985 and later became ambassador to Hungary.

I tried to convince Palmer and other officials that what I had heard and seen in Moscow might have important implications for improved U.S.–Soviet relations. I naively asked, "Why do we need to continue spending hundreds of billions of dollars each year protecting ourselves from the Russians, if they are on the verge of emulating our economic and political systems?" Palmer listened attentively, said little, and offered me no encouragement.

The CIA invited me to their Virginia headquarters for a debriefing session, acknowledged their familiarity with the Soviet simulation studies, and dismissed them as being unimportant. Harvard Sovietologist Marshall Goldman, who often appears on national television predicting the fall of Gorbachev, laughed smugly at my account of the Soviet computer studies.

I also prepared a memorandum summarizing my findings in Moscow and sent it to Secretary of State George P. Schultz,

Secretary of Defense Caspar Weinberger, and National Security Advisor William P. Clark, each of whom acknowledged receipt of my memorandum in writing.

The response of Reagan administration officials to what turned out to be an important precursor of Gorbachev's radical reforms was one of complete indifference. They clearly had bigger fish to fry in 1982. They had no interest whatsoever in information that could potentially undermine the rationale on which the greatest peacetime military buildup in history was to be based. To them, ending the cold war was just not as important as what they had in mind for the next six years.

To cynics who claimed that what I saw in Moscow was of no consequence, in 1982 I wrote in *The New York Times* that, "it appears that someone in Moscow is listening to what these Soviet economists are saying. Maybe we should, too."[2] It was not until my May 1985 visit to Moscow that I learned who had, in fact, been listening to these economists—Yuri V. Andropov and Mikhail S. Gorbachev.

In response to my query as to why these Soviet economists were engaged in this challenging research, they responded, "We have very big economic problems in the Soviet Union." They then proceeded to define some of these problems, which included a stagnant economy, inefficient agriculture, an inadequate supply of consumer goods and services, a serious technological gap with the West, a rigid political structure, a police-state mentality, a high death rate, and an increasingly alienated population.

The message from these pragmatic technocrats to their party bosses was clear. Unless the Soviets were willing to consider major structural changes in the economic mechanism similar to those being implemented by China and Hungary, then the economy was likely to continue to stagnate. Anything short of a Hungarian-style, market-oriented socialism would be inadequate to deal with the myriad economic problems faced by the Soviets.

When Yuri V. Andropov announced a package of "economic experiments" on 26 July 1983, the objective of which was to introduce decentralized management in all of the companies belonging to five industrial ministries, there was a solid scientific basis underlying these experiments. Under the decree from the Central Committee, which established these experiments, plant managers were given wider authority over their budgets, with greater discretion in matters of investment, wages, bonuses, and retained earnings, all of which had been tightly controlled by the supervisory ministries and Gosplan in the past.

The Andropov experiments began on schedule on 1 January 1984. One month later Andropov died, and Konstantin V. Chernenko presided over their implementation until his death in March 1985. Although Chernenko had little to say about them during his year in power, he did nothing to impede their progress. Most American experts scoffed at the Andropov experiments, considering them only cosmetic changes rather than much-needed structural changes.

These experiments were the logical consequence of nearly twenty years of scientific research by such well-known Soviet economists as V. S. Nemchinov, L. V. Kantorovich, Nikolay Fedorenko, and Abel G. Aganbegyan. Academician Aganbegyan, one of Gorbachev's principal economic advisors, was one of the most active economists involved in developing models to simulate the introduction of Hungarian-style economic reforms in the Soviet Union.

On 21 March 1985, ten days after Mr. Gorbachev came to power, former Duke University President Terry Sanford and I organized a conference on "East–West Trade and Joint Ventures" at a time when no one in the United States was interested in U.S.–Soviet trade. On the day that Chernenko died, I received four telephone calls from Moscow reassuring me that the Soviet delegation still planned to participate in the conference. Seventeen Soviets and Eastern Europeans showed up—a clear signal that it was no longer business as usual in Moscow.

Six weeks after Gorbachev came to power, I met with company managers and government officials involved with the economic reforms in Moscow, Leningrad, and Tbilisi. By that time the number of ministries participating in the economic experiments initiated by Andropov had been increased from five to twenty-one—one-third of all of the Soviet ministries. When asked why the experiments had been extended to include all of the enterprises in sixteen additional ministries, Soviet officials indicated that the experiments had been quite successful. Company managers who participated in the experiments reported increased output and efficiency, reduced production lead times, lower costs, higher profits, increased benefits and wages, and significantly improved employee morale. Not bad for the first year by almost any standards.

In June of 1985, I tried once again to convince the CIA, the Reagan administration, and a number of well-known journalists that all of the signs in Moscow pointed toward radical reform. Without exception their responses ranged from icy silence to polite skepticism. *Washington Post* editor Robert G. Kaiser[3] and Brookings Institution economist Ed A. Hewett scoffed at these ideas as naive and uninformed. They both had invested heavily in the view that the Soviet Union would never change. In his 1988 book *Reforming the Soviet Economy*,[4] Hewett viewed serious economic reform in the Soviet Union as a most unlikely scenario.

To help him de-Stalinize the Soviet Union and open the closed society, Gorbachev turned to a team of high-level economic strategists to lay the groundwork for additional reforms announced at the Party Plenum in June 1987 and at the All-Union Party Conference in June 1988. All of the economic reforms included in the new enterprise law, which went into effect on 1 January 1988, were based on recent simulation studies conducted by Soviet economists. Not until January 1989 did Gorbachev first publicly acknowledge the fact that the directions of his program for economic reform had been mapped out by more than one hundred economic studies by Soviet specialists before he came to power.

The fact of the matter is that most of Gorbachev's reforms have been the subject of intense simulation analysis for a long period of time. When Sovietologists claim there is no well-defined strategy underlying Gorbachev's *perestroika,* they are denying the relevance of two decades of management-science research on which *perestroika* is firmly grounded. Indeed, *perestroika* is the most comprehensive, in-depth, management-science project ever implemented anywhere in the world.

Soviet economists now enjoy an important advantage that was not available previously. They have empirical data on the actual results of economic reform going back to the initial Andropov experiments in 1984. Prior to the death of Brezhnev in 1982 there was no meaningful empirical database that could be used by Soviet economists to validate their analyses.

But as Soviet dissident Boris Kagarlitsky has documented in his intellectual history of the Soviet Union since 1917 entitled *The Thinking Reed,* the pursuit of a liberal political agenda in the Soviet

Union was by no means limited to a handful of economists and social scientists.[5] Since the 1920s a significant number of Soviet artists, actors, writers, and film producers have been discreetly laying the groundwork for a more open and more liberal political system in the Soviet Union. Many of the ideas of these Soviet dissidents were very subtle and very sophisticated. There is no doubt that both Gorbachev and his wife Raisa were strongly influenced by the thinking of some of these progressive Soviet artists as well as the aforementioned economists. If Gorbachev had not appeared on the scene when he did, someone with similar thinking would surely have emerged from this loose network of like-thinking Soviet intellectuals to challenge the moribund Soviet system. But the Soviets were indeed very lucky that a leader with Gorbachev's enormous political skills did emerge from such an intellectually bankrupt environment.

Economic Reform

Gorbachev has been driven towards radical economic, political, and foreign-policy reforms by a combination of internal problems, which we have previously defined, as well as a number of international forces. Internationally, the Soviets have been influenced by the economic and foreign-trade strategies of Hungary, China, Japan, Sweden, Finland, and West Germany, as well as the foreign policy of the Reagan administration. All of these forces are quite independent of Gorbachev the man. Contrary to what we are told by Sovietologists, the economic reforms will continue with or without Gorbachev.

Prior to the collapse of communist regimes all over Eastern Europe in 1989, Hungary had served as an important prototype for Soviet economic reforms. Unlike 1956, when the Soviets used force to snuff out Hungarian initiatives, since 1985 the Soviets have been much more interested in emulating some of the Hungarian reforms. The fact that China successfully replicated the Hungarian experiment with a population one hundred times the size of Hungary in less than one-third the time not only validated the Hungarian experience in the eyes of Soviet leaders, but it greatly enhanced its credibility. Obviously, Hungary is no longer the only Eastern European country that has the Soviets' attention.

In no area are Gorbachev's reforms more radical than in international trade. His fundamental objective is to strengthen the Soviet economy and reduce international political tensions through a strategy of increased global interdependence based on bilateral trade between the Soviet Union and the rest of the world.

The Soviets must increase the quality and quantity of their exports to the West to finance their much-needed imports of consumer goods, technology, and foodstuffs. Imports help break the monopolistic stranglehold some Soviet enterprises possess over certain industries. More imports mean more competition in the domestic market.

If the new chief executive of a major company such as AT&T or IBM wants to introduce fundamental changes, he must come to grips with the company's culture—the attitudes, values, and customs of the firm's managers and employees. This is precisely the situation in which Gorbachev finds himself as he attempts to de-Stalinize the Soviet Union and open the closed society. If Gorbachev is to succeed, he must confront the culture of the largest risk-free society in the world. But that is exactly what he is doing, and he is doing it very effectively.

For many years the Soviet Union has borne the brunt of American jokes about the poor quality of their consumer goods. A 1985 Wendy's television commercial ridiculed Soviet fashions by featuring a matronly Soviet woman dressed in a drab, potato-sack-like dress. Cynics claim that Gorbachev's efforts to internationalize the Soviet economy are doomed to failure because of the Soviets' inability to produce world-class consumer goods. But there are signs that this may be changing.

To increase productivity, Gorbachev has offered financial incentives to motivate managers and employees alike. Previously such incentives met with only limited success, since there were no high-quality consumer goods available on which the Soviets could spend their extra rubles. French designer clothes and other consumer goods imported from the West help energize the reforms.

Which comes first: the production of world-class consumer goods or the use of high-quality consumer goods to encourage the production of improved-quality Soviet products? In no sense has Gorbachev completely sorted out this complex problem. However, he has taken some very interesting first steps.

Although Gorbachev has begun dismantling the centrally planned economy, he has yet to replace the old system with anything resembling a viable market-oriented economy. Soviet economists repeatedly point out that Gorbachev's real challenge is how to create new markets completely from scratch. There are no well-defined markets for factory supplies such as raw materials, machinery, or equipment for Soviet industrial enterprises. Wholesale and retail distribution networks simply do not exist. Financial markets are still in the embryonic stage of development. Although Gorbachev's political reforms are far more radical than those of the Chinese, the results of his economic reforms pale in comparison to the Chinese experience.

To achieve his overall objective of making the Soviet Union a more open and more prosperous society, Mr. Gorbachev is pursuing a strategy that combines many of the elements of market-oriented, democratic socialism with an international strategy based on multilateral cooperation and global interdependence.

Common Problems

The Soviet economy also has serious shortages of raw materials and energy, which give rise to production imbalances, unfulfilled production quotas, the need for Western imports, and rising costs. In addition, the Soviet economy now suffers from a number of new problems, including rising unemployment, inflation, a trade deficit, declining oil exports, strikes, a growing foreign debt, and an increasing government deficit.

Unlike the Chinese economic reforms introduced by Deng Xiaoping in 1978, which generated average annual GNP growth rates of 9 percent during the following decade, the Soviet economic reforms have resulted in few positive results. Under Gorbachev the Soviet economy now appears to be deteriorating even further. One bright spot in the Soviet economy is the 200,000 cooperatives that emerged between May of 1987 and year-end 1989. Over five million people were employed by cooperatives by early 1990. Private enterprise will soon be a fact of life in the Soviet Union.

During the 1980s, the United States chalked up a series of record-high trade and budget deficits. We now have the dubious distinction of being the world's largest debtor nation. As we noted in the story of Johnny and Sasha, the rate of growth of productivity in the United States slowed from an average of 3 percent per year between 1947 and 1973 to an average of only 1 percent since 1973. Not only are we experiencing productivity problems but product-quality problems as well. All too often the expression "Made in the USA" has come to be associated with substandard materials and shoddy workmanship.

Although our economy has demonstrated an impressive ability to create an abundance of new jobs, wages have generally not kept pace with inflation. The rate of unemployment never dropped below 5 percent during the Reagan years.

Both the United States and the Soviet Union have serious agricultural problems. In our case the problem is overproduction—in sharp contrast to underproduction in the USSR. In 1987 the United States spent $26 billion on farm subsidies while thousands of farmers were being forced into bankruptcy by a combination of overproduction and falling farm prices.

Problems with Soviet agricultural production can be traced back to the czars in the eighteenth century and have persisted during every important period in recent Soviet history—World War I, the 1917 Revolution, War Communism, the New Economic Policy, Stalin, World War II, Khrushchev, and Brezhnev. Sixty years later, Soviet agriculture has never fully recovered from the forced collectivization schemes of Stalin in the 1930s.

The Soviets' agricultural problems stem from two primary sources—excessive centralization of agriculture and an extremely harsh climate. Inefficiency, waste, fertilizer shortages, transportation bottlenecks, and a lack of incentives are all characteristics of a rigid, unwieldy system that gives all too little attention to the feelings and attitudes of individual managers and workers. When these problems are compounded by short growing seasons and erratic rainfall, then frequent production shortfalls are the rule.

In response to the disastrous 1988 harvest, Gorbachev called for the dismantling of the state agricultural bureaucracy, the introduction of free markets, and lifetime leases to encourage private farming.

Private investment in plant and equipment is 10.2 percent of GNP in the United States in contrast to 17.0 percent in Japan. The average age of the U.S. industrial base is seventeen years compared to ten years for Japan. As a result of cutbacks in the rate of investment in plant and equipment in the United States and the Soviet Union, the rate of depreciation of equipment now exceeds the rate of investment in some industries. The failure to modernize key industries has contributed to the severity of several other major Soviet and American economic problems including productivity and product quality. It has also led to shortages of consumer goods in the USSR.

Both the United States and the Soviet Union have large supplies of crude oil and natural gas, which have not encouraged efficiency. Indeed, many economists believe that the Soviets would have been forced to reform their economic system much sooner, if the price of crude oil had not increased so dramatically in the 1970s. The precipitous price increase enabled the Soviets to put off *perestroika* for nearly a decade.

The Soviets had their 1986 nuclear disaster at the Chernobyl power plant. The United States has absorbed a $100 billion economic burden from abandoned nuclear-power plants and nuclear plants that were completed at costs substantially higher than alternative technologies. The future of nuclear power in both countries remains problematic at best.

In spite of the fact that it invests a large share of its GNP in research and development and graduates more engineers each year than do countries in the West, the Soviet Union continues to suffer from a technological gap with the West. Although the Soviets are particularly skilled at basic research, science, and mathematics, they experience consistent problems in transforming basic research into nonmilitary products and applications. Even though they have achieved significant technological breakthroughs in military and aerospace research and engineering, few of these achievements seem to have spilled over into the industrial sector of their economy. Some of their most notable technological deficiencies include computer hardware and software, process-control systems, and energy-related equipment.

But the United States has also begun to experience some technology problems of its own as evidenced by the fact that some high-tech imports now exceed exports. At least part of the blame is directly attributable to President Reagan's military spending spree.

In 1988, government and industry each spent $61 billion on R&D in the United States. But 69 percent of the Federal government's share went to military research in contrast to fifteen years earlier when government R&D was evenly divided between civilian and military purposes. In Japan only 4.5 percent of government R&D is allocated for defense. The corresponding figure for West Germany is 12.5 percent.

Since 1981, Federal spending for military R&D increased by 78 percent while civilian R&D spending declined 27 percent. Civilian R&D spending has remained at about 1.8 percent of GNP in the United States for two decades. Meanwhile Japan has increased civilian R&D spending to 2.8 percent of GNP and West Germany to 2.6 percent.

In the past, jet aircraft, computers, and computer chips were important commercial spin-offs of military R&D. But today's sophisticated weapons seem to have considerably less commercial relevance. There have been no major commercial breakthroughs generated by the B-1 bomber, the Stealth bomber, or the Strategic Defense Initiative.

The U.S. government has also demonstrated a penchant for investing in high-tech disasters such as the $4 billion nuclear breeder reactor program, the synfuels program, and uranium enrichment plants. President Reagan supported programs calling for the development of an $8 billion space station, a $8 billion superconducting supercollider, and a $46 billion research program for determining the chemical sequence of the genetic instruction set. The space station is now expected to cost $120 billion. The scientific community is deeply divided over the socioeconomic benefits of these multi-billion-dollar technologies. There is also evidence to suggest that a number of sophisticated technologies may have been oversold. These include manned space flights, the space station, and artificial intelligence. Furthermore, microcomputers are now so widespread in American business that their use has been utterly trivialized. In some cases they are being used by high-paid executives to deal with extremely mundane problems.

For over sixty years the Soviet economy survived with a truly primitive monetary system in which state-owned enterprises received literally all of their operating funds from the state monopoly bank, Gosbank. Until recently, Soviet enterprises could receive no funds whatsoever from either private or international sources abroad. The tightly controlled ruble is still not convertible on global money markets. But all of this has begun to change under *perestroika*. The Soviets have taken significant steps to monetize their economy, including the introduction of venture capital banks, commercial banks, checks, credit cards, and foreign joint ventures. They have expressed an interest in joining the World Bank, the International Monetary Fund, and the General Agreement of Tariffs and Trade. They have also introduced private cooperatives, employee-owned shares of state-owned companies, and a progressive personal-income tax. A stock market, a convertible ruble, free capital markets, and the elimination of price controls are sure to come. But monetizing the Soviet economy has also created inflationary pressures and an increasing budget deficit.

The U.S. economy, on the other hand, is plagued by some quite different financial problems, including huge annual budget deficits, a $3 trillion national debt, mounting foreign debt, a record number of bank failures, uncollectible Third World debt, and the $500 billion bailout of the savings and loan industry. Although the economy took the 19 October 1987 stock-market crash in stride, merger mania, leveraged buyouts, golden parachutes, short-run profits, and stock-price performance continue to be more important to Corporate America than innovative new products, product quality improvements, increased efficiency, participatory management, and long-term strategic planning.

Because there are so few consumer goods available in the Soviet Union, savings banks hold deposits equal to $1,700 for every man, woman, and child. Soviet workers save nearly half of their annual salaries. Americans have one of the lowest savings rates among the industrialized nations of the world. Savings represent only 3.9 percent of disposable income in the U.S. in comparison to 5.6 percent for Great Britain, 12.2 percent for West Germany, and 16.6 percent for Japan.

The biggest impediments to the implementation of the Soviet economic reforms are not Marxist-Leninist ideology, the *nomenklatura* (self-perpetuating party elites), or the government bureaucracy, but rather Soviet managers' lack of experience with market-oriented management practices. Inadequate management training is a very serious problem, which the Soviets have not confronted in any systematic fashion thus far. Most Soviet managers have no experience with such basic managerial functions as accounting, finance, marketing, or organizational development. We have previously described a number of serious American management problems in the story of Johnny and Sasha.

Some economists believe that the key to revitalizing the U.S. economy lies not with participatory management, foreign trade, or a national industrial policy but rather with a reduction in our defense burden. Some even go so far as to suggest that there may be an inverse relationship between high military spending and economic performance.[6] In a recent study, Joshua S. Goldstein has challenged the American myth that the preparation for war benefits the economy. Professor Goldstein argues that the military competes with and limits economic growth. His studies show that for every 1 percent of GNP allocated to military defense, overall economic growth is reduced by about one-half of a percent. He sees a linkage between Japan's relatively low military burden and its economic success—a fact which has influenced China to make huge cuts in its military budget.[7]

The CIA estimates that the Soviet Union spends $15.5 billion annually on military and economic assistance to Afghanistan, Angola, Cambodia, Cuba, Ethiopia, Nicaragua, and Vietnam. At the Malta summit, Secretary of State James Baker III hypocritically presented the Soviets with a paper spelling out the benefits to the Soviet economy of diverting this $15.5 billion to domestic programs.[8] The Bush administration has shown no interest in this type of analysis for the U.S. economy.

Overall Soviet defense spending fell by 4 to 5 percent in real terms in 1989 according to the CIA. In addition, over four hundred defense plants and two hundred research organizations increased production for the civilian sector in 1989.

Power Sharing

By broadening the base of participation of the Soviet people in the economic and political system, Gorbachev hopes eventually to turn the Soviet economy around. The key to participation is empowerment. Unless people feel they have a psychological and economic stake in the system, then *perestroika* will surely fail. Power sharing and tension reduction are aimed squarely at the problems of Johnny and Sasha.

In September 1988 Mr. Gorbachev reorganized the Central Committee of the Communist Party. The significance of these radical changes went unnoticed by Sovietologists. By creating six new Central Committee policy-making commissions, Gorbachev was emulating a sophisticated management style used by only a handful of very successful Western companies, such as IBM, Shell Oil, Dow Chemical, Federal Express, and Burroughs Wellcome.

The traditional single-boss, single-command hierarchical structure of the Soviet government has been replaced by a more flexible participatory-management system that combines a multi-boss, multicommand matrix with interdisciplinary management teams. This approach to strategic management was first introduced in the United States in 1968 by Dow-Corning to overcome some of the problems of hierarchical organizations including business interdependence, alienation, turf disputes, and organizational inflexibility.[9]

The real power of matrix management lies in the fact that it enables the CEO to maintain tight organizational control while decentralizing decision making and broadening the base of participation in the strategic-planning process. Paradoxically, through power sharing the CEO gains even more control over the organization—a point which has not escaped Gorbachev's attention.

IBM turned to matrix management in 1972 to deal more effectively with foreign competition and the antitrust charges brought against it by the Justice Department. The CEO of Burroughs Wellcome used a similar approach to take control of the company in 1986, change the corporate culture, and make the company more market oriented.

The Central Committee commissions are analogous to corporate strategy teams and reveal Gorbachev's strategic priorities—agriculture, socioeconomic development, legal and political reform, ideological revision, organizational development, and foreign affairs. The objectives of these commissions are (1) to define government strategies, (2) to coordinate the transfer of political power from government ministries to individual enterprises and local governments, and (3) to support the decision making of more autonomous state-owned enterprises and local governments and discourage central government intervention in their affairs.

The matrix-like organization provides Gorbachev with a powerful mechanism to coordinate and integrate the complex strategies required to change the Soviet culture. The strategy teams are consistent with Gorbachev's nonconfrontational management style.

Unlike many political leaders who often subject their adversaries to ridicule and intimidation, Gorbachev attempts to co-opt his adversaries through strategies based on mutual gain.

Through empowerment Gorbachev is attempting to encourage the Soviet people to assume more risk and responsibility for their personal lives in exchange for more personal freedom and the promise of an improved standard of living. He continues to maintain tight control over the Soviet government by increasingly sharing political power with enterprise managers, local Party officials, ethnic minorities in such places as Estonia and Azerbaijan, and Russian republic leader Boris Yeltsin. Power sharing and tension reduction are the foundations on which *glasnost* and *perestroika* are firmly based. Without power sharing there will be no empowerment. Without broad-based empowerment, the Soviet Union will cease to be a significant player in the global political arena.

The New Congress of Peoples Deputies—the supreme government body of the Soviet Union—provides further evidence of Gorbachev's commitment of power sharing. It consists of 1,500 deputies elected from territorial and national districts and 750 selected by Communist Party Committees, trade unions, youth, artists, and other organizations. The New Congress selects the members of the National Legislature—the Supreme Soviet—and elects the president.

Throughout 1988 and 1989 Soviet authorities demonstrated a high degree of tolerance for grass-roots political organizations such as the Moscow People's Front, the Democratic Union, and Democratic Perestroika. Some of these organizations have begun functioning as de facto political parties.

Then in February 1990, while Sovietologists and the American media were warning that the end was near for Gorbachev, the Central Committee of the Communist Party agreed to surrender its historic monopoly of power in the Soviet Union, create a Western-style presidency and cabinet system of government, and open the door to multiparty political pluralism. The Central Committee repudiated Article 6 of the Soviet Constitution, which granted the Communist party its monopolistic position. New legislation legalizes alternative political parties and grants them equal rights with the Communist party.

Article 6 of the Soviet Constitution

THE LEADING AND GUIDING FORCE OF Soviet society and the nucleus of its political system, of all state organizations and public organizations, is the Communist Party of the Soviet Union. The CPSU exists for the people and serves the people.

The Communist party, armed with Marxism–Leninism, determines the general perspectives of the development of society and the course of the domestic and foreign policy of the USSR, directs the great constructive work of the Soviet people, and imparts a planned, systematic and theoretically substantiated character to their struggle for the victory of Communism.

All party organizations shall function within the framework of the Constitution of the USSR.

At the July 1990 Communist party congress, Gorbachev pushed power sharing one step further when he reorganized the Politburo. By increasing the membership of the Politburo from twelve to twenty-four members and including representatives from each of the fifteen Soviet republics, Gorbachev broadened his power base significantly. In much the same way as he reconstituted the Central Committee, Gorbachev transformed the Politburo into a matrix-like organization defined along functional and geographic lines. Indeed, this was by far his most laudable accomplishment at the party congress. For the first time in Soviet history, every republic is now represented on the Politburo. This is particularly important when many republics are pressing the Kremlin for independence.

Just because power sharing has worked for some very large multinational corporations does not mean it will work in Moscow. Power sharing is very risky business.

Democratic Socialism

In addition to the sweeping political reforms already introduced by Mr. Gorbachev in the Soviet Union, between August and December of 1989 every Eastern European government made significant shifts away from Stalinism and Marxist-Leninist ideology toward what Gorbachev calls democratic socialism. The people of the German Democratic Republic not only brought down

Communist hard-liner Erich Honecker, but the Berlin Wall as well. Hungary, Poland, Czechoslovakia, Bulgaria, and Romania each took giant steps towards democracy and political pluralism.

Although every Eastern European country has become more democratic and more market oriented, what is likely to emerge in the Soviet Union and Eastern Europe is a type of democratic socialism—not American-style capitalism. The real differences between capitalism and socialism lie not so much with the question of who owns a nation's industrial enterprises, but rather in the extent to which individual citizens participate in the decisions affecting their personal lives.

It is Stalinism that has been defeated—not socialism. The very essence of socialism is participatory democracy, not state ownership of the means of production. Arguably, the only thing wrong with socialism in the Soviet Union and Eastern Europe is that it has never ever been tried. Until very recently, all of the Warsaw Pact nations were totalitarian states, not social democracies.

Austria, Canada, Finland, and Sweden—particularly Sweden— are among the countries to whom the Soviet Union and Eastern Europe are looking for role models as they attempt to break away from the shackles of Stalinism. They are among a handful of countries that consistently achieve high income levels while not ignoring the plight of the poor and less fortunate.

During the 1970s the Swedish economy was adversely affected by the 1973 OPEC oil shock, excessive government spending, and dissatisfaction among workers concerning their subordinate position in the workplace. Sweden experienced declining competitiveness, rising unemployment and inflation, and falling consumer incomes.

Beginning with a 16 percent devaluation of the krona in late 1982, Sweden embarked on a painful process of industrial restructuring aimed at reducing unemployment and inflation by increasing exports and raising capital spending by business. The Swedish economy improved on practically all fronts during the 1980s in contrast to its rather lackluster performance during the 1970s. Gross domestic product (GDP) grew twice as fast during the 1983–87 period as it did during the 1970s. Unemployment dropped from a peak of 3.5 percent in 1983 to less than 2 percent in 1990. Although the rate of inflation declined by 4 percent between 1983 and 1987, it shot back up in 1990 amid other economic problems in Sweden including labor unrest, slowed economic growth, and a widening current-account deficit.

A striking change has been the abandonment of "sunset" industry subsidies. The ship-building industry, which employed twenty-eight thousand in the mid-1970s, has been phased out over ten years, leaving no unemployment behind.

But Sweden is a tiny country of 8.4 million people with a strong base of shared societal values in contrast to the Soviet Union, which has a population of 285 million spread over fifteen heterogeneous socialist republics. Therefore, one must be somewhat cautious in generalizing from the Swedish experience to the Soviet Union.

One of the Soviets' most serious problems is their technological gap with the West. Although highly skilled at basic research, they have difficulty in translating it into consumer goods. The Swedes are much stronger in converting technology into marketable products. The market-oriented Swedish approach to research differs markedly from the inflexible, centralized Soviet approach. Also, Sweden is not a member of the Consultative Group Coordinating Committee, which tries to block the flow of Western technology to the Soviets.

A major obstacle to Soviet reform is management's inexperience in decentralized, market-oriented work practices. The retraining of Soviet managers and workers represents a monumental challenge. But the Swedes have been successful in retraining smokestack-industry employees and helping them reenter the work force.

Cooperatives represent a clever way of injecting new life into the Soviet economy by circumventing Soviet industrial ministries. The new Soviet law on cooperatives provides even more flexibility to tens of thousands of new cooperative business, including restaurants, auto-repair shops, consulting firms, and home-repair businesses. The Swedes have a lot of experience with cooperatives.

Sweden's nonconfrontational management style also spills over into the field of foreign relations. Through a foreign policy based on nonalliance during peacetime and neutrality during war, Sweden managed to stay out of both world wars and has remained at peace for over 175 years. Although it has a relatively strong defense program, it spends about half as much as the United States does when expressed as a percentage of GNP. It is one of the most generous countries in the world in terms of foreign aid to Third World nations. Sweden also has a long history as a peacemaker. For example, Sweden played a constructive role in formulation a "mutual recognition" strategy in the conflict between Israel and the PLO and a "mutual disengagement" strategy aimed at winding down the Angola–Namibia war.

Sweden has carved out an important niche in the global marketplace that avoids some of the pitfalls of capitalism and socialism. The Kremlin is paying attention to the Swedes. Maybe the United States should too.

Exactly what form democratic socialism will take in the Soviet Union and Eastern Europe still remains to be seen. However, what appears to be emerging is a pluralistic, participatory approach to politics and property ownership. In addition to state-owned enterprises, there will be private enterprises, cooperatives, and enterprises owned by local municipal governments. Both government and industry will be far more decentralized than in the past. There will be multiple political parties representing a full spectrum of political opinion. Communist parties will be reconstituted along the lines of social-democratic parties in Western Europe.

Economic Conversion

The ravenous appetite of our military-industrial complex has not only contributed significantly to our huge national debt but also to our serious productivity problems and our record trade deficits. In spite of the dramatic improvement in U.S.–Soviet relations, the Bush administration remained cool to the idea of a "peace dividend" in 1990. However, public and congressional debate over possible reductions in defense spending heated up considerably in 1990. This debate raises two fundamental questions. First, who should decide what is the proper level of defense spending for the United States in response to the changes in East–West relations? Second, if it is appropriate to reduce our commitment to military defense, then how should we go about transforming our economy from a defense-dependent economy to a peacetime economy?

One thing is for sure, these decisions should *not* be made only by the Defense Department. If they are left to the Congress, then the usual pro-defense lobby will carry the day and nothing will change.

The President should appoint a high-level White House commission to help plan and coordinate the transition from a cold war economy to an economy that reflects the new global order. The commission should be appointed for a single five-year term, help define defense and domestic priorities, and facilitate the orderly transition to a less militarily dependent economy.

The commission might identify those military projects that can be cancelled or reduced. It could also propose industries, infrastructure projects, and social-welfare projects that deserve priority attention and either government or private funding. In Japan, the Ministry of International Trade and Industry (MITI) identifies those industries which the government intends to encourage and helps arrange public and private financing for them. Infrastructure projects might include highway and bridge repairs, a high-speed railway passenger network, public housing, and improved air-traffic-control systems. The commission might also recommend that some defense-related funds be reallocated to support public education, the war on drugs, the homeless, and medical care for the poor.

The membership of the commission should be broad-based with representation from business, labor, the Pentagon, the poor, and various minorities. The primary objective should be to provide guidance in converting the U.S. economy to a more efficient civilian-driven economy that will be more responsible to the needs of the American people and better able to compete in the international marketplace.

Although there is conservative political opposition in Moscow to scaling back the Soviet military, there is no Soviet equivalent of the Committee on the Present Danger or any group approaching the American military-industrial complex in terms of political power. Since Soviet weapons manufacturers are state-owned, they are not driven by the profit motive to maintain their present position. Until recently labor unions in the USSR were government controlled and had little power to influence major policy decisions.

However, the reductions in the number of Soviet troops stationed in Eastern Europe are causing Gorbachev some big headaches in terms of unemployment and demand for housing. Returning soldiers find themselves unemployed, without adequate housing, and with a complete loss of the social status previously afforded Soviet military people.

Regrettably, the 1990 Persian Gulf crisis may have pushed economic conversion in the United States to the back burner for an indefinite period of time.

6

Lack of Competitiveness

U.S.–Soviet Trade

Both the United States and the Soviet Union are paying a high price for their inability to compete effectively in the international marketplace. Since the days of Lenin the Soviets have maintained a strong interest in trade with the West even though until recently they had little that the West wanted to buy other than crude oil, natural gas, and minerals. Unlike the United States, political ideology has never been a problem for Soviet trade officials in their trade relations.

China's foreign trade responded dramatically to Deng Xiaoping's "open door" policy towards the West. Between 1978 and 1988 Chinese trade increased from $20 billion to $103 billion. Foreign trade reforms were not introduced by Mr. Gorbachev until January 1987—two years after he came to power. Between 1985 and 1989 Soviet foreign trade only increased from $170.5 billion to $224 billion. During this same period the Soviet Union's balance of trade shifted from a $4.0 billion trade surplus in 1985 to a $5.4 billion trade deficit in 1989.

But the United States is also having very serious trade problems of its own. The U.S. trade deficit exceeded $100 billion in 1989 for the sixth consecutive year. The $106 billion 1989 trade deficit was roughly matched by the $57 billion Japanese trade surplus and the $53 billion West German trade surplus. As a result of America's huge trade deficit, it's not surprising that an increasing number of U.S. companies are looking for new markets in the Soviet Union and Eastern Europe. Intense competition in the West, combined with severe import restrictions imposed by Third

World nations straining under huge debts to U.S. banks, have made this necessary.

In 1988, Eastern Europe, including the Soviet Union, was the fastest-growing market for the United States. American exports to the eight Eastern European socialist countries soared 53.7 percent.

The Soviet Union is one of the very few countries with which the United States consistently has a trade surplus. This surplus shrank in 1986 and 1987 because the sharp drop in the price of oil reduced foreign currency available to the Soviets to buy American goods. In these two years, trade between the two superpowers averaged a paltry $2 billion per year, down from a high of $4.5 billion in 1979. However, in 1988, U.S.–Soviet trade increased 70 percent to $3.4 billion before reaching a record high of $5.0 billion in 1989 primarily as a result of increased Soviet grain purchases. Sino–American trade in 1989 was over three times as much as U.S.–Soviet trade. The Chinese exported $12 billion worth of goods to the United States in 1989 while buying $6 billion in return.

The Soviet Union offers the United States an untapped consumer market of over 285 million people, as well as a highly concentrated market for large-scale contracts. It also has vast reserves of hydrocarbons and energy, which make it an increasingly attractive trading partner as the U.S. supply of crude oil continues to tail off.

Since January 1987, most Soviet state-owned enterprises can now trade directly with the West. Foreign companies may own up to 100 percent of the equity in Soviet joint-venture companies. Repatriation of profits, reinvestment tax incentives, third-country operations, and expropriation protection are all part of the package. Special trade zones, new financial and banking institutions, and a freely convertible ruble are likely in the near future.

Corporate giants such as Dow Chemical, Abbott Labs, Pepsico, and Occidental Petroleum have traded with the Soviets for years. More-recent entries into the Soviet market are Combustion Engineering, McDonald's, Chevron, Pizza Hut, Baskin-Robbins, Ben & Jerry's Ice Cream, Eastman Kodak, Coca-Cola, Johnson & Johnson, and RJR Nabisco. It is now possible for much smaller American firms such as Merrick Engineering of Nashville, Tennessee—which has thirty-eight employees—to do business in the Soviet Union. My two favorite American firms operating in

Moscow are Lafitte's Landing Louisiana Cajun Restaurant and Delta Catfish of Indianola, Mississippi.

The power of the international marketplace is one of Gorbachev's most important instruments of change. He is much more interested in exporting Soviet-made goods and services rather than communism.

From the Soviet side the two biggest obstacles to increased trade with the United States are the lack of convertibility of the ruble and the unfamiliarity of Soviet managers with Western trade and management practices.

The Soviets took an important initial step toward ruble convertibility in November 1989 when they reduced the value of the ruble from $1.60 to 16 cents for foreigners in the Soviet Union and Soviets traveling abroad. All Soviet economists now talk openly about the problem of convertibility. The issue is no longer whether the ruble will become convertible but rather when will it happen, and by what mechanism. The Council for Mutual Economic Assistance (CMEA) has begun trading in hard currency at real market prices.

But if there is a single most important deficiency of *perestroika*, it is the Soviet Union's complete inability to come to grips with the monumental task of reorienting Soviet managers to a more market-like economy. The entire world of Soviet managers has been turned on its head, but these managers have been given virtually no new training nor new managerial skills to cope with these radical changes.

The Soviet approach to management education is completely piecemeal and woefully inadequate to meet the challenges of *perestroika* and the globalization of the Soviet economy. All too much attention is being devoted to American business schools—most of whom have little or nothing to offer Soviet managers. A typical delegation of Soviet management educators will visit the business schools at Harvard, MIT, Columbia, Duke, and Stanford with the objective of signing a protocol agreement to take back to Moscow as a kind of trophy. Most of these agreements are not worth the paper on which they are written. The Soviets refuse to pay for management education in hard currency. Neither side is committed to anything.

There are a handful—and only a handful—of American business schools that may actually be able to help Soviet managers.

These include the business schools at Oklahoma City University and the University of South Carolina. Oklahoma City University has an impressive track record of training managers in the People's Republic of China, Hong Kong, Malaysia, and Singapore. Also, Clemson University has recently started an MBA program in Moscow to train Soviet managers.

Those Soviet managers who want to specialize in international business should not come to the United States at all. Rather, they should go to the London Business School, INSEAD near Paris, the Stockholm School of Economics, or the Helsinki School of Economics. The state of the art of international management education in the United States is abysmal.

From the U.S. side, the major impediments to increased U.S.–Soviet trade are American ignorance, arrogance, and residual anti-Soviet paranoia. Our government has created some truly formidable obstacles to increased U.S.–Soviet trade, including export controls, import controls, financial controls, and other political and legal constraints. The Jackson–Vanik amendment linking Soviet most-favored-nation status to Jewish emigration and the Pentagon's irrational, anti-Soviet technology-transfer policies are cold war anachronisms.

If we mean what we say about wanting to encourage the Soviet Union to become a more open, market-oriented society, then why don't we offer them more positive encouragement rather than continuing to impose endless government restrictions on U.S.–Soviet trade? If we truly believe in the power of the free market, why don't we give it a chance to work in the Soviet Union?

In my opinion, the Soviet Union should seriously consider the possibility of backing away from its aggressive pursuit of trade with the United States until 1992. Instead it should concentrate its energy and its limited financial resources on its more friendly Western European, Japanese, and Third World trading partners. My advice to the Soviets is, "Don't be so eager to trade with the United States. Let American businessmen come to you," which they surely will do—particularly if they are squeezed out of Western Europe in 1992.

Take foodstuffs, for example. Soviet agriculture officials should buy more grain from Canada, China, Argentina, and India, and less from the United States. It's much better to pay hard currency to Soviet farmers to encourage Soviet grain production than to subsidize American farmers who support politicians like Senator Jesse Helms who always vote against the Soviet Union.

As for consumer goods, West Germany, Sweden, Finland, and Japan offer superior quality products and better service than can be provided by most American firms.

High technology can be purchased easily from Sweden, Finland, and Austria, who are not members of COCOM. West Germany and Japan should be offered positive encouragement to sever their ties with COCOM.

British, West German, Italian, and Japanese banks are much more reliable sources of credit than are American banks. The big risk in doing business with American banks is the fickle nature of the U.S. Congress when it comes to any policies related to the Soviet Union.

It's high time for the Soviet Union to reconsider its irrational obsession with trading with the United States at any price. It just might be surprised at the American response. By distancing itself from the U.S. market in the short run, the Soviet Union may reap substantial benefits in the future both from the United States and its other trading partners.

Both the United States and the Soviet Union will face a formidable foreign-trade challenge in 1992 when the twelve nations of the European Community (EC) unite as a single market. The EC represents $4 trillion in potential buying power and is America's most important trading partner. The U.S. Commerce Department estimates that trade between the United States and the EC could reach $1 trillion annually. If the United States and the Soviet Union are to have mutually beneficial trading relationships with the EC, they will both have to get their respective houses in order.

Unreliable Trading Partners

One claim often made by those who are opposed to any kind of U.S.–Soviet trade is that the Soviets are not reliable trading partners. Not only is this assertion blatantly false, but it is American companies, not Soviet companies, that have frequently failed to meet their contractual obligations to the Soviets.

The United States is one of the few countries in the world that consistently uses trade sanctions as a way of imposing its political will on other nations. If the U.S. Congress does not approve of the political behavior of a particular country, then it slaps trade sanctions on the straying nation regardless of any previous commitments that may have been made to that country by American companies.

During the period of détente, which began in 1972, the Nixon administration not only liberalized trade with the Soviets, but actively promoted Soviet trade through subsidized export credits and other interventionist measures. The 1972 U.S.–Soviet trade agreement called for expanded trade and mandated most-favored-nation tariff treatment, which required congressional approval. President Nixon determined that trade with the Soviets was indeed in the national interest and between 1972 and 1974 the Export–Import Bank granted approximately $500 million in credits to the Soviets to purchase U.S. exports. During 1972 the U.S.–USSR Joint Commercial Commission was established and the so-called North Star Consortium (involving Tenneco, Texas Eastern, and Brown and Root) was organized to study and discuss the development of a major Soviet gas pipeline involving financial and technical support from private U.S. companies.

The Export–Import Bank trade credits were short lived. The U.S. Congress saw fit to discontinue these credits to the Soviets in 1974 with the passage of the Jackson–Vanik amendment, which linked Export–Import Bank credits to Soviet Jewish emigration policies. Soviet confidence in the integrity of American business deals was further shaken in 1978 when President Carter revoked a license to Armco, Inc., to build a $400 million speciality steel plant in the Soviet Union. Carter also restricted the sale of oil and gas equipment to the Soviets and slapped them with a grain embargo after the 1979 Soviet intrusion in Afghanistan. The cancellation of the North Star Consortium by the U.S. government, the grain embargo, and President Reagan's 1982 gas pipeline sanctions sent a clear signal to the Soviets that they could not count on American companies to honor their contractual commitments. Before Reagan imposed sanctions against the Soviet gas pipeline, Caterpillar had 80 percent of the Soviet market for heavy-duty earthmoving equipment; Komatsu of Japan had only 20 percent. As a result of the sanctions, Komatsu's market share jumped to 80 percent, and nearly fifteen thousand jobs were lost at Caterpillar. As for the pipeline—it was completed ahead of schedule.

Not only do the Soviets honor their trade commitments with the West, but until very recently they have enjoyed such a good credit rating that Western banks were eager to lend them billions of dollars at below-the-market interest rates. They were considered to be a very safe credit risk. Recently, some Western bankers have begun tightening credit and charging the Soviets higher interest rates despite Moscow's sizable assets and substantial gold reserves. Some banks have become concerned over the rising Soviet hard-currency debt, the uncertainty surrounding the Soviet economy, and payment delays experienced by some Soviet creditors.

High-Tech Paranoia

Restrictions on the export of American technology to the Soviet Union are not new. For the first seven years the Reagan administration adopted an increasingly restrictive policy, which a National Academy of Science panel criticized for being "not generally perceived as rational, credible and predictable."[1]

Under Jimmy Carter, export controls were used sparingly, as punitive sanctions to support his administration's human-rights policy. Dresser Industries, Sperry-Rand, Armco, and Control Data were among the relatively few companies denied export licenses by the Carter Commerce Department.

What distinguished the Reagan administration's policy from that of previous administrations was the bitter ideological and political turf war between the Pentagon and the Commerce Department over technology-transfer policy. The feud also involved a broader dispute between business and government, and between the United States and its allies, over what items were of strategic value to the Soviet Union. Former Assistant Secretary of Defense Richard Perle demanded—and got—tough export controls on virtually every kind of technology, whether military-related or not. The Commerce Department, on the other hand, advocated a more moderate policy that would impose export restrictions on technologies determined to have direct military applications. In September 1987, the Defense Department accused Commerce of deception and bungling for allowing a Soviet-controlled shipping company in West Germany to buy an advanced computer from a California-based company, National Advanced Systems. (The Soviet company wound up buying a Japanese-made Hitachi instead of an IBM computer.)

Under Reagan the Pentagon did not limit its export control activities to American companies. It lobbied the sixteen-nation Consultative Coordinating Committee (COCOM), which regulates Western multilateral trade controls, to adopt a more hard-line position against the transfer of technology to the Soviet Union. But COCOM's members—including all NATO countries except Iceland and Spain—were not able to reach a consensus on rules and procedures. Western European members tended to favor much more limited export controls than the Pentagon, covering only those exports that are directly associated with significant military applications. The allies pressed the United States to cooperate in winnowing out items that are so widely available as to make controls useless. In exchange, the United States demanded that other COCOM members improve enforcement.

The harassment of small U.S. firms that export high-tech goods to the Soviet bloc was an example of how Pentagon policy under Reagan made companies less competitive, even as the nation's trade deficit in electronic equipment increased in the mid-1980s.

One of the most interesting examples of the Reagan administration's high-tech paranoia involved a proposal from Boston entrepreneur Alan F. Kay to help develop computer systems that would enable the Soviet planning agency, Gosplan, to become more market-oriented. Kay wrote to the U.S. Commerce Department and asked whether an export license was needed to hold a seminar in Moscow for Gosplan officials, at which he would describe the software he'd designed. He received a letter from the Office of Technology and Policy Analysis indicating that the seminar would require an export license since it "presents a significant risk to our national security."

Other examples of the Pentagon's attempts to impede the flow of Western technology to the Russians are its policy of restricting Soviet scientists' access to international scientific conferences and to formerly classified scientific information. In May 1985, as a result of Pentagon pressure, the organizers of an international conference on laser and electro-optical systems classified select papers to keep them from Soviet and East European participants.

Critics of U.S.–Soviet trade claim that the only reason the Russians are interested in trade with the West is to obtain technology to achieve military superiority. The Russians are often depicted by the Pentagon as scientific incompetents who must either buy or steal all of their technology from the West. But the thirty-year history of the Soviet space program is impressive evidence of their achievements in science and technology. Some of the best mathematicians and scientists in the world are Russians. They have state-of-the-art technology in medicine, lasers, space technology, steel production, and non-nuclear power engineering. We are the beneficiaries of Soviet advances in coal gasification, welding, and electromagnetic casting and metallurgical processes. Soviet-bloc countries hold over five thousand U.S. patents, and some of their technology is even used by Pentagon contractors to develop weapons systems, including the Strategic Defense Initiative.

Therein lies an important reason for their interest in joint ventures with the West. The Russians are particularly eager to gain access to Western marketing, production, and financial expertise. It is a myth, cultivated by the Reagan administration, that we have the power to deny the Russians access to our technology. It is virtually impossible for the United States to police the export policies of neutral countries such as Austria, Finland, and Sweden. It is even more difficult to monitor technology shipped to the Third World. Through Soviet-owned companies and representatives in the West, it is easy for Soviet technicians to observe, use, and evaluate Western technology in a completely open and legal manner.

One result of the Reagan administration's efforts to curtail the shipment of microcomputers to the Soviet bloc was the creation of a thriving new industry in Eastern Europe—privately owned manufacturing companies producing clones of American computers. Many types of high-tech equipment that are restricted by export controls are readily available in the Soviet Union and Eastern Europe.

According to the National Academy of Sciences study mentioned previously, the Reagan administration's effort to crack down on the diversion of technology to the Russians essentially failed and cost the U.S. economy over $9 billion a year. The belief that export controls are unduly restrictive, even counterproductive, is gaining ground in both political parties and among military and intelligence experts. In fact, there is substantial evidence to suggest that Reagan's obsession with denying the Soviet Union access to Western technology may inadvertently have strengthened the hand of the Russians technologically. Scientists in Moscow routinely rely on what Harvard Business School professor Michael Porter calls "market signals" from the Pentagon to help formulate their own technological priorities. They give the highest priority to projects that are most closely related to the technologies that the Pentagon tries hardest to deny them.

One way in which the Russians have responded to the Pentagon's full-court technological press has been to encourage innovation by offering their scientists new incentives. Soviet scientists and investors can now reap further benefits from their scientific discoveries by starting their own private management consulting firms. Many Soviet officials hope that these reforms will reduce the emigration of scientists to the West.

As a result of our nation's huge trade deficits, increasing pressure is being put on the Bush administration by high-tech manufacturers to relax export controls on nonmilitary technology. In March 1989, the Commerce Department did, in fact, loosen controls on computers and medical-equipment exports to the Soviet Union and Eastern Europe. With increased market pressure it has become even more difficult for the Bush administration to conceal the fact that Reagan's technology-transfer policy was ill-conceived and not in the best interest of the American people. Fearing a palace revolt among the other COCOM members, who are anxious to trade with the recently liberated Eastern European nations, in 1990 the Bush administration further relaxed COCOM restrictions on exports to the Soviet Union and Eastern Europe.

The Jackson–Vanik Amendment

It is arguable that the Jackson–Vanik amendment to the Trade Reform Act of 1974, passed by the Congress in response to pressure from Israel, did more to chill U.S.–Soviet relations and end détente than either the Soviet intervention in Afghanistan or the declaration of martial law in Poland. It linked most-favored-nation (MFN) status for the Soviet Union and Export-Import Bank financing of U.S.–Soviet trade to Soviet emigration policies—

specifically to policies affecting Soviet Jews. As a result, Soviet imports were subject to full tariff rates, which put them at a substantial disadvantage compared to countries selling comparable goods that enjoyed MFN status. Under this amendment, the Export-Import Bank was not permitted to participate in U.S.–Soviet trade so long as the Soviets denied their citizens, particularly Jewish citizens, the right to emigrate or imposed more than a nominal penalty on any citizen as a consequence of his or her desire to emigrate.

Since the enactment of the Jackson–Vanik amendment, not only has our Soviet foreign-trade policy been based on human rights, but our foreign policy has been preoccupied with this singularly divisive issue. The heart of the matter was the treatment of Soviet political dissidents—Jewish dissidents—who want to emigrate to the West. Both Presidents Carter and Reagan made the Soviet treatment of Jews the linchpin of their foreign policies towards the Soviet Union. This issue enraged Soviet leader Brezhnev, who claimed that the United States was interfering in Soviet affairs. In an unsuccessful attempt to deflect American public opinion away from Soviet human-rights abuses, Soviet leaders would often admonish the U.S. government to spend more time trying to solve its own human-rights problems—unemployment, homelessness, poverty, racism, violent crime, and drug abuse.

THE JEWISH EMIGRATION ISSUE

On 17 May 1948, only three days after Israel became an independent nation, the Soviet Union established diplomatic relations with Israel. However, it broke off ties when Israel refused to withdraw from the lands it had captured in 1967 during the Six-Day War, in which the Soviets had sided with Egypt and Syria. Shortly thereafter, all of the Soviets' Eastern European allies except Romania followed suit and cut diplomatic relations with Israel.

Between 1968 and 1989 over 365,000 Jews emigrated from the Soviet Union to the West. Indeed, the vast majority of all of the Soviet emigrants over the past twenty years have in fact been Jews.

Until very recently the Israeli government and American Jewish leaders maintained that another 400,000 wanted to leave. The Soviets claimed that most of the Jews who desired to leave had already done so, and that those who had applied for exit visas had received them, with the exception of those who were said to possess "state secrets" and had been turned down for national security reasons. Most Americans were skeptical of this line of reasoning, since some Soviet Jews had been denied visas stemming from classified research that they did over fifteen years ago. Such research could hardly constitute a threat to Soviet national security today.

In 1979, Jewish emigration increased dramatically, reaching a new high of 51,320. The Soviets fully expected President Jimmy Carter to respond to this high rate of Jewish emigration by granting the Soviet Union some relief from the Jackson–Vanik amendment. Carter was so preoccupied with Iran and the Soviet invasion of Afghanistan that he failed to respond at all. The Soviets were so annoyed by Carter's inaction that their position quickly hardened. Jewish emigration decreased precipitously over the next three years and averaged only 1,066 emigrants per year between 1983 and 1986. Not surprisingly—and with some justification—this added fuel to the charges of anti-Semitism that had been leveled against the Soviets.

ANTI-SEMITISM

There are approximately 1.5 million Jews in the Soviet Union, of whom a half million or so are thought to be practicing Jews who believe in the Jewish faith. The number of synagogues in the USSR is unknown.

The main thrust of the charges made against the Soviet Union by such organizations as the National Conference on Soviet Jewry and the Union of Councils for Soviet Jewry is that Soviet Jews have been singled out by Soviet authorities as the object of political persecution based on religion. Jewish leaders argue that Soviet Jews have been imprisoned, discriminated against, and prevented from emigrating primarily because of their Jewishness.

Anti-Semitism is an undeniable and deplorable fact of life in the Soviet Union and pre-dates the Bolshevik Revolution by several centuries. I have personally experienced it in Moscow. The anti-Semitic activities of the Soviet political organization Pamyat are widely publicized by the American media. There is no doubt that anti-Semitism has played a role in Soviet emigration practices over the past twenty years. Soviet Jews have been denied visas to emigrate to the West, and some have been punished and indeed imprisoned for having attempted to leave the Soviet Union.

THE BRAIN DRAIN

In reality, the use of the expression "possession of state secrets" was a euphemism for the Soviets' paranoid fear of the loss of some of their best scientists to the West, if they had opened the emigration flood gates too wide too soon. Many of the most distinguished Soviet scientists, scholars, and artists are Jewish. No doubt, if given the opportunity, some, but by no means all, might have headed for the West.

Given the Soviet Union's strength in basic research and science—particularly in space-related research—an open-door emigration policy could have resulted in a bidding war for Soviet scientists among American, Western European, and Japanese high-tech and aerospace companies. After martial law was declared in Poland in 1981, there was a mass exodus of many of the best Polish physicians, scientists, and engineers to the West. The effects of this severe brain drain have hampered the Polish economy.

What Jewish leaders called a Jewish emigration problem may, in fact, have been exactly what Soviet leader Mikhail S. Gorbachev said in his 1987 interview just prior to the Washington summit with Tom Brokaw on NBC News—a "brain drain" problem. Yes, Soviet Jews, their friends, and their families have been punished for attempting to leave the Soviet Union, but in many cases they were punished and denied visas because of the threat which their departure posed to the Soviet economy—not because they were Jewish. Repugnant though it may have been, Soviet authorities were much more interested in the fact that refusenik Natan Sharansky was a computer scientist than in his Jewishness.

Furthermore, the Soviet Union had a good reason to be skittish about the possible loss of well-educated Soviet scientists and engineers to Israel. Between 1980 and 1987 approximately 117,000 Jews immigrated to Israel, but during that same period 94,000 Jews emigrated from Israel. With its forty-year war with its Arab neighbors, Israel has a very serious under-population problem. As Israeli leader David Ben-Gurion told the American Jewish community shortly after the creation of the state of Israel, "What we need is Jews."[2] That Soviet Jews were increasingly attracted to

Israel after the Six-Day War in 1967, did not go unnoticed by Soviet authorities. But their real concern was the loss of scientists to Israel, not the fact that many of the scientists happened to be Jewish.

In no sense am I condoning the Soviet Union's abhorrent emigration policies. Discrimination on the basis of profession is no less obnoxious than religious discrimination. But our challenge to the Soviets on this issue should have been based on a more complete understanding of the problem and not merely on the symptoms. I believe that the evidence supports my hypothesis that Soviet emigration restrictions were more deeply rooted in "brain drain" paranoia rather than anti-Semitism.

But Gorbachev is now offering Soviet intellectuals positive incentives to remain in the USSR, and he has simultaneously relaxed Soviet emigration policies and created new ways to reward Soviet scientists for their accomplishments. Among the positive inducements to motivate scientists to stay in the Soviet Union are higher pay, the possibility of receiving patent royalties from their inventions, and the opportunity to start their own private management consulting firms. When scientists are given a piece of the economic and psychological action, they are less likely to be enticed away by lucrative financial offers from Western companies.

RECENT EXPERIENCE

During 1985 and 1986, Gorbachev's first two years in power, Jewish emigration remained essentially unchanged at the 1,000 level. However, it jumped to 8,155 in 1987 and to 19,343 in 1988 before reaching a new all-time high of 71,509 in 1989. By year-end 1988 virtually all of the well-known Jewish refuseniks had been permitted to leave. They included Natan Sharansky, who emigrated to Israel, and physicist Yuri F. Orlov, who was granted permission to emigrate to the United States as part of the deal the Reagan administration made with the Soviets to free American journalist Nicholas Daniloff and Soviet physicist Gennadi Zakharov. American industrialist Armand Hammer arranged for geneticist David Goldfarb and his wife to emigrate to the United States. Soviet cybernetics specialist Aleksandr Lerner, one of the best-known crusaders for Jewish emigration remaining in Moscow, was allowed to emigrate to Israel, as were Jewish activist Ida Nudel and scientist Vladimir S. Slepak. Lerner and Slepak had to wait seventeen years for permission to leave the Soviet Union.

In December 1986, the most famous political dissident in the Soviet Union, the late Dr. Andrei D. Sakharov, was permitted to leave Gorky, where he had been in exile since 1980. Not only did he return to his home in Moscow and resume his work as a physicist at the Soviet Academy of Sciences, but he was allowed to travel to the West and speak openly with the press.

Permission was granted to six young Soviet Jews to study for the rabbinate in the United States with the understanding that they would return to lead Soviet synagogues. The Soviet Union's first officially sanctioned Jewish cultural center opened in Moscow in February 1989. Yiddish is now taught there.

Diplomatic relations between Israel and the Soviet Union and Eastern Europe are clearly on the mend. Bulgaria, Czechoslovakia, Hungary, and Poland have restored full diplomatic relations with Israel after having broken them after the 1967 war. Although the Soviet Union has recognized the Palestine Liberation Organization as a legitimate independent state, it continues to inch toward the restoration of diplomatic ties with Israel. Gorbachev has called the absence of official diplomatic relations with Israel "abnormal."

Clearly the Soviets want and need improved diplomatic relations with Israel. In addition to their interest in Israeli trade and technology, the Soviets understand very well the important role that Israel plays on the international stage. Israel has too much political and economic clout for the Soviet Union to continue to remain estranged from such an influential nation.

Having distanced themselves from some of the more militant Arab nations, such as Iraq, Syria and Libya, the Soviets have signaled their interest in playing the role of a proactive force for moderation and peace in the Middle East. They have backed away from their confrontational strategies of the past and have indicated a willingness to cooperate with the United States in seeking peace in the Middle East. This was particularly evident in the 1990 Persian Gulf crisis.

In an ironic turn of events, by the end of 1988, U.S. immigration authorities, not the Soviet government, had become the biggest impediment to the emigration of Soviet Jews to the United States. Thousands of Soviet Jews are now being denied permission to enter the United States as refugees because they cannot demon-strate "a well-founded fear of persecution" in the Soviet Union. In 1990, Soviet Jews were arriving in Israel at the rate of ten thousand per month.

Although the Soviets have relaxed their emigration laws con-siderably, the United States continues to have very tough laws restricting immigration into the United States. This is nothing new. When the Nazis were killing thousands of Jews each day at Auschwitz in 1944, only 5,606 refugees, mostly Jews, were allowed into the United States.[3]

The Arab–Israeli War

Throughout the Reagan presidency, every time Secretary of State George Schultz and Soviet Foreign Minister Eduard Shevard-nadze met and every time President Reagan and General Secre-tary Gorbachev met, the Soviet human-rights issue was always at the top of the agenda. Although Reagan and Schultz were no doubt genuinely concerned about Soviet human-rights abuses, I believe there may have been another factor that contributed to the attention devoted to this emotionally charged issue, namely, U.S. financial support for Israel.

The total cost of the forty-year Arab–Israeli War has been estimated to be over $3 trillion. Each year Israel and the Arab countries spend on average $32 billion on military defense.[4] Since 1948, the United States has provided Israel with over $46 billion in economic and military aid.[5] Since the 1979 Camp David agree-ment was signed between Egypt and Israel, U.S. financial aid to Israel has averaged $3.1 billion annually. Average U.S. aid to Egypt comes to $2.3 billion.[6]

Prior to the Six-Day War in 1967, Israel enjoyed broad-based political support among Christians and Jews in the United States. Americans were attracted to Israel because of its Biblical significance, its experiments with democracy and its strategic importance in the Middle East. In the eyes of most Americans, Israel stood on the moral high ground in its conflicts with its neighbors. However, American public support for Israel began to erode after the Six-Day War, in which Israel captured the West Bank from Jordan, the Gaza Strip from Egypt, and the Golan Heights from Syria. Furthermore, Israel's economic dependence on the United States increased dramatically after the 1973 Yom Kippur War. These events posed a very serious strategic problem for Israel—how to persuade the U.S. Congress to continue supporting the Israeli military machine, which was becoming increasingly expensive to operate, when American public opinion was shifting away from Israel? The answer lay in the Soviet Union.

Between 1951 and 1967, before the Soviet Union broke off diplomatic relations with Israel, fewer than 12,000 Soviet Jews emigrated to the West (table 6–1). After the Six-Day War, Soviet Jews began to take more interest in their Jewish heritage and to express renewed interest in the Jewish nation. With considerable encouragement from Israel, Soviet Jews began applying for emigration visas in large numbers, beginning in 1969. Between 1969 and 1974, the year the Jackson–Vanik amendment was passed, 104,119 Soviet Jews emigrated from the Soviet Union (table 6–2).

Table 6–1
Jewish Emigration from the Soviet Union:
1951–1967

Year	Number of Jewish Emigrants
1951	186
1952	56
1953	39
1954	26
1955	123
1956	460
1957	1,314
1958	720
1959	1,353
1960	1,917
1961	216
1962	184
1963	304
1964	530
1965	887
1966	2,027
1967	1,416
TOTAL	11,758

Source: Martin Gilbert, *Sharansky: Hero of Our Time.*
New York: Viking, 1986.

Table 6–2
Jewish Emigration from the Soviet Union:
1968–1989

Year	Number of Jewish Emigrants
1968	230
1969	3,011
1970	1,044
1971	13,022
1972	31,681
1973	34,733
1974	20,628
1975	13,221
1976	14,261
1977	16,736
1978	28,864
1979	51,320
1980	21,471
1981	9,447
1982	2,688
1983	1,314
1984	896
1985	1,140
1986	914
1987	8,155
1988	19,343
1989	71,509
TOTAL	365,628

Source: Union of Councils for Soviet Jews.

There were persistent reports of Soviet anti-Semitism and persecution of Jewish dissidents during this period.

The Soviets initiated legal proceedings against Jewish activists in several cities throughout the Soviet Union in 1972. An odious exit tax was imposed on those wishing to emigrate, putatively to cover the cost of their education in the Soviet Union. Over one million Americans petitioned President Richard Nixon in 1972 to intervene on behalf of Soviet Jews during the first Nixon–Brezhnev summit. American and Israeli Jewish leaders began to step up their pressure on the Soviet Union to permit more Soviet Jews to leave.

It was against this background that the late Senator Henry Jackson and his protege Richard N. Perle teamed up with liberal pro-Jewish and pro-human rights groups on the one hand and right-wing anti-Soviet, anti-détente groups on the other to put pressure on the Soviet Union to liberalize its emigration policies. The result was the passage of the Jackson–Vanik amendment in 1974.

The Jackson–Vanik amendment was the beginning of the end of détente. It put the Soviets clearly on the defensive and further reduced the level of trust between the two superpowers. It also served to reinforce Israel's strong anticommunist image in the Middle East and restore some of the luster it had lost as a result of the Six-Day War. By working together with the United States to put an end to Soviet human-rights abuses, Israel once again gained the respect of the American people and the financial support of the Congress.

But Israel's price for helping the United States contain communism appears to have no upper limit. At present we are spending over $860 per person annually on the 3.5 million Jews living in Israel. Since Israel has the highest per-capita debt in the world, its very survival is totally dependent on U.S. support.

For national-security reasons our government does not publish the amount of financial aid that we provide Israel each year. For example, the Pentagon does not report the dollar amounts for Israel's Strategic Defense Initiative contracts. Even less information is available on American support for Israel's nuclear weapons arsenal. Although the United States currently provides Israel with grants of $3 billion annually, total U.S. government support for Israel is conservatively estimated to exceed $5 billion annually.[7]

A recent study by Mohammed Rabie has shown that Israel is the largest foreign-aid recipient in history, having received twice as much U.S. aid since 1948 as all of Latin America and three times as much as Africa. The Reagan administration alone gave Israel $13.5 billion in military aid and $10 billion in economic aid. Even though Israel spends 27 percent of its GNP on defense, its economy continues to experience one crisis after another with no signs of recovery.[8]

The Jackson–Vanik amendment enjoyed strong bipartisan support in the Congress—particularly among those with strong feelings against Soviet human-rights abuses. But it was also the initial salvo of a fourteen-year pattern of anti-Soviet activity that effectively destroyed détente, killed the SALT II Treaty, helped elect Ronald Reagan president, contributed to the rationale underlying his unprecedented military spending spree, and pumped billions of dollars of military aid into Israel. All of this was done in the name of protecting freedom, democracy, and human rights. In my opinion, this strategy had more to do with money, raw political power, and greed rather than human rights either in the Soviet Union or in Israel. Not everyone who supported the Jackson–Vanik amendment agreed with the anti-Soviet tactics. However, the Jackson–Vanik amendment did prove to be an effective tool in destabilizing U.S.–Soviet relations. Whether unwittingly or not, Israel benefitted from the deterioration in U.S.–Soviet relations and the attention focused on human rights by the Jackson–Vanik amendment.

The political force behind this anti-Soviet strategy was the Committee on the Present Danger (CPD). It has maintained a consistently pro-Israel bias since its inception and has served as a public forum for some of its members to criticize Soviet emigration policies. Among the more outspoken CPD members on the Jewish emigration issue were Reagan administration arms-control negotiators Kenneth L. Adelman, Max M. Kampelman, and Eugene V. Rostow, as well as National Security Council adviser Richard Pipes, Richard N. Perle, and writers Midge Decter and Norman Podhoretz.

From the time of his arrest in 1977 and his conviction on espionage charges in 1978, to the time of his release in February 1986, cyberneticist Natan Sharansky was by far the best known Soviet Jewish refusenik. The Sharansky case and the bizarre circumstances surrounding it were so emotionally charged that we will probably never know the exact nature of Sharansky's relationship to the CIA and the U.S. government. Sharansky was effectively used before and after his release by the Israeli lobby and the CPD in their quest for more aid for Israel and increases in the Pentagon's budget.

DOUBLE STANDARD

On 1 June 1990 at the Washington summit, President George Bush once again denied MFN status to the Soviet Union pending codification by the Supreme Soviet of Moscow's emigration policy. Bush also hinted that the granting of a waiver of the Jackson–

Vanik amendment might also be contingent on the Kremlin's policy towards Lithuania.

The fact that Bush had renewed China's MFN status during the previous week did not go unnoticed by Gorbachev in light of the Tiananmen Square massacre, which took place one year earlier. In a meeting with congressional leaders, Gorbachev angrily noted the hypocrisy of continuing to deny the Soviet Union MFN status while granting it to China.

As on many other occasions, the Soviets had met all of our preconditions for a change in American policy only to learn that we had arbitrarily raised the stakes. But the real issue had little to do with human rights.

At the time Bush turned down the Soviets on MFN, the Israeli government was in a state of chaos and was continuing to lose political support in Washington as a result of its inhumane treatment of the Palestinians living in the occupied territories. In addition, both the Soviet government and neighboring Arab nations were becoming visibly annoyed by Israel's policy of forcing recent Soviet Jewish emigrants to live in the occupied territories. Essentially Israel is using Soviet Jews as pawns in their war with the Arabs.

Once again Israel has found it politically expedient to use the Soviet Union and Eastern Europe as scapegoats to deflect American public opinion away from its own irresponsible behavior. The Lithuanian issue and charges of increased anti-Semitism in the Soviet Union and Eastern Europe are being effectively employed by the Jewish lobby in the United States to keep Gorbachev on the defensive. Regrettably, President Bush and Secretary of State Baker caved in to this pressure from Israel. Not only did they do Gorbachev a great disservice by denying the Soviets MFN status, but they apparently failed to realize that increased trade is beneficial to both countries—not just to the Soviet Union. To add insult to injury, the United States broke off its discussions with the PLO in June 1990 in response to a barrage of attacks put forth by Israeli political leaders.

When Israel invaded parts of Egypt, Jordan, and Syria in 1967, the United States chose to look the other way. Yet when Iraq invaded Kuwait, we sent more than three-hundred thousand troops to the Persian Gulf. For their support of his Persian Gulf policy, Bush finally granted the Soviets a Jackson–Vanik waiver in December 1990.

7

Declining International Influence

Shattered Illusions

In spite of its massive military buildup in the 1970s and early 1980s, the Soviet Union has little to show for its efforts in terms of international political influence. Of the 164 nations in the world today, the Soviets can claim to have significant influence in no more than eighteen and in many of those—particularly in Eastern Europe—their influence is clearly on the wane. Four of these countries—Afghanistan, Ethiopia, Mozambique, and Vietnam— are among the very poorest and most desperate in the world. Without exception, all of the Soviets' Eastern European allies have very serious economic problems, which contributed to the collapse of their communist governments in 1989. Only Czechoslovakia and Hungary appear to be capable of standing on their own feet. Although the German Democratic Republic (GDR) was the Soviets' most affluent ally, it was heavily subsidized by West Germany and enjoyed many of the privileges of memberships in the European Community.

The economic and political costs of Leonid Brezhnev's ill-conceived foreign policies far outweighed their benefits to the Soviet Union. Until recently, the Soviets were spending $5 billion annually on Cuba; $3.5 billion on Vietnam; another $3 billion on Angola, Ethiopia, and Mozambique; and $1 billion on Nicaragua.

The perception of never-ending Soviet advances and devastating U.S. setbacks since World War II is a myth perpetrated by the far right and American Sovietologists. The Soviet Union suffers from a lack of staying power and an inability to accumulate influence anywhere in the world. The only countries where the Soviets have been successful in gaining influence since the 1970s are completely impoverished. In addition, the Soviets have suffered major setbacks in China, Indonesia, Egypt, India, Iraq, and Afghanistan. Today there are no successful Marxist-Leninist states anywhere in the world. Prior to Gorbachev, Soviet foreign policy was an unmitigated disaster.

The Soviet invasion of Afghanistan in 1979, the declaration of martial law in Poland in 1981, President Ronald Reagan's anti-Soviet rhetoric, the downing of Korean Air Line flight 007 in 1983, and Soviet aid to the Nicaraguan Sandinistas all contributed to a rapid deterioration in U.S.–Soviet relations in the 1980s. Relations between the two superpowers were based on a never-ending cycle of fear and distrust of each other combined with a heavy dose of tough talk and macho pride.

Soviet relations with Western Europe suffered as a result of the war in Afghanistan, Poland's crackdown on Solidarity, and Brezhnev's unsuccessful attempts to divide NATO over deployment of cruise and Pershing missiles.

The Soviet Union has not been a significant player in the Middle East since it split with Israel after the Six-Day War in 1967 and its military advisors were expelled from Egypt in 1972. Throughout the 1980s the Soviets were aligned only with the most militant Arab nations—Libya, Syria, Algeria, South Yemen, and the PLO. However, the presence of Soviet troops in Afghanistan, an intensely Islamic country, did little to enhance the Soviet image in the Arab world. Also, indecisiveness during the 1982 Israeli invasion of Lebanon was a setback for Soviet–Arab relations. However, the removal of Soviet troops from Afghanistan, improved Soviet–Israeli relations, and the constructive role played by the Soviets in ending the war between Iran and Iraq have all served to enhance the Soviet Union's credibility in the Middle East.

In each of the three African nations in which the Soviet Union has significant influence—Ethiopia, Mozambique, and Angola— the Soviets are attempting to cut their losses by reducing military aid, downplaying revolutionary tendencies, and encouraging negotiations among warring factions. Although Ethiopia and Mozambique continue to be economic and political disasters, significant progress has been made in bringing the civil war in

Angola to an end. The Angola–Namibia accords negotiated by Angola, Cuba, South Africa, the United States, and the Soviet Union called for the withdrawal of all Cuban troops by 1991, the withdrawal of South Africa from Namibia, and the political independence of Namibia. The Soviets have indicated that they plan to discontinue supplying arms to the African National Congress, the formerly banned black resistance movement in South Africa. Finally, in 1989, the Soviet Union dispatched its first diplomatic mission to South Africa since the two nations cut diplomatic ties over thirty years before.

Early on, Gorbachev began to recognize the deleterious consequences of the Soviets' Third World activism on U.S.–Soviet relations—particularly their support of Cuba and Nicaragua. Cuba and Nicaragua represented a form of token opposition to the fact that the Soviet Union is surrounded by NATO missile bases, including those in Turkey, which lies on the Soviet Union's southern border. Although the Soviet presence in Latin America has always been minimal in comparison with our presence in Western Europe, right-wing American politicians supported by the Cuban–American lobby insisted that it represented a major threat to U.S. national security. Nothing could have been further from the truth.

As Philip Brenner has pointed out in *The Christian Science Monitor*, in many ways Cuba has become "the Soviet Union's Israel."[1] Gorbachev's 6 April 1989 speech in Havana was an exercise in diplomacy nudging Fidel Castro towards *perestroika*. It was not by chance alone that the Soviets have reduced economic aid to Cuba and discontinued arms shipments to Nicaragua. The Soviets have also reduced their support of guerrillas in El Salvador, Guatemala, and Honduras.

Sino–Soviet relations have improved significantly since 1960, when Khrushchev withdrew all of the Soviet engineers and technicians who had been working in China in the 1950s. As a result of border disputes and ideological differences between Khrushchev and Chairman Mao, political relations between the two countries remained in a deep freeze until 1982, when Brezhnev invited China to end their twenty-year estrangement. Deng Xiaoping then imposed three conditions on the normalization of Sino–Soviet political relations—that the USSR withdraw its troops from Afghanistan, reduce its military presence on the Chinese border, and discontinue its support of the Vietnamese occupation of Cambodia. When all three of these conditions had been satisfied, the Chinese invited Gorbachev to Beijing to meet Deng and diplomatic relations were resumed.

Two issues continue to divide the Soviet Union and Japan—the Kuril Islands and technology-transfer restrictions. The Japanese insist that a necessary condition for improved Japanese–Soviet relations is the return of the Kuril Islands occupied by the Soviets since the end of World War II. These tiny islands off the northern coast of Japan are Japanese ancestral burial grounds and the site of important Soviet military outposts for protecting Soviet submarines in the Sea of Okhotsk. The Soviets are eager to have access to Japanese technology, which is currently denied them because of COCOM export control restrictions.

The real problem that Gorbachev faces in foreign affairs stems from the fact that in a closed society such as the Soviet Union was, the whole concept of "foreign policy" represented a contradiction in terms. It was extremely difficult to formulate and implement a viable foreign policy for a country that insisted on such tight controls on the flows in and out of the country of literally all information, people, trade, and capital. To have stable diplomatic and economic relations between two countries necessitates a certain degree of openness and flexibility in relations between the two countries—something which had not existed in the Soviet Union for over sixty years. For the Soviet Union to become a major force in international economic and political relations, Gorbachev had no other choice than to open the door to the outside world.

But what about the U.S. side of the foreign policy equation? At one level there is no basis for even comparing U.S. and Soviet international influence. U.S. influence is so strong throughout the world that Soviet influence appears to be minuscule by comparison.

But there are some clear signs that we have paid a high price for Ronald Reagan's narcissistic, Rambo-style foreign policy and that our international influence is slipping even though we remain by far the strongest military power in the world. A relatively minor international incident that took place in Turkey in May 1989 illustrates the nature of the problem. Even though Turkey, which is a NATO member, received $563 million in U.S. military and economic aid in 1989, it refused to allow U.S. military officials to examine an advanced Soviet fighter that had been flown to Turkey by a defecting pilot. The Turkish decision deprived the United States of a significant intelligence coup.

In 1986 France refused to grant U.S. bombers permission to fly over French territory enroute to Libya to bomb Tripoli. Then in 1988, the Spanish government asked the United States to reduce the size of its NATO forces stationed in Spain and remove three squadrons of F-16s. The Danes and Norwegians have never been enthralled by nuclear weapons, and Greek participation in NATO remains tenuous at best. Some Germans are expressing increasing displeasure with the forty-five-year occupation of their country by American troops and the continued presence of U.S. nuclear weapons.

In Latin America, Reagan did everything possible short of a direct U.S. invasion of Nicaragua to bring down the Sandinistas. The only difference between Reagan's tactics in Nicaragua and those employed by the Soviets in Eastern Europe was that the Soviets were more successful. However, Reagan did succeed in driving the Marxists out of power in tiny Grenada—a move which did little to improve U.S. relations with Latin America. In March 1988 Reagan sent 3,200 American troops to Honduras claiming that a Nicaraguan invasion was imminent. The Hondurans were unimpressed.

In a dramatic example of American gunboat diplomacy in Latin America President Bush sent twenty-four thousand troops to Panama in December 1989 to oust military strongman General Manuel Antonio Noriega. In El Salvador the U.S.-backed government has lost popular support and appears to be no closer to winning the war against the guerrillas.

In South Korea, the United States is frequently the target of sometimes violent student demonstrations. Recently, 261 American Peace Corps volunteers were forced out of the Philippines by communist insurgents. We are paying high-priced ransom to continue operating the Clark Air Force Base and the Subic Bay Naval Base there. We will probably have to relinquish one of these huge military installations during the 1990s.

In the Middle East we have had no success in bringing an end to the forty-year Arab–Israeli war because of our closed-minded support for Israel. The United States bears considerable responsibility for the complete destruction of Lebanon, which was brought on by the 1982 Israeli invasion, which had the blessings of the Reagan administration. In part, the 1983 invasion of Grenada was aimed at diverting public attention away from the 241 U.S. servicemen who were killed in the bombing of the Beirut Marine headquarters. In spite of Reagan's tough talk and his arms-for-hostages deal with Iran, nine Americans remained hostages in the Middle East and terrorist attacks against the United States continued through the final days of the Reagan administration. (More recently, our bellicose Persian Gulf policy has received only modest support from our allies and moderate Arab nations.)

U.S. intervention in the Third World during the 1980s was based on the "Reagan Doctrine," which claimed that the United States had the right to intervene in any country where there was an opportunity to fight either the Soviet Union or communism. Under the assumptions of the Reagan Doctrine the U.S. invasion of Grenada, military aid to the contras in Nicaragua, and the bombing of Libya were fully justified. In all cases, the Reagan Doctrine stood above the United Nations and international law. The corollary of the Reagan Doctrine was that the Soviet Union had no legitimate interests whatsoever in the Third World, and it must reconcile itself to giving up its recently acquired positions in the Third World.

What was so interesting about the Reagan Doctrine was its similarity to the Brezhnev Doctrine—a doctrine which President Reagan vehemently denounced over the years. Ironically, the Brezhnev Doctrine was much more limited in scope than the Reagan Doctrine. The former applied only to socialist countries whereas the latter is global in scope. One of the principal attributes of the Reagan Doctrine was its flexibility. It enabled President Reagan, without any apparent sense of irony, to proclaim his duty to wage war on terrorism in Libya at the very moment he was seeking $100 million in military aid from Congress to export terrorism, via its contra clients, into Nicaragua. Thus, at a time when Gorbachev was pulling the Soviet Union back from its Third World adventures, the Reagan Doctrine provided limitless opportunities for the United States to impose its form of government on literally any country in the world. But the Reagan Doctrine did not win any more converts to freedom and democracy than the Brezhnev Doctrine won over to communism.

To add insult to injury, Sony Chairman Akio Morita and Japanese Liberal Democratic Party politician Shintaro Ishihara in their provocative book *The Japan That Can Say "No"*, offered the United States some unsolicited criticism of American trade and management practices. The authors not-so-subtly suggested that it was time for Japan to begin flexing its trade and technological muscles and that the United States was likely to come out on the short end of such a power play. In relatively abrasive language, Morita and Ishihara admonished the United States to clean up its economic act. Before the English version of the book was formally published in the United States, it drew a lot of flack from both business and government.

Global Interdependence

In terms of international relations, Gorbachev's objective is to bring the Soviet Union into the international mainstream of global politics and foreign trade. To increase the Soviet Union's political, economic, and technological interdependence with the rest of the world, Gorbachev is pursuing a strategy based on multilateral trade, political cooperation, and the principle of "reasonable defense sufficiency."

In his relations with the United States, Western Europe, and Japan, Gorbachev's attention is focused on trade and technology. With Eastern Europe, Afghanistan, Angola, Mozambique, Cambodia, Cuba, and Nicaragua, his strategy is to cut his losses and save face. We shall now examine some of the implications of Gorbachev's strategy of global interdependence on international organizations, Europe, the United States, the Far East, the Middle East, and the Third World.

INTERNATIONAL ORGANIZATIONS

In a complete reversal of roles, the Soviet Union announced in October 1987 that it was paying all its outstanding debts to the United Nations including nearly $200 million for peace-keeping operations that it had previously refused to support. This action by the Soviets combined with a number of big successes for the UN in 1988 prompted President Reagan to soften his opposition to the United Nations, and the United States began paying its UN bills as well. In May 1990, the Soviets were granted observer status in the General Agreement on Tariffs and Trade and joined the newly established European Bank for Reconstruction, which will provide aid to help revive Eastern Europe's economy. As we have previously noted, the Soviet Union is also interested in membership in the World Bank, the International Monetary Fund, and the European Community.

EASTERN EUROPE

Gorbachev's 25 October 1989 visit to Helsinki just prior to the collapse of the Berlin Wall gave further credence to the view that the name of the game in Eastern Europe was indeed *Finlandization*. While in Helsinki Gorbachev denounced the Brezhnev Doctrine, which ostensibly gave the Soviets the right to intervene in the affairs of another socialist country such as Czechoslovakia in 1968. Over the weekend following the 2–3 December 1989 Malta summit the GDR's entire communist government resigned, Czechoslovakia announced a new cabinet including noncommunist members for the first time since 1968, and the Soviets joined their other Warsaw Pact allies in condemning the 1968 Soviet invasion of Czechoslovakia.

Not so long ago Finlandization was a dirty word used by the American political right to refer to the spread of Soviet influence in the West. In his 1980 book *The Present Danger*, neoconservative Norman Podhoretz warned of the "Finlandization of America, the political and economic subordination of the United States to superior Soviet power."[2]

More recently, Finlandization has been used to describe the increased political and economic independence from Moscow enjoyed by Eastern Europe.

Finns don't cotton to the new use of Finlandization any more than they did to the conservative version ten years ago. They are quick to point out that unlike the rest of Eastern Europe, they have maintained their political independence since 1917. Although the Soviets annexed a piece of Finland during World War II, the rest of Finland has remained free of Soviet occupation.[3]

The 1948 Treaty of Friendship, Cooperation, and Mutual Assistance between Finland and the Soviet Union mostly assures a stable and mutually profitable bilateral trade relationship between the neighboring countries. The impressive performance of the Finnish economy is due in no small part to its trading relationship with the Soviet Union. The treaty is based on Finnish neutrality and assumes no military relationship whatsoever between the two countries.

Only once since the end of World War II have the Soviets attempted to exert undue political influence over Finland. In 1961, Nikita S. Khrushchev tried to pressure the Finns into high-level diplomatic meetings stemming from Soviet concerns about West Germany. The Finns cleverly negotiated their way out of this diplomatic squeeze-play and once again preserved their independence.

Whether Finlandization is an appropriate description for what is happening in Eastern Europe may still be an open question. But one thing is for sure: By year-end 1989, the political, economic, and military linkages between the Eastern bloc and the Soviet Union bore no resemblance to the form they had taken six months earlier.

In the first free election in Poland in almost a half a century, on 4 June 1989, Solidarity achieved a decisive majority vote in a parliamentary election. Then on 19 August, Tadeuz Mazowiecki, a senior Solidarity political leader and a well-known Roman Catholic, became the first noncommunist prime minister of Poland since the late 1940s.

In January 1990 Poland embarked on a radical free-market strategy of economic reform, including market-determined prices, the privatization of state-owned industries, and a convertible currency. Inflation and acute shortages of food and consumer goods were soon replaced by a substantial decline in economic output, rising unemployment, and increasing labor unrest. The shops in Warsaw are now full of meat and produce that few Poles can afford to buy. With its $40 billion debt to the West the future of the Polish economy continues to look bleak. Thus far the Solidarity government has failed to demonstrate that it has either the sense of vision or the political skills to lead Poland away from forty-five years of communism. Even with the multi-billion dollar combined-aid package from West Germany, France, Japan, and the United States, the Polish economy may not survive the shock treatment approach to capitalism that it has embraced.

For the foreseeable future, Poland is likely to remain one of the least stable countries in Eastern Europe. Indeed, its very survival as an independent nation could be in jeopardy. In the event the

Polish economy does collapse, "Who will bail out Poland?" Gorbachev has made it quite clear that the Soviet Union has neither the resources nor the desire to save the Polish economy. President George Bush's niggardly response to Poland's economic plight hardly suggests that Poland can count on the United States to turn its economy around. Neighboring Czechoslovakia has too many economic woes of its own to be able to offer much assistance to Poland. Only a unified Germany appears to have the resources and the political and economic incentives to save Poland.

In October 1989 Hungary disbanded the Hungarian Socialist Workers Party (Communist party) and replaced it by the Hungarian Socialist Party, which was summarily driven from power by free elections held in the spring of 1990. Hungary's decision to allow thousands of East Germans to flee to West Germany in September of 1989 led to the collapse of the Honecker government in the German Democratic Republic and the opening of the Berlin Wall.

Three months before the Berlin Wall opened on 9 November 1989, the official party line in Washington was that East Germany would be the toughest nut to crack in Eastern Europe. Our government, the press, and most Sovietologists assured us that there was virtually no chance for political or economic reform in the German Democratic Republic. Yet within a period of less than six weeks, Gorbachev visited East Berlin, Erich Honecker was sacked, the Berlin Wall crumbled, and the German Democratic Republic was having serious discussions with West Germany about reunification.

It was not by chance alone that when the Hungarians opened their borders to the fleeing East Germans, both Warsaw and Prague followed suit. That the Soviet troops stationed in East Germany showed so little interest in the dramatic changes taking place there, suggested that Gorbachev was not just a casual observer of the East German revolution. And that a few days later the East German scenario was replicated in Czechoslovakia with a minimum of violence, provided further evidence that Gorbachev's tension-reduction and power-sharing strategies were taking hold in Eastern Europe as well. Then, as if this were not enough, the Bulgarian communists kicked out long-time party boss Todor I. Zhivkov and began accelerating the pace of reform, and aging Romanian dictator Nicolae Ceausescu was driven out of power and shot by a firing squad. Even nonaligned communist Albania is now showing signs of breaking with Stalinism.

Referring to Eastern Europe, Gorbachev has said that, "Each people, choosing socialism, decides itself on the forms, ways and methods of constructing the new society that suit its historically formed ethnic values, economic possibilities, and spiritual potential."[4] Against this background, then what does the future hold for the Council for Mutual Economic Assistance (CMEA) and the Warsaw pact?

Most of the Eastern European countries as well as the Soviet Union appear to be much more interested in forging a relationship with the European Community before 1992 rather than in attempting to resuscitate CMEA. There are few, if any, economic or political incentives to motivate CMEA members to prolong its life.

As for the Warsaw Pact, its days are numbered as well. As far back as 18 April 1986, Gorbachev began calling for "the simultaneous disbandment of the Warsaw Treaty and NATO, or at least the military organizations of both alliances to begin with."[5] If Gorbachev follows through on his strategy to demilitarize Europe and help create a "common European home," then the justification for the continued existence of the Warsaw Pact will soon fade away.

The reunification of Germany is a major threat to both NATO and the Warsaw Pact, for it undermines the entire rationale on which they were based in the first place.

Thus, in Eastern Europe Gorbachev has once again redefined what had previously been perceived as a zero-sum problem and transformed it into a non-zero-sum problem in which everyone wins. Rather than being remembered as the Soviet leader who presided over the death of communism in Eastern Europe, he is more likely to be remembered as the father of democratic socialism in Eastern Europe.

WESTERN EUROPE

In July 1986, while hosting French President François Mitterrand in Moscow, Gorbachev first played his European card and began calling for a "Europe for Europeans." Gorbachev has become increasingly forceful in his pleas for an end to the division of Europe.

Although American cynics claim that Gorbachev's primary aim is to dismantle NATO, I believe that his agenda in Europe is based mostly on economic concerns. Gorbachev must demilitarize Europe so that he can reduce his own costly military commitments to Eastern Europe. He is much more interested in the trade and technology potential of the $4 trillion economy of the European Community than he is in NATO. He is also interested in the $640 billion economy of the European Free Trade Agreement countries—Austria, Switzerland, Norway, Sweden, Finland, and Iceland—all of whom are neutral (except Norway) and have tariff-free trade with the rest of Western Europe.

However, if Gorbachev is successful in breaking the hammer-lock control that the United States maintains over Western Europe through its NATO forces, then he can simultaneously increase trade with Western Europe and significantly scale down the size of his army in Eastern Europe, both of which actions would be of enormous economic benefit to the Soviet Union.

UNITED STATES

By early 1986 Gorbachev's foreign-policy objective towards the United States was becoming increasingly obvious: To reduce the level of tension between the Soviet Union and the United States and negotiate a comprehensive arms-control agreement with the United States covering conventional forces, nuclear weapons, and space-based weapons. Gorbachev not only wants a major arms-control agreement with the United States, but his task of revitalizing the Soviet economy will be much easier if he can reduce the level of Soviet military spending.

By the time of the Malta summit in December 1989, Gorbachev was well on his way to convincing the Bush administration that it was in the interest of the United States for him to be successful in his efforts to implement political and economic reform in the Soviet Union and Eastern Europe.

As Gorbachev's personal popularity continued to increase in the United States, the level of distrust that Americans felt towards the Soviets has declined as well. As evidence of Gorbachev's success in reducing tension with the United States, there is increased political pressure on the Pentagon to cut back on military programs and expenditures.

FAR EAST

In July 1986, in a speech made in Vladivostok, on the Pacific coast of the Soviet Union, Gorbachev made it clear that China, Japan, and the Pacific Basin were major targets of Soviet foreign policy. In May 1989 Gorbachev reestablished diplomatic relations with China. Gorbachev had little to say about the Tiananmen Square uprising, which took place a few days after his departure from Beijing. Sino–Soviet trade has increased sharply in recent years.

The Japanese model for economic development has not only captured Gorbachev's attention but it is strongly influencing his foreign-trade policy. The Soviets are particularly anxious to tap into Japanese technology as a means of neutralizing the effects of the U.S. embargo on the export of U.S. technology to the Soviet Union. Although the Japanese do sell some technology to the Soviets, they are members of COCOM as a result of U.S. coercion. The COCOM restrictions limit the extent to which they can sell technology to the Soviets.

A sticking point in Soviet–Japanese relations is the occupation by the Soviet Union of the Kuril Islands. The real question is whether or not the Soviets would be prepared to turn over the Kuril Islands to the Japanese in return for improved access to Japanese technology. One way or another, the Soviets must find a strategy to break the Pentagon's technological embargo against them. The recent book *The Japan That Can Say "No"* hints that Japan may be willing to cooperate with the Soviets in finding ways around the American-imposed technological embargo.

In general, Gorbachev has signaled his strong interest in expanding the Soviet Union's economic influence in the Pacific Basin including such countries as Thailand, the Philippines, Malaysia, Singapore, South Korea, Taiwan, and Indonesia. In June 1990, Mr. Gorbachev met South Korean President Roh Tae Woo in San Francisco thus ending over forty years of estrangement between the Soviet Union and South Korea. A few months later the Soviets established diplomatic relations with South Korea.

MIDDLE EAST

As further evidence of Gorbachev's break with the Soviet Union's xenophobic past, consider the case of the Middle East, where the

Reagan administration successfully managed to deny the Soviets a position of influence in the peace process. In a policy reversal, the Bush administration has encouraged Soviet efforts to end the Arab–Israeli war.

All of the Soviet Union's Eastern European allies have restored diplomatic relations with Israel, and the Soviets are expected to do the same. Through Israel the Soviets hope to gain a position of influence in the Middle East peace process and purchase sophisticated technology.

Until recently the biggest hurdle to overcome in Israeli–Soviet relations was the Soviet Union's policy on Jewish emigration. With over seventy thousand Soviet Jews immigrating to the West in 1989, this issue has effectively been laid to rest.

Not only has the Soviet Union strengthened its diplomatic relations with moderate Arab nations such as Qatar, Bahrain, and Saudi Arabia, but it has distanced itself somewhat from more militant Arab countries. For the first time, in August 1986, the Soviets reduced their oil exports to the West by 6 percent in support of OPEC's efforts to stabilize the world price of crude oil. The knee-jerk reaction of the Reagan administration to the Soviet Union's decision to lease three oil tankers to Kuwait in 1987 precipitated a crisis in the Persian Gulf and a huge U.S. military buildup there. Later, the Soviets cooperated with the Reagan administration and the United Nations to help bring about an end to the Iran–Iraq war. They also condemned the Iraqi annexation of Kuwait.

THIRD WORLD

In no area is the complete failure of Soviet foreign policy more evident than in the Third World. Without exception, the economies of all of the Soviet Union's Third World clients can be described as basket cases. These include Afghanistan, Angola, Cuba, Ethiopia, Mozambique, Nicaragua, North Korea, and Vietnam. In addition to their poverty, these countries share two other characteristics. They each have relatively repressive governments and require substantial amounts of foreign economic assistance. With each of these countries the Soviets are attempting to pare their losses.

Not only have these countries proven to be an economic drain on the Soviet Union, but they have consistently been a political embarrassment as well by providing evidence that the Soviets were still interested in exporting Marxist-Leninist revolutions.

The Soviets have withdrawn their troops from Afghanistan and have admitted that their 1979 invasion of their neighboring country was not only ill-conceived but illegal as well. They participated in the wind-down of the war in Angola. Economic support for Cuba and Nicaragua has been reduced, and military aid to Nicaragua has been discontinued. In addition, the Soviets have put pressure on Vietnam to end their war with Cambodia and have encouraged North Korea to make peace with South Korea. And in South Africa, the Soviet Union has been playing a conciliatory role in facilitating negotiations between the government and the previously outlawed African National Congress.

In the not too distant future—under considerable pressure from the White House—the Soviet Union will agree to discontinue all military aid to Cuba and Latin America. In return, the United States may provide the Soviet Union with limited economic assistance tied to specific economic reforms, and also end its thirty-year economic boycott of Cuba. In addition, the United States must assure Gorbachev that it will not participate in or support a repeat performance of the 1961 Bay of Pigs invasion of Cuba. Castro will be allowed to stand or fall without Soviet military support and without American intervention.

As for the Soviet Union's future relations with Third World nations, the emphasis is on trade and technology. The Soviets are actively pursuing relations with the larger, more affluent Third World countries such as Argentina, Brazil, India, and Mexico, while giving lip service to the needs of the more impoverished Third World countries such as Ethiopia and Mozambique.

Downsizing

President Mikhail S. Gorbachev has offered the Baltic republics the Soviet equivalent of a leveraged buyout. His message to defiant republics is, "If you don't like it here, you are free to go—but at a price."

Gorbachev understands that the Soviet Union—not unlike many large American companies as well as China, India, Brazil and possibly the United States—is unmanageable in its present form. It is too big and contains too many heterogeneous republics, ethnic minorities, religions, and nationalities to be effectively managed by the Kremlin or any other single authority. The newfound freedom of Eastern Europe has raised the expectations of Soviet minorities and nationalities who feel they too should be granted independence from Moscow.

Since the days of Henry Ford and Alfred P. Sloan, Jr., mass production, assembly lines, and specialization of labor have been assumed to lead to increased efficiency, lower costs, and higher profits in American manufacturing companies. The recent experience of industrial giants such as Chrysler, General Motors, and IBM suggests that once a company expands beyond a certain size, further increases in scale may actually reduce efficiency, raise costs, and lower profits.

As American companies have continued to grow, the rate of growth of productivity has been declining for three decades. Today's well-educated, affluent workers resent authoritarian management and work inefficiently in repetitive assembly-line jobs designed for poor, ignorant blue-collar workers of the 1940s who respected military-style authority.

But this is similar to the problem Mr. Gorbachev faces in the Soviet republics. Without military force it will be impossible to manage Azerbaijan, Lithuania, Moldavia, and Tadzhikistan where there is serious ethnic and nationalistic unrest. Surely the Soviets have learned that military authority is not a viable option for governing a nation that aspires to global influence.

While providing the republics with a legal secession mechanism, Gorbachev will also offer them economic incentives and political concessions to stay. Departing republics must pay relocation costs for their citizens who want to remain in the Soviet Union. They must also compensate the Soviets for state-owned property—mines, oil fields, factories, public utilities, highways, schools, hospitals, et cetera.

The Baltic republics will seek financial aid from the West to buy their way out of the Soviet Union. Others may have second thoughts about the economic and political risks of going it alone. The political and economic upheavals in Poland and Romania have not gone unnoticed. Armenian Christians may fear the consequences of being surrounded by Moslem nations—Azerbaijan, Iran, and Turkey. Not unlike belligerent teenagers, some republics may have less enthusiasm for secession once it is permissible.

The population of the Baltic republics plus Armenia, Azerbaijan, and Georgia is only twenty-three million out of a total Soviet population of 285 million. The Ukraine has over fifty million people. If all of the non-Russian republics were to secede, the remaining Russian republic would still be the largest country in the world in terms of geographic area and have a population of 150 million.

Secession could impose significant economic costs on the Soviet Union. Azerbaijan is a major oil-producing and petrochemical region. The Ukraine is the Soviet bread basket.

Gorbachev will try to persuade each republic to stay, seek reasonable compensation from those who elect to leave, but stop short of military intervention to block their secession. Ultimately, if the political costs of a republic remaining in the union outweigh the economic benefits, then it will be allowed to leave.

Throughout the world Gorbachev is cutting his losses with a foreign policy based on tension reduction, power sharing, and global interdependence. How could he possibly choose a different strategy for dealing with the republics? The alternative to downsizing the Soviet Union is political, economic, and military chaos.

When a republic such as Estonia leaves the Soviet Union, Gorbachev will pursue a cooperative relationship with the emerging nation similar to the mutually profitable relationship that the Soviets enjoy with Finland. He will most likely propose a loose-knit confederation with former republics similar to what may emerge in Eastern Europe based on trade and mutual security rather than the presence of Soviet troops. Gorbachev has no interest in replicating the disastrous Warsaw Pact experience with a group of alienated republics.

Downsizing the Soviet Union is truly a radical strategy that will not play well with Russian nationalists, but does Gorbachev really have any other choice?

But what about the United States? Isn't there considerable evidence to suggest that it too has become too large to be managed by a Washington-based central government? Just as the Kremlin has found it impossible to manage the Soviet economy from Moscow; the Congress has experienced the futility of trying to legislate strategies for dealing with such problems as poverty, homelessness, racism, drug abuse, crime, child abuse, acid rain, and a failing public-education system.

These problems simply do not lend themselves to top-down solutions imposed by a higher authority. Their solutions require the bottom-up participation of those affected by them as well as a sense of community connecting those who have been victimized with those in a position to influence their solution.

The United States is so large and so diverse that the problems of Los Angeles and Chicago bear little resemblance to those of Texas, Vermont, Oregon, or the Mississippi Delta. Furthermore, the people living in Richmond, Virginia, couldn't care less about the problems of the people living in Harlem and vice versa.

Is it any wonder that our Congress has so much difficulty trying to reach a consensus on anything? It is unrealistic for one legislative body to represent the interests of so many heterogeneous states, ethnic minorities, political ideologies, and religious sects. That confusion rules on Capitol Hill is hardly surprising.

What is conspicuously absent in the United States these days is a well-defined sense of community or feeling of connectedness linking our fifty disjoint states. This is in contrast to such tiny countries as Austria, Finland, Norway, Sweden, and Switzerland, which not only enjoy a very high standard of living but a real sense of community.

Consider, for example, the fact that only a few of the small towns in our country have any railroad passenger service whatsoever linking them to the rest of the nation. Fifty years ago most towns and villages had regular passenger train service. When I used to visit my grandfather in a tiny Mississippi village in the 1940s, the most important event each day was the arrival of the Gulf Mobile & Ohio passenger train—*The Rebel*—which made regular stops there. We have spent so much money promoting energy-inefficient, high-polluting automobiles that we virtually destroyed rail passenger service. Amtrak has done a remarkable job of trying to bring back passenger train service in spite of the Reagan administration's efforts to drive it out of business.

In the 1860s eleven Southern states did secede from the Union and formed the Confederate States of America. They were finally dragged kicking and screaming back into the Union after military defeat, occupation, and Reconstruction. Nearly one hundred years later Southern segregationists argued that racial integration could never be forced on the South by Washington. Not unlike the Soviet Union's attempt to impose communism on the Baltic republics, forced integration has neither eliminated segregation nor racism.

While there are many more African-American elected officials in the South than there were thirty years ago, most of the public schools in the major Southern cities are predominantly African-American—the whites having fled to private segregation academies and all-white suburban public schools. Although there are many affluent African-Americans living in Atlanta, Richmond, and Raleigh-Durham; many parts of Alabama, Louisiana, Mississippi, and South Carolina resemble Third World countries. Most of the African-Americans living in the rural South today are not only poor, but very poor. Maybe the states-rights advocates of the 1950s and 1960s were right. It may indeed be impossible to impose top-down social reforms on a state, region, or nation. Certainly that is an important lesson from the Eastern European experience over the past forty-five years.

In spite of all of the patriotic hype of the Reagan years, four major threats have helped hold the Union together during the twentieth century—World War I, the Great Depression, World War II, and the Soviet Union.

With the reduced Soviet threat, is it possible that in the not-too-distant future, one or more American states may conclude that the cost of financing its share of the Union's $3 trillion debt exceeds the benefits derived from our defense-burdened government? What if states start asking some very tough questions about the cost/benefit ratios of federal programs aimed at reducing poverty, drug abuse, crime, and environmental pollution? What would be the congressional reaction if Texas or Oregon were to declare their independence just as Lithuania did? Would congressional reaction be any different from Gorbachev's reaction to the secession movement of the Baltic republics?

8

Global Development

So long as the United States and the Soviet Union continue spending $1.5 billion a day defending themselves from each other, a host of global problems go unattended including regional wars, terrorism, poverty, hunger, disease, drug abuse, and environmental pollution.

For far too long the United States and the Soviet Union have given only lip service to many of these problems. However, some of them have now come back to haunt the two superpowers—particularly the United States. Just as the cold war doesn't pay anymore, ignoring global problems in an increasingly interdependent world doesn't pay either. Neither superpower can continue sitting idly by while serious harm is inflicted on much of the world without bearing part of the cost. In a surprising turn of events, Third World debt, AIDS, drug addiction, and environmental pollution now provide the impoverished nations of the world with increased political leverage to confront the superpowers.

War and Terrorism

As recently as 1988 there were still twenty-five wars being fought throughout the world—more wars than in any previous year on record. A study by World Priorities estimated that by 1988, seventeen million people had lost their lives in all wars, rebellions, and uprisings since the end of World War II.[1]

Five of these wars had either ended or were winding down by 1990. They are the wars in Afghanistan, Angola, Cambodia, and Nicaragua and the war between Iran and Iraq. With the exception of the Iran–Iraq war, each of these wars was linked to the East–West conflict. But neither communism nor capitalism appeared to be winners in any of them. The only real winners were the international arms merchants who supplied the opposing factions. Through 1987, in Afghanistan 85,000 Afghans and 14,000 Soviet troops had lost their lives, in the Iran–Iraq war 377,000 died in eight years, in Angola and Namibia 213,000 lives were lost since 1975, in Cambodia and Vietnam 54,000 people died since 1979, and 30,000 in Nicaragua since 1981.[2]

In addition to being the greatest military superpowers in the world, the United States and the Soviet Union are the world's largest suppliers of arms to the rest of the world. However, Third World countries such as Brazil and China are also becoming major players in the international arms market. After sliding to their lowest point in years in 1989, U.S. and Soviet arms sales to Third World nations increased again in 1990 in anticipation of major new agreements to reduce conventional forces in Europe. Weapons that would have to be destroyed under pending arms-reduction treaties are being sold off to Third World governments by both superpowers.[3]

Although the threat of nuclear war between the United States and the Soviet Union has been significantly reduced, the possibility of nuclear attack from other nations remains a threat to both superpowers. Even though only three other nations—China, England, and France—openly admit to having nuclear weapons, an additional eleven nations are believed to have nuclear arsenals or have taken steps to develop such weapons. These are Israel, India, Pakistan, South Africa, Argentina, Brazil, Iran, Iraq, North Korea, Taiwan, and Libya. In addition, over twenty developing countries now have ballistic missiles.

Not unrelated to regional wars is another common threat to the United States and the Soviet Union—political terrorism. During the 1980s, most of the terrorist attacks throughout the world were aimed at the United States. Many were directly related to the Arab–Israeli war in the Middle East. However, more recently the Soviets have also become the target of frequent airline hijackings and terrorist attacks. For example, in 1988 Iranian rioters attacked the Soviet Embassy in Teheran throwing rocks and firebombs and attempting to break into the compound. Terrorism also has the potential to poison improved U.S.–Soviet relations.

Both nations share a common interest in reducing the incidence of terrorism—particularly in the Middle East.

Our one-sided foreign policy biased towards Israel has played a significant role in Middle Eastern terrorism. Even though there are fewer than six million Jews in the United States, their ability to influence U.S. foreign policy is without equal. Through the highly effective Jewish lobby in Washington, Israel has exerted an inordinate amount of influence over our foreign policy in the Middle East. I know, from very painful firsthand experience, that to criticize our uncompromising support of Israel is to make oneself vulnerable to charges of anti-Semitism.

We are told whether or not we can provide military aid to Arab countries, whether the Palestine Liberation Organization can open an office in Washington, and whether PLO Chairman Yasir Arafat can enter the United States to address the United Nations. Under increasing Israeli pressure to do so, the United States recently broke off its dialogue with the PLO. In January 1990, the U.S. State Department informed the United Nations Food and Agriculture Organizations (FAO) that we would pay only $18 million of our $61.4 million 1989 assessment to the Rome-based agency as a result of disputes over FAO's support for the PLO.[4]

The fact that prior to 1990 there was no serious effort in Congress to repeal the Jackson–Vanik amendment even though the Soviets had made significant progress in cleaning up their emigration policies is further evidence of the influence that Israel wields in Washington. If the Jackson–Vanik amendment were as effective as Jewish leaders claim, why did it take sixteen years to resolve the problem? Is it possible that the problem might have gone away much sooner if there had been no such punitive legislation passed by our Congress? Isn't it quite likely that the Jackson–Vanik amendment actually exacerbated the problem?

Throughout the 1980s, after each Middle East bombing, hijacking, or other Arab terrorist attack aimed at the United States, the Reagan administration's response was to call for punitive action and revenge against the culprits. No interest was expressed in trying to understand the root causes of Arab terrorism. No one dared to ask the obvious question, "To what extent does our myopic pro-Israel foreign policy contribute to Middle East terrorism?"

The bombing of Pan American World Airways Flight 103 on 21 December 1988, which killed 259 people, was a vivid reminder that the American approach to terrorism based on tough talk is not very effective. Perhaps by working together as they did to end the Iran–Iraq war, the United States and the Soviet Union can begin to sort out the root causes of political terrorism and take some joint action to deal with them. However, the recent events in the Persian Gulf provide little room for optimism in this regard.

In his farewell address in 1796 President George Washington warned us of the inherent dangers of blindly siding with one nation when he said,

> . . . a passionate attachment of one nation for another produces a variety of evils. Sympathy for the favorite nation, facilitating the illusion of an imaginary common interest in cases where no real common interest exists, and infusing into one the emnities of the other, betrays the former into a participation in the quarrels and wars of the latter without adequate inducement or justification. It leads also to concessions to the favorite nation of privileges denied to others, which is apt doubly to injure the nation making the concessions by unnecessarily parting with what ought to have been retained, and by exciting jealousy, ill will, and a deposition to retaliate in the parties from whom equal privileges are withheld.

With the thaw in U.S.–Soviet relations, Israel's influence on U.S. foreign policy appears to be on the wane. To justify further U.S. military aid, Israel is going to have to find a new enemy to replace the Soviet Union—a role which Iraq seems all too willing to play. In the meantime the Israeli government and American Jewish leaders continue to level charges of anti-Semitism against the Soviet Union and Eastern Europe.

In early 1990 American Secretary of State James Baker III and Soviet Foreign Minister Eduard A. Shevardnadze began turning up the heat on Israel and the PLO respectively to negotiate more seriously a resolution of their differences. Improved U.S.–Soviet relations have already made it much more difficult for Israel and the PLO to continue playing the United States and the Soviet Union off against each other as they have in the past so as to maximize the flow of superpower military and economic aid. It remains to be seen whether President George Bush is strong enough to propose significant cutbacks in U.S. aid to Israel. Such a step would go a long way toward bringing an end to the Arab–Israeli war, thus reducing Arab terrorism.

While turning up the heat on the Arabs and the Israelis, the superpowers should turn down the heat in Central America. Latin Americans should be allowed to sort out their own political differences without the fear of intervention by either the United States or the Soviet Union. While the Soviets have significantly reduced their role in Latin America, we have not. If anything, our role has actually increased in Panama, Colombia, Bolivia, and Peru. Keeping our nose out of Latin America seems to be a very bitter pill for the United States to swallow. Unfortunately, we have neither the political will nor the self-discipline to keep our hands off small Central American countries.

Poverty, Hunger, and Disease

Of the 5.3 billion people in the world over 500 million are hungry and more than two *billion* suffer from malnutrition. Ruth Leger Sivard's World Priorities study found that 14 million children die of hunger-related causes each year, 100 million people have no shelter whatsoever, 1.3 billion do not have safe drinking water, and 800 million adults cannot read or write.[5]

According to Archer Daniels Midland CEO Dwayne Andreas, providing a nutritionally adequate diet to the world's hungry is not an impossible dream, but an achievable goal. Feeding the world's hungry is a much more cost-effective way of increasing the likelihood of political stability than expenditures on military defense.[6]

Yet a recent study by the United Nations Children's Fund (UNICEF) found that the Third World nations of Africa, Asia, and Latin America are spending half of their annual budgets on military defense and the servicing of their huge external debts. The study also found that the combined military expenditures of both industrialized nations and Third World nations exceeds the total annual income of the poorest half of the world. Diverting only 5 or 10 percent of this huge sum to more human concerns could have substantial impact on global poverty.[7]

At the core of the problem of global poverty is an excessive rate of population growth. According to the United Nations Population Fund, the world's population will reach 6.25 billion by the end of this century. Although Third World countries have the highest population growth rates, they are only a part of this complex problem. In discussing a recent study by the UN Population Fund, its executive director Dr. Nafis Sadik noted that while the industrialized nations contain less than 25 percent of the world's population, "they consume 75 percent of the energy used, 79 percent of all commercial fuels, 85 percent of all wood products, and 72 percent of all steel production."[8]

On the other hand, the tiny West African country of Burkina Faso—unknown to most Americans—with a population of 8.3 million has an annual per capita income of only $120. Only 11 percent of the children in Burkina Faso attend school and there is only one physician available for every 57,180 persons in contrast to the United States where there is one doctor for every 470 persons.

To appease its right-to-life supporters, the Reagan administration withdrew U.S. government support for many Third World family-planning programs. The real question is whose lives are these pro-life advocates trying to save? Surely it is not the lives of millions of children who die of malnutrition and disease each year?

When in 1982 the first cases of AIDS were reported around Kasensero, Uganda, few Americans were particularly concerned about the incidence of Third World disease. However, today it is a quite different story. In 1989, 300,000 people had died of AIDS worldwide. Nearly 800,000 Ugandans tested positive for the HIV virus in December 1989. About one in eight Ugandans is infected with AIDS in contrast to one in two hundred in the United States. The Soviets have acknowledged an increasing number of AIDS cases in their country as well. In the largest hospital in Warsaw, over one-third of the drug addicts admitted for treatment tested positive for AIDS. AIDS is a global disease that has reached epidemic proportions in some parts of the world. It is not likely to go away without a unified U.S.–Soviet effort in collaboration with Third World partners.

Because people infected with the AIDS virus are unusually susceptible to tuberculosis, the incidence of TB has increased dramatically in those areas of the United States where there are a large number of AIDS cases. There were so few cases of TB in the United States twenty years ago, that public health officials confidently predicted the near-elimination of the disease by the year 2000. Unfortunately for the people of the United States and the rest of the developed nations of the world, the Third World disease AIDS carries with it a deadly Third World side effect—tuberculosis.

While the U.S. Congress and the White House cynically debate whether or not there should be a "peace dividend," how big it should be, and how we should spend it, millions of people living in impoverished Third World countries are dying of hunger, malnutrition, and disease. What can possibly be the moral justification for continuing to spend hundreds of billions of dollars protecting ourselves from an impotent enemy—the Soviet Union— while allowing masses of innocent people to die as a result of our arrogance and deliberate neglect? For an untold number of people who once lived in Africa, Asia, Latin America, and the Middle East, the cold war end game did not come soon enough. The lingering stench of their misery and premature deaths is the real legacy of the cold war.

The deaths of millions of people from malnutrition and disease cannot be explained by a lack of resources or inadequate technology. The affluent nations of the world have the resources and the technology to eradicate poverty and reduce the incidence of disease in most Third World countries. What is missing is the vision, political will, and commitment to reallocate funds from military security to the pressing needs of the world's poor.

The end of the cold war is going to make it much more difficult for us to pretend that hunger and disease do not exist. For forty-five years, we and the Soviets have chosen to look the other way except when aiding a particular developing country served our own respective cold war agendas. Unfortunately, the problems not only did not go away, but they got worse.

Drug Abuse

There is an obvious relationship between Third World poverty and America's ever-increasing drug problem that went virtually unnoticed by the Reagan administration. Reagan was so preoccupied with his cowboy, gunslinging approach to the drug problem that he failed to realize that the key to the international drug market is the huge income gap between the United States and Third World countries. One way or another, we are going to pay our dues to countries like Afghanistan, Thailand, Mexico, Panama, Bolivia, Brazil, Mexico, Colombia, and Peru. If we continue to refuse to help them economically, they will seek other options. One very profitable alternative is the U.S. drug market. While right-wing politicians successfully bash all forms of foreign aid, we end up subsidizing Third World nations through the international drug market. One advantage of this form of foreign aid is that we do not have to fear the possibility of corrupt foreign politicians siphoning off American tax dollars. In the international drug market, the foreign drug lords get all of the profits.

Also, our feeble attempts to induce Latin American governments to cooperate with us in stopping the flow of drugs play right into the hands of left-wing politicians in countries like Colombia, Bolivia, and Peru. Why should they help us solve this problem? Eliminating drug traffic will simply reduce their already-low incomes even further. To put it bluntly, there is nothing in it for them.

Since the Soviets have recently admitted that drugs are becoming a Soviet problem, they too may find it useful to consider the foreign-aid implications of the international drug market.

Environmental Pollution

Acid rain, the greenhouse effect, and all forms of air and water pollution are global problems generated by the major industrial nations of the world and are now being exacerbated by the economic-development needs of the Soviet Union, Eastern Europe, and the Third World. Not only are acid rain and global warming very serious problems in North America and Western Europe, but they are being increasingly acknowledged as equally serious problems in the Soviet Union and Eastern Europe. The Soviets did not even begin discussing pollution until the late 1980s, and their plans for dealing with it are no less anemic and underfunded than those of the United States.

The United States and the Soviet Union are responsible for nearly 50 percent of the deadly carbon dioxide buildup in the atmosphere—the principal cause of global warming. The approach of the Reagan and Bush administrations to acid rain and global warming is to study these problems, pretend they do not exist, and do nothing to solve them.

It is now clear that Eastern Europe is an ecological disaster. Ninety percent of the trees in East Germany are either sick, dead, or dying. Budapest's air is twice as polluted as that of London in the 1950s. Half of Poland's water is so polluted that it is unfit even for industrial use. Eighty percent of Poland's deep wells are polluted and a quarter of its soil is too contaminated for safe farming. The Vistula River, from which Warsaw gets all of its drinking water, is a lifeless open sewer—one of the most polluted rivers in the world. The architectural wonders of Cracow are being rapidly destroyed by the air pollution produced by Polish smokestack industries, which have no pollution abatement equipment whatsoever.

A quarter of Czechoslovakia's rivers contain no fish. The poor quality of Eastern European coal leads to degradation of soils, damage to forests, and the acidification of surface and ground water. In over one hundred cities in the Soviet Union, people are exposed to levels of industrial pollution that are ten times greater than safe health norms.[9]

Mortality rates are up all over Eastern Europe and pollution-related illnesses such as cancer, heart disease, and skin diseases are on the increase. Recent Soviet studies have established a "clear-cut relationship" between the level of air pollution and the rate of illness of the resident population.

There is no doubt that one of the benefits that the people of the Soviet Union and Eastern Europe hope to realize from the end of the cold war is the increased availability of consumer goods. But of more fundamental importance is their very survival, which is by no means assured with the present levels of air, water, and soil pollution. What stake do we have in helping the Soviets and Eastern Europeans deal with their pollution problems? A very big stake! The effects of air and water pollution know no political boundaries. The impact of global warming and the greenhouse effect will be felt by capitalist nations and socialist nations alike.

While the wealthy industrial nations of the West admonish countries like China, Brazil, and Mexico to assume more responsibility for the global environment, no one seems to want to bear the cost of expensive antipollution equipment and policies. Arrogant American environmentalists chastise the Brazilian government for the overdevelopment of the Amazon rain forest, but offer no alternative development strategies or financial resources to help Brazil develop its economy. The world is also facing mounting problems of water scarcity. Environmental pollution and water shortages are but two more examples of global problems that do not lend themselves to the cold war, zero-sum approaches of the past.

Global Development Strategies

Although Japan's economy is only half the size of that of the United States, Japan has become the world's largest donor and lender of economic aid to developing countries. In 1988 Japan spent a little more than $10 billion on foreign aid, which represented 0.32 percent of GNP and one-third of what it spent on defense. The United States spent thirty times as much on defense as it did on foreign aid—a little less than $10 billion, or 0.22 percent of GNP. In July 1989, Japan announced a $43 billion aid package of grants and loans to improve the global environment and to stimulate economic growth in countries ravaged by poverty, hunger, and indebtedness.[10]

The 1990 U.S. foreign-aid budget amounted to $14.6 billion, of which $3 billion was earmarked for Israel, which with a per capita GNP of $7,000 is hardly a developing country. An additional $2.3 billion was allocated to Egypt and only $900 million for the rest of Africa, $1.0 billion for Central America, and $200 million for all of South America.

Unfortunately, these paltry sums reflect the deep suspicion that most Americans have for foreign aid. A recent New York Times/CBS News poll found that 83 percent of Americans would find cutting foreign aid to be an acceptable means of reducing our budget deficit. Cutting foreign aid was preferable to reducing any other form of government spending as well as increasing taxes. Only 64 percent of those surveyed felt that cutting military spending was an acceptable method for lowering the deficit.[11]

As long as the United States and the Soviet Union continue to divert such huge amounts of resources into military defense, global problems such as poverty, AIDS, drug abuse, and environmental pollution will persist.

During the late 1970s and early 1980s, when Western banks were anxious to lend money to developing nations at double-digit interest rates, many Third World Countries piled up huge debts to American, Western European, and Japanese banks. Third World debt was $1.3 trillion at year-end 1989—one-third of which was owed by Latin American nations. Brazil and Mexico owed $120 billion and $107 billion respectively.

The economic effects of this debt burden have become absolutely crushing. According to the World Bank, average income in the middle-income developing countries—particularly in Latin America—has been reduced by one-seventh since 1980 as a result of the debt burden. For the very poorest countries—primarily in Africa—income has been reduced by one-quarter. Furthermore, the poorer countries are transferring their wealth to richer, developed nations in record amounts.

There is also increasing concern that the economic crisis generated by the Third World debt problem could precipitate a political crisis in Latin America and a return to authoritarian rule. One result of the debt crisis that affects both the United States and the Soviet Union is the inability of Third World countries to increase their imports from the United States and the Soviet Union. Both the United States and the Soviet Union need new markets for their exports. But Third World nations are so strapped for cash and hard currency that they cannot afford to import anything. However, in January 1990, the Bush administration pledged to cancel debts of $735 million owed by twelve sub-Saharan African countries. The per-capita incomes of these countries range from a low of $150 in Zaire to a high of $390 in Ghana.[12]

If U.S.–Soviet relations continue to improve, there will be increased opportunities for superpower cooperation in confronting some of the global problems defined in this chapter. A significant slow-down in the arms race could free up additional resources to be used to reduce some of the human suffering caused by these problems.

What is called for is a new U.S. global-development strategy targeted primarily at Third World countries. This strategy should be based on three principles: (1) multilateral cooperation, (2) significant host-country participation, and (3) reduced military aid.

MULTILATERAL COOPERATION

Since the 1945 Bretton Woods agreement, three institutions have defined the rules of international trade and commerce—the International Monetary Fund, the World Bank, and the General

Agreement on Tariffs and Trade. For the first twenty-five years after Bretton Woods, the United States dominated the world economy and the policies of these three institutions. But a lot has changed during the past two decades. U.S. economic dominance is being challenged by Japan and West Germany. The Soviet Union and Eastern Europe are pressing for full participation in the Bretton Woods institutions. Hungary and Poland are already participating. Third World nations are raising some very tough questions about these institutions as well. These include questions related to the equitable distribution of benefits, increased participation in decision making, sharing of industrial research and development, economic stability, and environmental protection.[13]

It remains to be seen whether these institutions will survive the political and economic pressures being set loose by the new global order resulting from the changes taking place in the Soviet Union and Eastern Europe. The United States will be an important participant, but increasingly it will have to share economic and political power with Japan, Western Europe, the Soviet Union, and possibly China.

The United States can afford to do substantially more for Third World countries than it has in the past. In the future we should cooperate more effectively with multilateral development organizations such as the United Nations, the World Banks, and the International Monetary Fund. The combined economic and political resources of the United States, Japan, Western Europe, and the Soviet Union could go a long way toward reducing the scope of global poverty, disease, and environmental pollution.

Davidson College economist Charles E. Ratliff, Jr., has come up with an innovative idea for financing Third World development. He has proposed the creation of a World Development Fund that would have the power to levy taxes and make expenditures to transfer resources from affluent industrialized member nations to less-affluent Third World members.

As envisaged by Ratliff, the World Development Fund would be a supernational authority established by treaty among member nations. Participation in the management of the Fund would be roughly equal for affluent members and Third World members, with net-gainers playing a crucial role in the expenditure and auditing decisions. The aim of this feature is to ensure that net-payers do not meddle in the internal affairs of net-gainers.

With universal membership and an international income tax yielding 1 percent of the Gross World Product, the Fund would raise approximately $160 billion annually. Expenditures would be allocated to Third World member nations principally on the basis of needs and resources but also on such bases as uniqueness of projects and possibility of long-run payoff.

There are several advantages of the Fund when compared with existing foreign aid programs. First, Fund outlays would be economically driven rather than politically motivated, as is the case with most unilateral aid programs. An equal voice for net-gainers and net-payers should reduce the risk of economic considerations being crowded out by political considerations. Second, net-gainer countries would not be politically obligated to specific donor countries, as is currently the case. Third, by providing a more stable and predictable source of funds, Third World countries could engage in long-range planning. Fourth, since development assistance would be provided by *all* nations, net-gainers would have more freedom and self-respect.

Two economists, one Soviet, and the other American, have proposed that the two superpowers discontinue their Third World rivalry and cooperate on foreign-aid projects. American University economist W. Donald Bowles and Elena Arefieva of the Soviet Institute of the World Economy and International Relations have proposed a number of U.S.–Soviet joint ventures in Third World countries, including natural-disaster emergency relief, reforestation, water supply, energy, technical education, health care, and urban construction. Under these proposals, Third World countries would be transformed from battlegrounds for superpower influence into areas of superpower cooperation.

Finally, since the 1950s the United States and the Soviet Union have spent billions of dollars on our own separate space-exploration projects. Much of the space-race competition was fueled by the cold war and the military implications of the control of space. At long last, the Soviets and the Americans are beginning to talk about joint space ventures so as to reduce the combined cost of our space programs.

HOST COUNTRY PARTICIPATION

Other than direct contributions of food and medical supplies to alleviate short-run crises, U.S. foreign aid should be increasingly oriented toward participatory technical and managerial assistance. There should be less emphasis on giveaway programs and more effort to train and involve local managers and administrators in the solution of their own problems.

The Paris-based Aga Khan Network, the largest and most respected private development organization, has been particularly successful in implementing "bottom up" development strategies in some twenty-five Third World countries. The Aga Khan approach is based on a relatively simple formula that emphasizes self-sufficiency, technical assistance, good management, and a thorough knowledge of the local situation.[14] The American-based Save the Children organization has a similar operating philosophy.

To assist company managers in Third World economies adapt to the rapidly changing global environment, our government should help launch an "International Management Corps." The idea of an International Management Corps (IMC) draws on the experience of three existing programs. The International Executive Service Corps sends retired U.S. executives to Third World countries as management consultants. The Soros Foundation supports the training of Hungarian and Soviet managers. And the Peace Corps sends Americans to work in developing countries around the world.

An increasing number of large American companies such as McDonald's, IBM, and Intel are offering their senior executives sabbatical leaves of up to three months to recharge their batteries away from the day-to-day office routine. Some of these companies may be willing to allow their executives to serve as consultants to Third World companies for short periods of time. Typically a consultant would be assigned to the general manager of a particular firm.

The IMC would serve as a broker that attempts to find qualified American consultants to meet the needs of specific Third World businesses. The process would begin with the manager of a particular company submitting a written request to the IMC for a consultant with certain specific skills. The IMC would then attempt to find such a consultant in the United States.

The consultant would be paid a regular salary in dollars by his or her employer. However, the client company would be required to pay the local expenses for the consultant as well as a consulting fee in local currency only. The consulting fees would be paid into a management-education fund for supporting management education in the host country. Each host country would have an advisory board to make recommendations on how to spend the funds made available to its own management education fund. The education fund could be used to support management-education institutions, programs, and activities in the host countries.

A second dimension of the IMC involves direct financial support in dollars for Third World managers and management students who want to study in the United States. Applications for IMC financial support would be submitted to the respective host-country education fund for competitive evaluation. The IMC and the host country would share the dollar cost of each financial award according to some previously agreed matching formula. For example, for every dollar spent by the host country for management education abroad, the IMC might provide two dollars in matching support.

The benefits of the IMC to Third World managers are clear. They would gain access to sophisticated American management expertise at a relatively low cost. Funds would also be generated in local currency to support management education within the host country. In addition, company managers would be provided with increased opportunities to study in the United States. American managers, on the other hand, will gain valuable experience in the practical realities of doing business in Third World countries. This experience should prove to be particularly beneficial to American companies that are considering the possibility of trading with these countries or entering into joint ventures with them.

The IMC is a relatively inexpensive way in which the United States can offer technical assistance to the Third World. It should have some appeal to the Bush administration since it rests solidly on two fundamental tenets of the administration—volunteerism and free enterprise.

REDUCED MILITARY AID

In addition to placing more emphasis on multilateral cooperation and host-country participation in its Third World development strategies, the United States should cut back on its military aid and arms sales to Third World nations. As we noted before, arms sales to Third World nations by both superpowers shot upward in 1990 in anticipation of European arms-control agreements.

Hopefully, over the long run there will be less incentive for the world's two largest arms dealers to continue shipping instruments of death to disadvantaged Third World countries, who can't afford them in the first place. A recent United Nations study concluded that if the Third World were to reduce military expenditures by only 2.5 percent and spend the extra money on food, health care, and improved living conditions, then the lives of six million children would be spared each year.[15]

The Eastern European Wringer

In an unexpected turn of events, it now appears that, at least in the short run, Third World countries are likely to suffer reductions in foreign investment, loans, and economic aid as a result of the rapidly changing situation in Eastern Europe. As international lending agencies, foreign aid programs, and private foundations redirect their support to Eastern European countries, some of their funds will be diverted from Third World projects. For example, the U.S. Agency for International Development and the Peace Corps already have projects in Poland and Hungary. The United Nations is facing similar pressures to allocate funds on the basis of the degree to which a country has been democratized rather than on its economic needs. Over the long run, Third World countries should still benefit from increased superpower cooperation in meeting the challenge of global development problems. However, in the short run, some of the resources that might otherwise have been allocated to the Third World may find their way to Eastern Europe. More recently, Third World oil importers have been confronted with the devastating effects of skyrocketing oil prices precipitated by the Persian Gulf crisis.

9

The Leadership Challenge

Our Leadership Gap

Within a matter of months after the end of World War II, the Soviet Union and the United States embarked on a cold war characterized by an endless series of hostile acts on both sides and an unprecedented military buildup. Among the more noteworthy cold war events were Churchill's "Iron Curtain" speech, George Kennan's "Mr. X" article, the Soviet blockade of West Berlin, the Hungarian revolution, the erection of the Berlin Wall, the Cuban missile crisis, the Prague Spring, the passage of the Jackson–Vanik amendment, the Soviet invasion of Afghanistan, and President Reagan's "evil empire" speech.

However, Mikhail S. Gorbachev's rise to power in 1985 ushered in a whole new approach to U.S.–Soviet relations. For over forty-five years the foreign-policy leadership of the United States and the Soviet Union could best be described as reactionary and destructive. Both U.S. and Soviet leaders were strongly influenced by World War II. The mentality of the Great Depression was a drag on the imagination of American leaders, while Stalinism took its toll on Soviet leaders.

Gorbachev and Bush are the first superpower leaders since World War II to substitute a more conciliatory approach to foreign policy for the traditional tit-for-tat cold war strategies. The Nixon–Brezhnev period of détente proved to be an all too short-lived exception to this rule. Both the United States and the Soviet Union have demonstrated a complete lack of imagination and creativity in dealing with each other over the years. This leadership

ship gap is the common denominator linking each of the eight U.S.–Soviet problems we have previously discussed.

Gorbachev's Management Philosophy

The past five years have witnessed the emergence of one of the most remarkable managers of the twentieth century—Mikhail S. Gorbachev. Cynics have claimed that Gorbachev has no strategy whatsoever and is merely shooting from the hip. But they know not from whence they speak. Like the best of his American corporate counterparts, Gorbachev combines a well-defined management philosophy with lots of hard work. As I pointed out in chapter 5, *perestroika* is firmly grounded on more than fifteen years of research with in-depth computer-simulation experiments.

OBJECTIVES

Gorbachev's objectives have remained remarkably consistent since 1985:

1. *Economy:* To improve the quality of life of the Soviet people by strengthening the Soviet economy, closing the technological gap with the West, and producing world-class consumer goods for domestic consumption and export abroad.

2. *Agriculture:* To become self-sufficient in agricultural products and foodstuffs.

3. *Democratization:* To introduce participatory democracy into the Soviet Union and Eastern Europe.

4. *Foreign Policy:* To strengthen the Soviet Union's diplomatic and trade relations with the international community of nations.

5. *Arms Reduction:* To negotiate a major arms-reduction agreement with the United States and its NATO allies covering conventional forces, nuclear weapons, and space-based weapons.

6. *Culture:* To change the culture of the Soviet Union in such a manner that in exchange for more personal freedom, individual citizens will be encouraged to assume more risk and responsibility for their individual lives.

STRATEGIES

By granting the Soviet people increased political freedom at the outset followed by the gradual introduction of economic reforms — in contrast to the Polish shock-treatment approach—Mr. Gorbachev may have paved the way for more serious, longer-lasting reforms than any of those being implemented by other socialist nations. His five strategies for bringing the Soviet Union into the global mainstream are:

1. *Tension Reduction:* Reduce tension and conflict at home and abroad through a nonconfrontational problem-solving approach based on open discussion, negotiation, and mutual trust.

2. *Power Sharing:* Through power sharing increase the psychological and economic stakes that the Soviet Union's stakeholders have in *perestroika*. Empower Soviet enterprise managers, labor unions, local government officials, ethnic minorities, socialist republics, religious groups, Eastern European nations, and Third World allies.

3. *Democratic Socialism:* Broaden the base of political and economic participation of the Soviet people in the policymaking process of decisions affecting their lives using Sweden, Finland, Austria, and Canada as models.

4. *Global Interdependence:* Through multilateral trade, political cooperation, and the principle of "reasonable defense sufficiency" increase the Soviet Union's political, economic, and technological interdependence with the rest of the world.

5. *Downsizing:* Reduce the Soviet Union to a more manageable size by divesting itself of those republics for which the political and economic costs of their staying in the USSR outweigh the benefits.

Under Gorbachev, the Soviet Union has become more open, more democratic, more market-oriented, less risk-averse, and more outward looking. What truly differentiates Gorbachev from most politicians is his well-defined vision of the future—not only for his own country, but for the world. Unlike many politicians who rely exclusively on an ad hoc management style, Gorbachev's

well-honed strategies reflect years of research and analysis.
Whether dealing with the United States, Eastern Europe, China,
the Baltic republics, or disgruntled Soviet consumers, Gorbachev
always takes the long view.

Gorbachev, who has learned much from American corporate
leaders, may be able to return the favor. His nonconfrontational
approach to conflict resolution, power sharing, and participatory
management could prove to be quite useful to American executives in labor–management negotiations, business–government
strategies, and stockholder relations.

Our Denial of *Perestroika*

Since 1961, the cold war has been epitomized by the presence of
the Berlin Wall. Yet during the very week in which the GDR opened
its borders to the West and the wall came crashing down, the U.S.
Congress was putting the finishing touches on a $296 billion mili-
tary-spending bill. In spite of the sweeping changes that took place
in Eastern Europe and the Soviet Union in 1989, the Congress did
not begin pressing the Pentagon for significant cutbacks in major
U.S. military programs until the second half of 1990.

In virtually every field of endeavor, including economics, law,
politics, human rights, religion, culture and foreign policy, the
Soviets have acted precisely as American politicians have demanded since the early 1950s. By the end of 1990, the Congress
had made only token cuts in the defense budget, had yet to repeal
a single anti-Soviet trade law, and was threatening additional
trade sanctions. Among the anti-Soviet trade bills pending in the
Congress in 1990 were bills dealing with human rights, slave labor,
tied-financing, technology transfer, and anti-dumping. As always,
the aim of these bills was to destabilize the Soviet Union. Although
President Bush and Secretary of State James Baker III understand
that the Soviets are serious about *perestroika*, this message seems to
have eluded our congressional leadership.

Although President Gorbachev confidently proclaimed the end
of the cold war at his joint press conference with President Bush
following the Malta summit, Mr. Bush could not bring himself to
say the same. Regrettably, as Gorbachev began his sixth year in
power, influential people in our government, our national media,

and noted Sovietologists were still engaged in a broad-based denial of the significance of *perestroika*.

During Gorbachev's first three years in power, many Sovietologists repeatedly assured us that he was not for real. His economic and political reforms, his openness and candor, his attacks on Stalinism, his cuts in military spending, and his dramatic shifts in foreign policy were all said to be a sham—just further examples of communist propaganda. But when cold warrior Ronald Reagan finally had the opportunity to observe *glasnost* and *perestroika* first hand in Moscow in June 1988, Sovietologists were forced to change their tune.

For the next year or so the conventional wisdom among CIA, Pentagon, and academic Sovietologists was that Gorbachev was a one-of-a-kind Soviet leader who was trying to reform the Soviet Union, but he was bound to fail. Not only should we do nothing to enhance his chances of success, but rather we should continue our military buildup in anticipation of Gorbachev's eventual defeat. We were further warned that once Gorbachev was out of the picture, the USSR would soon revert to Stalinism. Trouble in Eastern Europe, ethnic unrest in the Soviet Union, and conservative political opposition in Moscow were the forces mentioned most often that would surely bring Gorbachev down.

These forecasts of gloom and doom are heightened each August when Gorbachev takes his annual vacation away from Moscow. Every August brings a flurry of rumors in the Western press that he is on his way out. "Where is Gorbachev?" "How long has it been since he was seen in public?" "What is the political significance of his long absence from Moscow?" "Is he terminally ill?" And each summer the answers to these questions are always the same. "Gorbachev is simply on vacation and his absence from Moscow is of no political significance whatsoever."

Similar rumors are generated before every important meeting of the Politburo and the Central Committee and each U.S.–Soviet summit meeting. Whether Gorbachev's days are numbered is a debatable point. But thus far his staying power has proven to be truly remarkable. He has already survived much longer than most Sovietologists such as Marshall Goldman ever led us to believe. Goldman has made a career of warning national television audiences of Gorbachev's imminent demise. One of these days Professor Goldman will no doubt be right.

The unrest in Eastern Europe not only failed to bring Gorbachev down, but he is generally credited with having paved the way for increased political freedom there. Contrary to what was predicted by Sovietologists such as Zbigniew Brzezinski and Richard Pipes, Gorbachev's hand was actually strengthened by the collapse of communism in Eastern Europe. Although it is impossible to predict the final outcome of the secessionist demands of Estonia, Latvia, Lithuania, and other Soviet republics, it is unlikely that Gorbachev will allow himself to be boxed into a corner by any of these republics. He is too flexible and too attuned to political power sharing to be brought down by dissident republics.

According to maverick Sovietologist Jerry F. Hough of Duke University, Gorbachev not only is "for real," but we have "grossly exaggerated the strength of conservatives in the Soviet Union." In a 1989 article in *Foreign Affairs* Hough said that "Gorbachev is a very skilled politician who knows what he is doing."[1]

American cynics seem to confuse their own needs for instant gratification with those of the Soviets, failing to realize that since 1917 the Soviet people have been promised more consumer goods. Gorbachev is actually using shortages of food and consumer goods to make the case to the Soviet people for price reforms and a convertible ruble. Unlike Poland where political leaders have from time to time surprised the Polish people with precipitous price increases, often followed by political chaos, Gorbachev spent over five years laying the ground work for flexible prices and a convertible ruble.

How long Gorbachev will stay in power remains uncertain. However, if the Soviet Union intends to remain a global superpower, then reverting to Stalinism is not a viable option with or without Gorbachev. *Glasnost* and *perestroika* are here to stay. All of the internal and external forces pushing the Soviets towards radical economic and political reform will still persist long after Gorbachev leaves the political scene. *Perestroika* is not the cause of Soviet economic and political problems but rather is an attempt to respond to the systematic neglect of these problems for over sixty years.

Our denial of *perestroika* reminds me of growing up in Jackson, Mississippi, during the 1950s. Nearly one hundred years after the war—the Civil War—few white Southerners acknowledged that the war was actually over. They were unwilling to admit that we had lost the war and that blacks deserved to be treated as human beings rather than as slaves. It was not until the late 1960s and early 1970s that white Southerners began to abandon some of their stereotypical views of blacks.

Is it any wonder that Americans find it equally difficult to believe that fundamental changes have taken place in the Soviet Union? For over seventy years, but particularly since the 1950s, we have been told repeatedly that "You can't trust the Russians." Anticommunism has been the driving force of our foreign policy since World War II. We are so conditioned to always assume the worst about anything the Soviets do or say that it is virtually impossible to view them in any other way.

Unlike the South, which lost the Civil War but continued to pretend otherwise for over one hundred years, the United States has actually won the ideological battle with Stalin-style communism. Ironically, while the Soviets certainly know that we won, some American politicians such as Vice President Dan Quayle and Senator Jesse Helms of North Carolina seem to be oblivious to this fact. Otherwise, why continue spending nearly $300 billion annually to protect ourselves from the Russians? Why do Radio Liberty and Radio Free Europe continue to beam their cold war messages into the Soviet Union and Eastern Europe?

Sovietologists still have only limited understanding of Gorbachev's management philosophy and style. A series of events that took place in 1987 and 1988 serve to illustrate the difficulty they have in grasping the essence of one of Gorbachev's most important strategic weapons—power sharing.

At the June 1987 Party Plenum, the Central Committee gave Gorbachev control of the Politburo and approved a list of new radical economic reforms, including self-financing of enterprises, decentralized decision making, and the election of factory managers by employees. Yet for six months before the Plenum, Sovietologists warned that Gorbachev was facing increased opposition to *perestroika* and forecast his demise. But where was the evidence that Gorbachev was facing such insurmountable obstacles? Just before the Plenum a small West German plane landed in Red Square. Two days later Gorbachev fired the defense minister and the commander of air defenses—hardly suggesting that he was dealing from a position of weakness.

In October 1987, Moscow party boss Boris N. Yeltsin was forced to resign after a speech before the Central Committee.

Sovietologists said this was evidence of Gorbachev's growing political problems—especially with No. 2 Communist Party official Yegor K. Ligachev. But it simply was not true. When a high-ranking official embarrasses a nation's leader, the official is likely to be fired. The Yeltsin affair was much ado about nothing.

Throughout Gorbachev's tenure in office, Ligachev was the darling of the American press until he was recently upstaged by Yeltsin who was elected president of the Russian republic. It was as though each new reform would surely be Gorbachev's last. If disillusioned Moscow politicians such as Ligachev or Yeltsin don't topple Gorbachev, he will certainly be ousted by the KGB or the Soviet military.

During the weeks preceding the June 1990 summit in Washington, American television and print media engaged in an unrelenting attack on Gorbachev and the shortcomings of *perestroika*. Over and over again each night we were told by the anchors of the national evening news programs about all of Gorbachev's problems—the Soviet economy, the Baltic republics, ethnic unrest, and the political threat posed by Boris Yeltsin. We were repeatedly warned that Gorbachev was in deep political trouble and that he desperately needed a deal with President Bush. Endless television interviews were conducted with disgruntled Soviet citizens. Rarely did our press mention Gorbachev's incredible record of success in opening up the Soviet Union and establishing positive linkages with the rest of the world. Instead the American people were treated to four weeks of anti-Gorbachev, anti-Soviet hype.

No mention was made by our media of the fact that the United States, unlike the Soviet Union, has no political game plan whatsoever for responding to the end of the cold war and the colossal political and economic changes sweeping across the world today.

A few weeks later, Gorbachev-bashing by the American media was further intensified during its coverage of the twenty-eighth Congress of the Communist Party in Moscow. Amid predictions that Gorbachev would be unseated as party chairman by unruly conservative opponents, Gorbachev actually strengthened his own political power by further diffusing the power of the party. Not only was he reelected party chairman, but he threatened to purge the party of conservative obstructionists.

In October 1990, with Gorbachev's support, the Soviet parliament approved the most radical set of economic reforms ever presented to the Soviet people. The following are among the far-reaching reforms scheduled over a two-year period:

- flexible prices;
- a convertible ruble;
- a money-and-banking system that includes a federal reserve system and a stock exchange; and
- the privatization of industry, retailing, agriculture, and housing.

Most of these reforms are long overdue, and their successful implementation is critical to the political survival of Mr. Gorbachev—as he duly noted at the party congress. Indeed, he volunteered to step down of his own accord, if the Soviet economy was not turned around within two years.

If Gorbachev is eventually brought down—as he may very well be—the United States will bear no small part of the responsibility for his fall from power. Our government has done little or nothing to help the plight of the Soviet economy. By refusing to remove discriminatory trade sanctions against the Soviets and denying them credit and economic aid, we may have made our gloomy forecasts of Gorbachev's demise a self-fulfilling prophecey. Regrettably, the Bush administration's approach to aid to Gorbachev may prove to have been too little, too late.

I believe we have to look for a psychological explanation for our continued denial of *perestroika*. No matter how much new evidence is presented of the depth and breadth of the truly radical Soviet reforms, we always demand more. Is it possible that our denial stems from the fact that we cannot bear the pain of admitting that we too need *glasnost* and *perestroika*? For forty-five years it has always been a lot easier to criticize the Soviet Union for every imaginable sin rather than to take a hard look at ourselves. America has lost its sense of direction, and our politicians and opinion leaders attempt to compensate for this loss by playing to American narcissism. A nation so obsessed with its own myths about freedom and individualism is naturally attracted to the politics of narcissism and repelled by the politics of cooperation, whether with the Soviet Union or any other nation. Gorbachev's message of tension reduction, cooperation, and trust has gone right over the heads of our press, our Sovietologists, and our Congress.

The United States Needs *Glasnost* Too

Within a matter of a few weeks during the fall of 1989, the Soviet government (1) admitted that the 1979 Soviet invasion of Afghanistan was not only ill-conceived but illegal; (2) acknowledged that the Krasnoyarsk radar station in Siberia was indeed in violation of the ABM Treaty; (3) denounced the Brezhnev doctrine; and (4) condemned the 1968 Warsaw Pact invasion of Czechoslovakia. These admissions of past guilt were by no means the only signs of increased candor and contrition expressed by Soviet leaders during the Gorbachev era. The Soviets have accepted responsibility for the tragic downing of Korean Air Lines flight 007 in 1983 and admitted that the 1986 Chernobyl nuclear accident was caused by gross incompetence and mismanagement. Former Soviet leader Joseph Stalin has been the object of endless attacks by the Soviet press—particularly since 1986. There is now open criticism of Vladimir I. Lenin himself.

The Soviets have acknowledged the 1939 secret agreement between Stalin and Hitler, which led to the involuntary annexation of the Baltic republics. Their role in the 1940 Katyn Forest massacre in which several thousand elite Polish officers were executed was revealed in *Moscow News*.

Unfortunately, the reaction of many American politicians and Sovietologists to these revaluations is a smug, "We told you so." How is it that we so passively accept all of these painful admissions on the part of Soviet leaders without any inclination whatsoever to take a serious look at ourselves. Are there no cold war skeletons in our closet? Why do we persist in avoiding the obvious question, "Doesn't the United States need *glasnost* too?"

Since 1945 Americans have been told by our political leaders that Harry Truman did the rest of the world a big favor by bombing Hiroshima and Nagasaki. As the story goes, the use of the bomb was necessary to end the war and avoid further bloodshed. But convincing research of War Department records by historian Gar Alperovitz casts serious doubts on the legitimacy of this claim. Alperovitz has shown that Truman knew that the United States had Japan on the run and that the unconditional surrender of Japan was imminent. Alperovitz argues that Truman's real motive in dropping the bomb was to make certain that the Soviet Union, which was about to enter the war against Japan, did not gain a foothold in China.[2] Truman's decision to unleash the atomic bomb was the first salvo of the cold war.

If Alperovitz's hypothesis is correct—and there is little evidence to suggest otherwise—then the American atomic bomb myth is at least as big a lie as any myth ever perpetrated by Stalin, Khrushchev, or Brezhnev. Yet one can hardly imagine President Bush or any other American president ever apologizing for such a colossal mistake.

As we have previously noted, our government brought thousands of Nazi war criminals into this country after World War II and set them up in prominent positions in the CIA, Radio Liberty, Radio Free Europe, and leading American universities. Not only did this disgraceful activity go virtually unnoticed by our press in the late 1940s and early 1950s when it was actually happening, but when it was finally exposed by Christopher Simpson in his 1988 book *Blowback* it was met by stony silence by our politicians, our press, and Sovietologists.[3] American Jewish leaders uttered hardly a whimper when *Blowback* was published.

If the Soviets had no legitimate reason to be in Afghanistan, we had even less justification for our involvement in the war in Vietnam, which took place half way around the globe from here. Although many Americans know that our role in Vietnam can be justified on neither moral nor national security grounds, few of our political leaders have been willing to say this publicly. And those such as Senator George McGovern who did take a strong stand against U.S. intervention in Vietnam later paid a high political price for challenging the myths on which our involvement was based.

While accusing the Soviets of being military expansionists and pathological liars, our government has shown no remorse whatsoever for its 1961 Bay of Pigs invasion of Cuba, the CIA's role in overthrowing the Marxist government of Chilean President Salvador Allende in 1973, our illegal mining of the harbor in Managua, President Reagan's invasion of Grenada and bombing of Libya, and more recently President Bush's use of massive military force to bring down Panamanian dictator Manuel Antonio

Noriega. In spite of recent evidence linking the CIA to the arrest of South African political activist Nelson Mandela nearly three decades ago during the Kennedy administration, once again the response of our government has been silence.

In July 1988 when the USS Vincennes shot down Iran Air flight 655 killing 290 people, the Pentagon not only refused to accept responsibility for the tragedy but attempted to shift the blame to Iran. Few Americans are willing to admit that the real reason for military intervention in the Persian Gulf was to support our oil import habit.

Our government much prefers to talk about Soviet human-rights violations rather than acknowledge some of our own unattended problems such as poverty, homelessness, high infant-mortality rates, and racism.

Sovietologists often refer to the self-serving politics of Stalin, Khrushchev, and Brezhnev as the "personality cult," but American politicians suffer from a similar malaise—the politics of narcissism and instant gratification. Knowing the low tolerance level the American people have for self-criticism, our politicians give us exactly what we want to hear from them—congratulatory self-aggrandizement. President Reagan's grasp of the politics of narcissism was without equal.

A Kinder America and a Gentler World

George Bush is the first American president since Franklin D. Roosevelt to have the luxury of being able to forge a foreign policy based on some objective other than stopping the spread of communism. Since 1945 our entire foreign policy and many of our domestic policies have been driven by unabashed anticommunism. On the one hand, this situation provides President Bush with an unprecedented opportunity to define a new vision of the future for the United States. On the other hand, it represents an awesome responsibility. He must come to terms with the fact that anticommunism has never been a vision of the future and never will be.

In both his presidential nomination acceptance speech and his 20 January 1989 inaugural address, President Bush called for a "kinder nation and a gentler world." His inaugural address suggested a management philosophy based more on pragmatism rather than anticommunist ideology. Not only did Mr. Bush use the word "love" three times in the speech, but there was not a single reference to the Soviet Union. Throughout the speech Mr. Bush repeated the phrase, "A new breeze is blowing." He also spoke of a need for volunteerism—"a thousand points of light"— and a need for "greater tolerance and easy-goingness about each other's attitudes and way of life." All of this was in sharp contrast to the macho, bombastic anti-Soviet rhetoric of Ronald Reagan whom George Bush served for eight years with unquestioned loyalty.

His first serious foreign-policy test occurred after the 4 June 1989 Tiananmen Square massacre in Beijing. His subdued response to this cruel disaster represented a significant departure from Ronald Reagan's cowboy-style diplomacy. He was unwilling to write off ten years of improved Sino–American relations no matter how reprehensible the Chinese actions might have been. In spite of strong congressional opposition, a year later President Bush extended China's most-favored-nation status for another year.

Mr. Bush has often been accused of being timid in his response to President Gorbachev's unprecedented reforms. I believe that "unimaginative" more accurately depicts his actual behavior. What is missing is a conceptual framework for visualizing the new world order as well as America's role in it. There is no clearly defined vision of the future for Europe, the Middle East, the Far East, or Central America or how the United States should relate to these important regions. There appears to be an excessive preoc- cupation with short-run political popularity rather than coming to terms with the new challenges and opportunities afforded by a rapidly changing global environment.

Unlike President Reagan, Mr. Bush seems to realize that no longer is it possible for the United States to speak with any cer- tainty for its allies. As the threat of conventional war in Europe becomes less likely, the massive U.S. military presence there is more difficult to justify. One senses a certain uneasiness as the United States tries to define a new niche for itself in Europe.

Although President Bush's policy toward the Soviet Union is far less bellicose than that of President Reagan, there is neverthe- less a certain ambivalence surrounding it. A bizarre nostalgia for the cold war remains in effect—a reluctance to let go of what

Undersecretary of State Lawrence Eagleburger has described as "a remarkably stable and predictable set of relations among the great powers."

While proclaiming at the Malta summit that the changes in Eastern Europe deserve "new thinking," Mr. Bush refused to talk about a "peace dividend" and dodged a question from the press as to whether he agreed with Mr. Gorbachev that the cold war was over. After promising Gorbachev a U.S.–Soviet trade agreement at Malta, Mr. Bush succumbed to pressure from the Jewish lobby and refused to grant the Soviets MFN status at the June 1990 Washington summit pending codification of Soviet emigration policies.

There must be times when the Soviets are truly confused about where Bush stands concerning U.S.–Soviet relations. In May 1989 when Gorbachev announced that he would withdraw five hundred nuclear weapons from Eastern Europe, Secretary of Defense Dick Cheney responded, "He has got so many ratholes over there in Eastern Europe that five hundred is a pittance." White House press spokesman Marlin Fitzwater dismissed the proposal as a "public relations gambit" perpetrated by a "drugstore cowboy."[4]

Although the State Department succeeded in partially muzzling the hardline anti-Soviet rhetoric of Deputy National Security Adviser Robert M. Gates, Vice President Dan Quayle is allowed to run amok, calling the Soviet Union a "totalitarian system" and stirring the political juices of right-wing diehards who don't want to see the cold war end. Although Quayle's drivel undoubtedly annoys the Soviets, he is able to appease the far right.

If Bush wants to drop Quayle from the 1992 presidential ticket, what better way to do it than to let Dan Quayle be Dan Quayle? By 1992 anticommunism may have become an irrelevant cliche—not unlike Mr. Quayle.

Other than occasional blasts at Panamanian strong man Manuel Antonio Noriega and Sandinista leader Daniel Ortega, President Bush's actions during his first ten months in office were generally consistent with the "kinder, gentler" philosophy articulated in his inaugural address.

However, in November and December of 1989, Bush abruptly dropped his low-key approach to foreign policy in favor of a return to Reagan's macho-style diplomacy. He dispatched the antiterrorist Delta Force to the San Salvador Sheraton Hotel ostensibly to free American hostages who were thought to have been taken by Salvadoran guerrillas. When the Delta Force arrived, there were no hostages to be found. While Bush was meeting Gorbachev in Malta, U.S. F-5 fighter jets from Clark Air Base in the Philippines were being used to intimidate rebel forces who were attempting to overthrow the government of Corazon Aquino.

Then on 20 December 1989, the U.S. military illegally invaded tiny Panama—the thirteenth time during this century—and overthrew the government of alleged drug trafficker and former CIA operative Manuel Antonio Noriega. Over twenty-four thousand troops and two Stealth bombers were required to bring down Noriega and install a U.S.-supported puppet government in Panama City. Twenty-six Americans lost their lives along with several thousand Panamanians in the bloody military assault ostensibly precipitated by the death of a single American soldier dressed in civilian clothes. Thousands were left homeless. Several days later, with the assistance of the Vatican Embassy in Panama, Noriega was kidnapped by U.S. authorities and taken to Miami to face criminal charges on his drug-related activities.

President Bush told the American people that Operation "Just Cause"—the Panamanian invasion—was necessary to protect American lives and the Panama Canal and to stop a major player in the international drug market. He then offered the Panamanians a few hundred million dollars for their losses.

Americans were euphoric over our aggressive intervention in Panama, just as they had been when President Reagan invaded Grenada and bombed Libya. President Bush's popularity soared in the polls. Most Americans love to see the United States play the role of global bully.

Like Mr. Bush said at Malta, "Well, you know these charismatic, macho, visionary guys—they'll do anything." So much for a kinder nation and a gentler world.

In his 1 January 1990 New Year's address to the American people President Gorbachev called for a "more calm and reasonable" world—an often-stated theme throughout his first five years in power.

New Year's Address to the American People

I suggest making the 1990s a decade of drawing the United States and the Soviet Union closer together on the basis of universal human values and a balance of interests, and together with all countries ridding the world of fears and mistrust, or unnecessary weapons, of outdated political concepts and military doctrine and artificial barriers between people and states.

The year 1990 could become a genuine turning point in the efforts to limit and reduce arms. We, on our part, shall do everything for that.

At the same time our two countries could do much for further improvement of the overall moral and political climate in the world. In this case one may have no doubt that we shall bring nearer the transformation of the world and will make it more calm and reasonable.

The 1990s may become a decade when freedom, democracy and equality will begin to be established on a global scale and in an increasingly irreversible way.

People may say that all these are long-known truths and age-old values. This is so, indeed. But never before were we prepared so well for implementing them as now, at the turn of the century. Let us work purposefully, patiently and with belief in their triumph.

Mikhail S. Gorbachev
1 January 1990

In February 1990, a few days after delivering the most humane State of the Union Message since the days of John F. Kennedy—a message aimed at making it easier for Gorbachev to reduce the number of Soviet troops in Eastern Europe—President Bush embarked on a saber-rattling tour of American military bases and SDI research labs to promote his huge military budget. Both Mr. Bush and Mr. Gorbachev are still shackled with cold war conservatism among their respective political constituents. Gorbachev has been far more successful in pulling away from Communist

Party conservatives than President Bush has in escaping the clutches of the political right wing of American politics.

Our challenge today is to take this democratic system of ours—a system second to none—and make it better.

A better America, where there's a job for everyone who wants one.

Where women working outside the home can be confident their children are in safe and loving care— and where government works to expand childcare alternatives for parents.

Where "Made in the U.S.A." is recognized around the world as the symbol of quality and progress.

Where every one of us enjoys the same opportunities to live, to work and to contribute to society. And where, for the first time, the American mainstream includes all of our disabled citizens.

Where everyone has a roof over his head—and where the homeless get the help they need to live in dignity.

Where our schools challenge and support our kids and our teachers—and where all of them make the grade.

Where every street, every city, every school and every child is drug free.

President George Bush
State of the Union Address
31 January 1990

A few months later, Mr. Bush was under a great deal of pressure from congressional leaders to punish the Soviets for intimidating Lithuania for its efforts to secede from the USSR. Both Democratic and Republican demagogues were urging him to punish the Soviet Union for its heavy-handed cutting off of oil and natural gas supplies to Lithuania. As was the case with China, Mr. Bush once again turned the other cheek and refused to be sucked into what was essentially a Soviet internal problem. To his credit, he recognized that improved U.S.–Soviet relations are far more important than placating a dissident Soviet republic that had overplayed its hand in international politics—a republic which will eventually be set free by the Soviet Union with or without U.S. intervention.

In spite of the barrage of American media attacks on Gorbachev and the Soviet Union prior to the June 1990 Washington summit, a great deal was accomplished during Mr. Gorbachev's meetings with Mr. Bush, not the least of which was a strengthening of the personal relationship between the two superpower leaders. As evidence of how far the Bush–Gorbachev relationship has evolved, Gorbachev was shown on national television driving President Bush's golf cart at the Camp David presidential retreat.

On the more substantive side, the Washington summit produced a number of important bilateral agreements covering such diverse topics as chemical weapons, nuclear testing, trade, the peaceful use of nuclear energy, U.S. grain exports, increased passenger and cargo airline service, student exchanges, and ocean studies. In addition, further progress was made towards conclusion of the START treaty dealing with strategic nuclear weapons and a START II treaty that would include reductions in multiple warhead missiles.

One of the most positive contributions made by the Bush administration to the cold war end game has been the very constructive and creative relationship that exists between Secretary of State James Baker III and Soviet Foreign Minister Eduard A. Shevardnadze. Already the Baker–Shevardnadze relationship has contributed significantly to a reduction in tension and hostility in such places as Iran, Afghanistan, Angola, Namibia, South Africa, Nicaragua, Cambodia, and Korea (North and South).

At the NATO summit held in London in July 1990, under the strong influence of President Bush, the alliance softened considerably many of its harsh cold war policies. In addition, President Gorbachev and other Eastern European leaders were invited to address NATO. In the meantime, Mr. Bush steadfastly refused to budge from his position of opposition to U.S. economic aid for the Soviet Union.

In spite of his campaign rhetoric expressing concern for the safety and well-being of children of working parents, President Bush vetoed a bill requiring large American companies to provide their employees with unpaid family leave time. The United States is one of the few countries in the world that does not require employers to offer their employees such protection—all of which leaves one wondering, "Who is the real George Bush?"

In the final analysis, our Persian Gulf policy and the White House battle with the Congress over the 1991 budget have demonstrated rather conclusively that "a kinder nation and a gentler world" and "read my lips; no new taxes" were, respectively, nothing more than meaningless clichés aimed at shoring up George Bush's political popularity.

A Vision of the Future

Even before the 1989 political shakeup in Eastern Europe, government leaders worldwide were having increasing difficulty coping with an unprecedented degree of risk and uncertainty. Only with substantial help from Mikhail Gorbachev did Ronald Reagan barely escape being the fifth consecutive president to be held in extremely low public esteem when he left the White House. International terrorism, the Iran–contra affair, the 29 October 1987 stockmarket crash, Daniel Ortega, and General Manuel Antonio Noriega all made Reagan's life difficult.

Without exception, Presidents Johnson, Nixon, Ford, Carter, and Reagan paid dearly for their inability to formulate a clearly defined vision of the future, a coherent set of national objectives, well-defined strategies, and an integrated process for coordinating these strategies. Vietnam, Watergate, OPEC, and Iran contributed to the demise of Reagan's four predecessors.

In addition to the uncertainties created by the Soviet Union and Eastern Europe, President Bush must confront rising oil prices, record-high trade and budget deficits, unstable financial markets, the savings and loan crisis, an increasing gap between the rich and the poor, a divisive labor–management climate, possible default on Third World debts, a serious drug problem, an AIDS epidemic, environmental degradation, and continued political unrest in Central America and the Middle East.

In response to the political changes precipitated by Mr. Gorbachev in the Soviet Union and Eastern Europe as well as other forms of global uncertainty, the American people should insist that our president have a clear national strategy.

As we have previously noted, during most of the Reagan years, the State Department, the Pentagon, the CIA, and the National Security Council each had their own independent foreign policy. Is it any wonder that the Reagan administration had so much difficulty in responding to Gorbachev's arms-control initiatives?

Although we encourage strategic planning by companies such as IBM, AT&T, and General Motors, most Americans view government planning as an anathema. But our government is certainly not devoid of planning. The Council of Economic Advisors, the Office of Management and Budget, the Congressional Budget Office, the Federal Reserve Board, and most government agencies all engage in planning. The issue is no longer whether or not to do government planning. Although the president does not control the Congress or the Fed, he should actively encourage the executive branch to march to the beat of the same drummer.

How should the United States respond to Gorbachev's economic, political, and foreign policy initiatives? What changes, if any, should be made in our diplomatic, military, and foreign trade policies towards the Soviet Union? How can we more effectively coordinate the activities of multiple government agencies in simultaneously attacking the demand *and* supply sides of the drug problem? What is needed is a problem-solving approach, guided by the President, that is capable of answering such tough questions.

Although President Bush has taken some important—yet very small—steps towards ending the cold war, neither the Republican party nor the Democratic party seems to have a very well defined cold war end game strategy. Two highly interdependent questions remain unanswered. First, how will we in fact go about reducing our commitment to military defense? Second, how will we go about reallocating the resources that are freed up as a result of the reductions in military spending?

In terms of transforming the U.S. economy from a defense-driven economy to a civilian economy, we may want to examine the role played by the Japanese Ministry of International Trade and Industry (MITI) in resurrecting the Japanese economy from the smoldering ashes of World War II and converting it into a global economic powerhouse. The types of business, labor, and government partnerships found in Sweden, Finland, and Austria may also be useful models for the United States to consider as it formulates its cold war end game strategy.

Each year the president delivers two reports to the Congress — the State of the Union address and the annual budget message. But in a large American company, the budgetary process would not begin without agreement among the senior executives on the company's objectives and strategies. In the case of our government, there is a missing report—the president's national strategy.

This is not a plea for Soviet-style planning or socialism, but rather a call for the president to articulate his vision of the future. The strategic plan should be brief and to the point—no more than three pages. It should outline the president's primary objectives and strategies for the nation and provide a framework for coordinating government agencies and evaluating their budget requests.

The Soviet Union is the most overplanned society in the world—the United States, the least planned. Just as top-down, centralized planning has not solved all of the Soviet Union's problems, so too the market does not seem to have solved all of our problems either. Our two countries should spend more time listening to each other. We both stand to gain from the experience.

Real Political Pluralism

Ronald Reagan often called for political pluralism in the Soviet Union and Eastern Europe. Then with lightning-like speed, political pluralism actually came to Eastern Europe in 1989, and the Soviet Union appears to be headed in the same direction.

Multiple parties are a fact of life in Western Europe. Today the countries that don't have strong multiparty political systems include the United States and a large number of Third World military dictatorships. Nationally, the United States has a single party masked as a two-party system—the Republican party. Minority parties are powerless.

Reagan's charisma alone cannot explain the Republicans' landslide victories in the 1980, 1984, and 1988. Notwithstanding Jimmy Carter's 1976 election, the Republican party has controlled our domestic and foreign policy agenda since 1968. Carter's victory was a fluke precipitated by the Watergate affair.

The Democratic party has not had an original idea since the Great Society and the Civil Rights Acts of 1964 and 1965. Nixon got us out of Vietnam, opened the door to China, and initiated U.S.–Soviet détente.

Carter's recognition of China was merely an extension of Nixon's policy. Assisted by National Security Council Advisor Zbigniew Brzezinski, Carter presided over the death of détente. Brzezinski—a right-wing Republican disguised as a Democrat— revealed his true political colors in 1988 by endorsing George Bush. He cynically transformed Carter's human-rights policy into a mechanism for destabilizing U.S.–Soviet relations. In 1980, Brzezinski drove Secretary of State Cyrus Vance out of the Carter administration, took control of Carter's foreign policy, and pro- vided the intellectual basis for Reagan's "evil empire" policy.

When the Republicans aimed their big guns at Carter in 1980, he became a born-again superhawk—a scenario replicated by Walter Mondale in 1984 and Michael S. Dukakis in 1988. All the Republicans have to do is bark at a Democrat for being soft on defense and he becomes a militant cold warrior. The most disgust- ing television spot in the 1988 campaign showed Michael Dukakis riding in an army tank wearing an undersized helmet.

That George Bush was able to label Dukakis a liberal was evidence of campaign manager James Baker's cleverness. The political philosophy of Dukakis was vintage Democratic me-too- ism—not political liberalism. His warmed-over Republican de- fense policy ignored all of Soviet leader Mikhail S. Gorbachev's sweeping reforms.

Even after its humiliating defeats, the Democratic party still has no well-defined strategies for arms control, U.S.–Soviet rela- tions, or winding down the cold war. It is so starved for foreign policy ideas that the highest priority is given to bashing China, Japan, and, more recently, Iraq.

The Democratic Congress goaded Mr. Bush into invading Panama and then basked in the glory of bringing down strongman Manuel Antonio Noriega. Not unlike the communist parties in Eastern Europe, the Democratic party is incapable of reforming itself.

Democrats supported most of President Reagan's pet military projects—the Stealth bomber, the Trident II submarine, the MX missile, and Star Wars. The only serious Democratic defection was resistance to aid for the Nicaraguan contras. Democratic Senators Bill Bradley, Albert Gore, Charles S. Robb, and Sam Nunn were usually in lockstep with Reagan's defense policies.

The military-industrial complex provides the glue holding our two parties so close together. Significant military budget cuts are unlikely unless a third party emerges with enough clout to take on the Pentagon, the CIA, and the defense industry. But third-party candidates will remain an illusive dream unless we simplify our voter registration procedures and ban paid political ads.

The inside money is nudging the Democrats to the right, claiming this is the only viable strategy for recapturing the White House. But this will surely fail, because the Republicans have the political center locked up. They have staked out all of the right positions on all of the important issues to play to the center and the far right.

The Democratic party's answer to right-wing think tanks such as the Heritage Foundation is the new Progressive Policy Institute whose aim is to bring the Party back into the political mainstream.

The Party has no vision of the future. Whether the issue is defense spending, Soviet trade, drugs, homelessness, health care, or AIDS, it merely emulates the Republican party. The comatose Democratic party is effectively brain dead and should be cut free of its life-support systems.

Isn't it high time we introduced real political pluralism in the United States? If pluralism is as good as we claim it is for Eastern Europe, why not try it in the United States? Why don't we replace the defunct Democratic party with two or three more open and participatory parties that can truly represent those disenfranchised by the Republican party? Who knows? We might all benefit from the experience.

Participatory Democracy

For all too many years the ground rules for competition between and within the Democratic and Republican parties have been based on political ideology and cold war anticommunist dogmas. As the cold war subsides, those Americans who did not participate in the benefits of Ronald Reagan's capitalist blowout of the 1980s are likely to demand a bigger piece of the political and economic action in the future. These include most working-class people, African-Americans, Hispanic Americans, the poor, and environmental activists, to mention only a few. Many of these disillusioned Americans are fed up with political ideology and frankly do not give a damn about such emotional issues as abortion, flag burning, and school prayer, which are used by conservative and liberal politicians alike to jerk our apathetic electorate around. They are much more concerned about our finding some practical solutions to such problems as poverty, homelessness, inadequate child care, drug abuse, violent crime, a badly crippled education system, and environmental pollution.

People like these are committed to the premise that Americans can find practical solutions to such problems, but that the people affected most by them should participate in their solution. Solutions should be sought that benefit *all* the people of our nation and not merely feed the old, retarding mythology, which has sustained visions of the past by starving the imagination of government and people alike. Many Americans desire to see our country achieve its full potential, to replace empty political rhetoric, so long the solace of our nation, with pragmatic dialogue, and to tell both the Democratic party and the Republican party that time is running out and that if they want to survive they must replace their ideological cold war–based politics with practical, hard-nosed programs capable of yielding positive, progressive solutions to our many socioeconomic problems.

Concerned Americans of either political persuasion and every ideological bent must therefore enter the decade of the nineties by asking themselves some very tough questions.

The first question is long overdue. "Can political ideology provide answers to the really pressing problems of the 1990s?" In reality, is it not the political, economic, social, and educational *institutions* of our society that serve to interpret and direct our lives? Does not their level of performance in large measure determine the "quality of life?"

One thing seems certain. Our institutions will face new demands in the 1990s. Former Kennedy–Johnson speechwriter Richard Goodwin has warned us that

> Many of our institutions, including our political parties themselves, are led by men who developed their ideas in response to earlier demands and are therefore unable to understand or cope with a newer set of problems. . . . When institutions and leaders are faced with demands they barely understand, their reaction is often to become rigid and defensive, and even angry. . . . A people suffering from institutions that can't respond, problems that are

mutually left untouched and the myriad of uncertainties in their own private and public existence must inevitably rise in protest.

No matter what label we use—alcoholic, drug addict, child abuser, rapist, murderer, or polluter—all are responses to and symbols of the institutional crisis in our nation. Our institutions are incapable of dealing with a society plagued by problems of alienation and meaninglessness as portrayed by the story of Johnny and Sasha.

What can be done to ameliorate the problem of institutional *obsolescence* without further contributing to the problem of *ideological isolationism?* Throughout this book we have examined some of the important political, economic, and social institutions of the United States and the Soviet Union. We have discussed Gorbachev's response to the problem of institutional obsolescence in the Soviet Union. We now outline an American cold war end-game strategy based on two simple premises. First, Americans should spend more time discussing our common problems and less time arguing political ideology. Second, Americans need to learn to ask the right questions about our government and its approach to problem solving.

Specifically, in evaluating any particular government policy we should ask three basic questions. What does the policy do for people? What does it do to people? How do people participate in the implementation of the policy?

But while planners, journalists, and academic visionaries dream of what America might become, our politicians in Washington continue their harangues against government inefficiency, the Japanese, the Soviets, abortion, flag burning, and anyone who has the audacity to challenge their self-serving, undemocratic ways. As Richard Goodwin has observed, "Asking many of today's institutions to respond to new needs is a little like putting a man on a windowsill and asking him to fly. Not only was he not built for flight but if you keep insisting he's likely to turn around and punch you in the nose." Institutions should serve the people—not vice versa. It is time for problem solving to replace political ideology as the focal point of American politics.

POLITICS

In response to the dual problems of institutional rigidity and political polarization, I believe it will be necessary to establish a new political party to challenge the Democratic and Republican parties and enable us to move beyond the cold war. Of much more importance than actually winning the presidency is the new party's ability to confront the conventional wisdom of the two dominant parties. It should work to raise the level of public consciousness of the importance of the six fundamental human concerns outlined in chapter 1—good health, economic security, meaning, knowledge, freedom, and empowerment.

In addition to appealing to the politically disenfranchised, the party should target disillusioned yuppies who have become bored with a life-style based on money, power, and the accumulation of material goods. Above all the party should be nonideological and firmly grounded on the principles of pragmatism and participatory democracy. It should attempt to broaden the base of political participation in the United States by simplifying voter registration, banning political advertising, and introducing real political pluralism by making it easier to organize new national political parties—even parties which may become its future competitors.

The party must come to grips with the mounting sense of alienation and powerlessness that encompasses virtually every aspect of American life. It must be cognizant of the fact that when people have no sense of meaning in their lives and lose confidence in their ability to shape their own destiny, they become frightened by the present. Their need to protect what they have can lead to fear and insecurity about everything. Indeed, that's what the cold war was all about from both sides and why it lasted so long.

ECONOMICS

The party should be favorably disposed towards the use of markets to allocate resources but still recognize that even markets have their limits when it comes to matters related to the distribution of income and wealth, health care, housing, education, public transportation, and environmental pollution. The acid test whether the market or the government should be the option of choice for dealing with a specific economic problem should be based entirely on pragmatic considerations rather than ideological concerns. The party should support the creation of a high-level commission similar to the Japanese Ministry of International Trade and Industry (MITI) to provide guidance in transforming the American economy from a bloated, military-driven economy to a more efficient peacetime economy that will be more responsive to the needs of the American people and be able to compete more effectively in a rapidly changing global economic environment.

SOCIAL WELFARE

With an eye toward countries like Austria, Finland, and Sweden, the party should support a broader social-welfare net than is presently the case. It should take a proactive approach to such problems as unemployment, poverty, homelessness, alcoholism, drug abuse, crime, and AIDS. For example, the party should support a national health-insurance program that would require employers either to provide their employees with adequate health insurance or to pay a tax to help finance such coverage through a public fund. More attention should be devoted to the demand side of such problems as alcoholism, drug addiction, and crime. Why do people take drugs and commit violent crimes? What are the alternatives to tougher law enforcement, which does not seem to work?

The party might also consider introducing a national public-service program similar to those found in Western Europe in which every American is obliged to spend a short period of his or her life involved in public service.

CONFLICT RESOLUTION

With regard to labor–management relations, business–government relations, foreign affairs, and international trade, the party should take its cues from three of Mr. Gorbachev's strategies— tension reduction, power sharing, and global interdependence. It is important for the party to encourage more participatory labor–management relations and more cooperative business–government relations that are not necessarily tied to specific government policies.

For example, through research, education, and moral suasion, the party might provide Corporate America and the American working class with some new models of labor–management relations based more on mutual cooperation and trust rather than confrontation and deception.

The party should also encourage the pursuit of nonviolent options for dealing with conflicts involving foreign affairs, terrorism, crime, and drug abuse.

FOREIGN AFFAIRS

High priority must be given to reshaping our foreign policies and defense policies so that they reflect the changing global political order and the end of the cold war. No one has asked us to play the role of global policeman in Central America, Europe, the Middle East, or the Far East—plus we can no longer afford to do so. Our approach to foreign affairs and international trade should become more cooperative and less confrontational. Not only should we encourage our foreign trading partners to pursue free trade policies, but we should practice what we preach and back away from our knee-jerk protectionist tendencies. Finally, our country should assume more responsibility for the solution of such global problems as hunger, poverty, Third World debt, disease, environmental pollution, and drug abuse.

We Need More Public Men and Women

Cold war policies predicated on yesterday's misperceptions stand little chance of success in tomorrow's world. The changing realities in the Soviet Union, Eastern Europe, and the rest of the world demand a fresh, new, human approach to international politics.

The eloquent words of Lucius Quintus Cincinnatus Lamar, one of the South's most gifted statesmen, in 1878 may be applicable today to both the United States and the Soviet Union: "The liberty of this country and its great interests will never be secure if its public men become mere menials to do the biddings of their constituents instead of being representative in the true sense of the word, looking to the lasting prosperity and future interests of the whole country."

I believe that history will show that Mikhail Sergeyevich Gorbachev was indeed a public man. Not only is he a world-class risk taker, but he is one of the very few political leaders of this century who consistently placed the interests of his country and the rest of the world ahead of his own self-interest. Above all, he hopes to avoid replicating American mistakes in a Soviet setting.

Both the United States and the Soviet Union need more public men and women to finish the cold war end game.

Postscript

The made-for-television Persian Gulf drama precipitated by Saddam Hussein's invasion of Kuwait contained all of the elements one might expect in a Tom Clancy post–cold war spy-thriller—a demonic enemy, suspense, political intrigue, military heroics, and Middle East oil. This action-packed TV series became an instantaneous success with American viewers in need of a new demon to replace the Soviet Union. President George Bush had no difficulty convincing a receptive American TV audience that Saddam Hussein was indeed the new Adolf Hitler.

The story began unfolding in late July when Soviet military advisors in Baghdad and the CIA learned of Hussein's plans to annex Kuwait. In spite of all of the joint U.S.–Soviet hand-wringing over Hussein's brutal attack on Kuwait, neither superpower did very much to dissuade him. Upon learning that the invasion was imminent, the Soviets remained silent, and the United States sent April C. Glaspie, our ambassador to Iraq, to London the day before it actually took place—clearly signaling that neither superpower was very concerned about Kuwait's fate.

But how could this be? If Secretary of State James Baker III and Soviet Foreign Minister Eduard A. Shervardnadze had written Tom Clancy's script for Hussein, they would not have changed one word of it.

By triggering a 100 percent oil-price increase, Hussein—with the help of the U.S.-led embargo of Iraq—may have done for the Soviets what no Western country would dare do, namely, finance the bailout of their economy. Soviet leader Mikhail S. Gorbachev has repeatedly indicated that the Soviet economy needs an infusion of nearly $25 billion in hard currency before it can see the light of day. If the price of oil remains over $30 per barrel compared to the 1989 average of $18, then Gorbachev will have his much-needed external financing in less than two years. Not bad for a neophyte capitalist!

Since the 1972 OPEC oil crisis, every American president has yearned for an excuse to establish an American military presence in the Persian Gulf. But this temptation has always been tempered by the threat of possible Soviet reprisals. Saddam Hussein provided George Bush with an excuse to send over 400,000 American troops, 50 warships, and 1000 warplanes to Saudi Arabia at the "invitation" of King Fahd. When the Soviets blinked at the heavy-handed U.S. invasion of Iraq, they not only reconfirmed the end of the cold war, but the end of alleged Soviet political and military influence in the Middle East.

So long as Kuwait remained in check, then Iraq controlled 20 percent of the world's proven oil reserves—a figure which would have jumped to 45 percent if Saudi Arabia were under Hussein's influence. But it is the United States—not Iraq—that now occupies Saudi Arabia and the United Arab Emirates. Given our proven ability to intimidate Mexico, Venezuela, and our NATO allies—Canada, England, and Norway—the United States now effectively controls over 51 percent of global oil reserves. If the Soviets join forces with us, then together we control nearly 60 percent of world reserves. The Soviet Union has the largest proven oil reserves outside the Persian Gulf and 40 percent of the world's natural gas reserves.

American troops will remain in the Persian Gulf for a very long time—perhaps until Saudi Arabian oil reserves run dry. Just as the Soviet Union found it in its interest to "protect" Eastern Europe from Nazi fascism after World War II, so too has the United States seen fit to protect the Persian Gulf from Arab "fanatics." Unfortunately, many moderate Arabs find American occupation no more appealing than Soviet occupation was to Eastern Europeans.

With the U.S. Congress on vacation during August 1990 and four television networks standing ready to glamorize his every military move, President Bush had carte blanche to do whatever he pleased in the Persian Gulf. There was virtually no dissent from either side of the political aisle from Congress. In theory Operation Desert Shield and the accompanying naval blockade of Iraq were a multilateral effort. In practice, our NATO allies, Japan, and moderate Arab states provided only a modicum of economic and military support. Desert Storm was, in reality, almost entirely an American show of force.

It was not by chance that both Germany and Japan used constitutional arguments to justify only token support for U.S. intervention in the Persian Gulf. They understood very well why Pan Am and TWA flights were usually singled out by Arab terrorists as their targets during the 1980s rather than Lufthansa or Japan Air Lines. Most Arabs equate America's foreign policy in the Middle East with Israel's militantly anti-Arab policies.

Oil is by no means the only benefit that has accrued to the Bush administration as a result of Hussein's brutal attack on Kuwait. Several of Defense Secretary Dick Cheney's favorite military projects, including the Stealth bomber and Star Wars, were in serious political trouble as a result of reduced Soviet–American tensions. Hussein not only injected new life into the moribund Soviet economy, but he helped preserve our $300 billion military-defense budget. He also provided the defense industry with a new lease on life and NATO with a much-needed new enemy to replace the Soviet Union.

On the domestic scene, public attention was diverted from the President's son's highly questionable business relationship with Denver's Silverado Savings and Loan Bank. The "no new taxes" campaign pledge was soon forgotten by all. Our huge budget deficit, the savings and loan scandal, and other serious economic problems were pushed aside in the interest of national security.

Reminiscent of Reagan, Mr. Bush traded on images of "freedom and democracy" to justify sending American troops to Saudi Arabia. Few Americans know that Saudi Arabia is a feudal monarchy in which women are not even permitted to drive automobiles. Kuwait and Saudi Arabia may be among our friends — but democratic they are not. Democracy exists mostly in the breach in the Middle East. The *Boston Globe* suggested that Bush's real agenda in the Persian Gulf was to make the United States safe for gas guzzlers.

At the apex of Soviet political power, it's hard to imagine communist propaganda ever being as effective as that of the American television networks in supporting President Bush's military policies in the Persian Gulf. For weeks CNN provided its American viewers live twenty-four-hour coverage of the Middle East equivalent of "cowboys and Indians." Americans were mesmerized by the one-sided patriotic hype. During the 1980s President Ronald Reagan was often shown on TV riding his horse on his ranch in California. To add drama to the Persian Gulf saga, Bush appeared frequently on TV during his August vacation making shoot-from-the-hip attacks on Saddam Hussein from his electric golf cart and his speedboat in Kennebunkport, Maine. He also made frequent trips between Kennebunkport and Washington on his own gas guzzler—Air Force One. In the meantime, Bush's oil patch buddies were having a real Texas-style blowout—laughing all the way to the bank about their friend—Saddam Hussein.

Among the big losers in the Persian Gulf crisis are Eastern Europe, oil-poor Third World countries, and possibly the state of Israel. Inefficient Eastern European countries hooked on cheap Soviet oil must now purchase crude oil at the world market price in real money. The effects of $30 per barrel crude oil on the economies of Eastern Europe and Third World oil importers could be devastating.

Since the 1973 oil crisis, Israel has very profitably played the role of our only true friend in the Middle East—the only country in the region that could be trusted to stand up to communism. The end of the cold war and the presence of U.S. troops in Saudi Arabia have significantly reduced Israel's strategic importance to the United States. Reduced American military aid to Israel might finally bring its leaders to the bargaining table with the PLO.

Although the cold war is finally over, our need for a bigger-than-life enemy seems to never end. At least for a while, Saddam Hussein was willing to fill this void. He played his role very well. Who will be the demon in Tom Clancy's next novel? Only time will tell.

Notes

Chapter 1. The Story of Johnny and Sasha

1. This chapter is based on an article by the author entitled "Redefining Corporate Motivation, Swedish Style," *The Christian Century,* 30 May 1990, pp. 566–69.

Chapter 2. The Pot Can't Call the Kettle Black

1. Bill Keller, "News Lurks on the Crime Blotter in Moscow," *The New York Times,* 18 December 1987.
2. "The Soviet Penal System," *Soviet East European Report* 7, no. 2 (10 October 1989).
3. Lawrence Mishel and Jacqueline Simon, *The State of Working America.* Washington, D.C.: Economic Policy Institute, 1988.
4. Mishel and Simon.
5. Louis O. Kelso and Patricia Hetter Kelso, "Why Owner-Workers Are Winners," *The New York Times,* 29 January 1989.
6. Milt Freudenheim, "Debating Canadian Health Care Model," *The New York Times,* 29 June 1989.
7. Richard D. Lamm, "Saving a Few, Sacrificing Many—at Great Cost," *The New York Times,* 2 August 1989.
8. Joseph A. Califano, Jr., "Drug War: Fool's Errand No. 3," *The New York Times,* 8 December 1989.
9. Richard Halloran, "Seoul Agrees to Buy 120 U.S. Fighters," *The New York Times,* 25 October 1989.
10. Carl Sagan, "The Common Enemy," *Parade Magazine,* 7 February 1988, p. 4.

Chapter 3. The Temple of Doom

1. Ralph K. White, *Fearful Warriors*. New York: The Free Press, 1984.
2. Boris Kagarlitsky, *The Thinking Reed*. London: Verso, 1988, p. 355.
3. White, p. 123.
4. Tom Gervasi, *The Myth of Soviet Military Supremacy*. New York: Harper & Row, 1986, p. 7.
5. V. L. Allen, *The Russians Are Coming*. Shipley, England: Moor Press, 1987, p. 79.
6. V. L. Allen, p. 77.
7. V. L. Allen, p. 85.
8. Christopher Simpson, *Blowback*. New York: Weidenfeld & Nicolson, 1988.
9. Zbigniew Brzezinski, *Game Plan*. New York: Atlantic Monthly Press, 1986, pp. 14–15.
10. Brzezinski, *Game Plan*, p. 19.
11. Brzezinski, *Game Plan*, p. 260.
12. Zbigniew Brzezinski, *The Grand Failure*. New York: Charles Scribner's Sons, 1989, p. 8.
13. Richard A. Stubbing, *The Defense Game*. New York: Harper & Row, 1986, pp. 12–13.
14. Richard Pipes, *Survival Is Not Enough*. New York: Simon and Schuster, 1984.
15. Daniel Chirot (editor), *The Origins of Backwardness in Eastern Europe*. Berkeley: University of California Press, 1989.
16. Jay Berman, "Time to Stop Treating Cuba Like an Untouchable," *The Christian Science Monitor*, 7 September 1988, p. 11.
17. Wayne S. Smith, *The Closest of Enemies*. New York: W. W. Norton, 1987.
18. John Spicer Nichols, "The Power of the Anti-Fidel Lobby," *The Nation*, 24 October 1989, pp. 389-92.
19. Tom Gervasi, *The Myth of Soviet Military Supremacy*. New York: Harper & Row, 1986, p. 24.
20. Gervasi, pp. 63–64.
21. Dwight D. Eisenhower, *Farewell Radio and Television Address to the American People*, 17 January 1981.
22. Gervasi, p. 38.
23. Karen Rothmeyer, "Scaife's Seed Money Helps New Right Blossom," *Common Cause* magazine, August 1981, p. 15.
24. Philip M. Boffey, et al., *Claiming the Heavens*. New York: Times Books, pp. 27–37.
25. Philip M. Boffey, pp. 28–29.
26. Christopher Simpson, *Blowback*. New York: Weidenfeld & Nicolson, 1988, pp. 99–101.
27. Fred Hiatt, "Perle's Distrust Shapes U.S. Policy," *Washington Post*, 2 January 1985.
28. Eric Alterman, "Wrong on the Wall, and Most Else," *The New York Times*, 12 November 1989.
29. Eric Alterman.

30. Eric Pace, "As U.S. Assesses East-Bloc Policy, Experts Differ on How Bold It Should Be," *The New York Times*, 19 November 1989.
31. Franklyn D. Holzman, "Politics and Guesswork," *International Security* (Fall 1989), pp. 101–31.
32. Lawrence J. Goodrich, "Peace Dividend Unlikely in U.S. Intelligence," *The Christian Science Monitor*, 11 December 1989.

Chapter 4. Military Overkill

1. "The U.S. Military After the Cold War," *The Defense Monitor* (Center for Defense Information) 18, no. 8, p. 4.
2. Paul Kennedy, *The Rise and Fall of the Great Powers*. New York: Random House, 1987.
3. Andrew Rosenthal, "Air Force Grounds B-1's After a Wing Punctures a Tank," *The New York Times*, 29 March 1989, p. 1.
4. John R. Kasich, "$600 Million per Stealth Bomber," *The New York Times*, 18 July 1989.
5. Richard W. Stevenson, "Northrop's 'Awesome' B-2 Gamble," *The New York Times*, 20 August 1989.
6. Philip M. Boffey, *et al.*, *Claiming the Heavens*. New York: Times Books, 1988, pp. 5–6.
7. Peter Dworkin, "Long Knives in the Laboratory," *U.S. News*, 29 February 1988, pp. 16–17.
8. Philip M. Boffey, pp. 12–22.
9. Zbigniew Brzezinski, *Game Plan*. New York: Atlantic Monthly Press, 1986, p. 262.
10. Warren E. Leary, "Report Depicts 'Star Wars' As an Unworkable System," *The New York Times*, 25 April 1988.
11. Tom Wicker, "Star Wars in Decline," *The New York Times*, 14 June 1988.
12. David E. Sanger, "Martin Marietta Selected for U.S. for Tests Simulating 'Star Wars,' " *The New York Times*, 23 January 1988.
13. John H. Cushman, Jr., "G.E. Wins 'Star Wars' Contract, *The New York Times*, 13 May 1988.
14. Andrew Rosenthal, "Tower Declares 'Star Wars' Shield Can't Be Complete," *The New York Times*, 27 January 1989.
15. Fran von Hippel and Thomas B. Cochran, "The Myth of the Soviet 'Killer' Laser," *The New York Times*, 19 August 1989.
16. "Nuclear Bomb Factories," *The Defense Monitor* (Center for Defense Information) 18, no. 4 (1989), p. 1.
17. "U.S.-Soviet Military Facts," *The Defense Monitor* (Center for Defense Information) 18, no. 5 (1988), p. 5.
18. "Nuclear Bomb Factories," p. 1.
19. Matthew L. Wald, "Retribution Seen in Atom Industry," *The New York Times*, 6 August 1989.
20. Gar Alperovitz, "Did We Have to Drop the Bomb?" *The New York Times*, 3 August 1989.

21. "Energy Projects that Failed," *The New York Times*, 12 December 1988.
22. "A Train of Disasters for Nuclear Power," *The New York Times*, 24 January 1984.
23. Michael Ross, "Trident II Doesn't Fly," *The New York Times*, 25 August 1989.
24. Daniel S. Greenberg, "High-Tech Extravaganza Dying," *Journal of Commerce*, 10 August 1989.
25. Thomas H. Naylor, "Is Finlandization the Answer?" *Chicago Tribune*, 5 October 1989.
26. "Soviet Compliance with Arms Agreements," *The Defense Monitor* (Center for Defense Information) 16, no. 2 (1987), p. 8.
27. Thomas H. Naylor, "How George Schultz Took Charge," *The Journal of Commerce*, 27 July 1988.

Chapter 5. Economic Uncertainty.

1. Thomas H. Naylor, "The Impact of Simulation on Soviet Economic Reforms," *Simulation*, August 1988, pp. 46–51.
2. Thomas H. Naylor, "A Menu of Options by Soviet Economists," *The New York Times*, 16 October 1982.
3. Robert G. Kaiser, Russia: *The People and the Power*. New York: Washington Square Press, 1984.
4. Ed A. Hewett, *Reforming the Soviet Economy*. Washington, D.C.: Brookings Institution, 1988.
5. Boris Kagarlitsky, *The Thinking Reed*. London: Verso, 1988.
6. Paul Lewis, "Military Spending Questioned," *The New York Times*, 11 November 1986, p. Y25.
7. Joshua S. Goldstein, "How Military Might Robs the Economy," *The New York Times*, 16 October 1988.
8. Michael R. Gordon, "U.S. Offers Moscow a Few Ideas on How to Improve Its Economy," *The New York Times*, 7 December 1989.
9. Thomas H. Naylor, *The Corporate Strategy Matrix*. New York: Basic Books, 1986.

Chapter 6. Lack of Competitiveness

1. Thomas H. Naylor, "The Ban that Boomeranged," *The Nation*, 19 December 1987, pp. 755–56.
2. Melvin I. Urofsky, *We Are One!: American Jewry and Israel*. New York: Anchor Press, 1978, pp. 265–66.
3. V. L. Allen, *The Russians Are Coming*. Shipley, England: Moor Press, 1987, p. 150.
4. David T. Mizrahi, "Cost of Conflict Soars from Billions to Trillions," *World Paper/Journal of Commerce*, April 1988, p. 5.

5. Mohamed Rabie, "U.S. Aid to Israel," *The Link*, May–June 1989, p. 12.
6. David T. Mizrahi.
7. Richard H. Curtis, "Choices Americans Don't Make for Themselves," *Washington Report on Middle East Affairs*, September 1989, p. 45.
8. Mohamed Rabie, pp. 13–14.

Chapter 7. Declining International Influence

1. Philip Brenner, "Cuba Is the Soviet Union's Israel," *The Christian Science Monitor*, 10 April 1989, p. 19.
2. Norman Podhoretz, *The Present Danger*. New York: Touchstone, 1989, p. 12.
3. Thomas H. Naylor, *"Is Finlandization the Answer?" Chicago Tribune*, 5 October 1989.
4. Mikhail S. Gorbachev, speech in Kiev on 23 February 1989.
5. Mikhail S. Gorbachev, speech to the East German Socialist Unity Party Congress in Berlin, 18 April 1988.

Chapter 8. Global Development

1. Ruth Leger Sivard, *World Military and Social Expenditures—1987–1988*. Washington, D.C.: World Priorities, 1987, pp. 29–31.
2. *Ibid.*
3. Robert Pear, "Prospect of Arms Pacts Spurring Weapons Sales," *The New York Times*, 25 March 1990, p. 12.
4. Paul Lewis, "U.S. Cuts Funds to U.N. Food Agency over PLO." *The New York Times*, 10 January 1990.
5. Ruth Leger Sivard, p. 25.
6. Dwayne Andreas, "Here's a Way to Outwit Hunger," *World Paper*, May 1987.
7. David R. Francis, "World's Children Need Peace Dividend," *The Christian Science Monitor*, 18 May 1990, p. 7.
8. Robert C. Cowen, "More of Us, More Problems," *The Christian Science*, 17 April 1990, p. 9.
9. "Stalin's Legacy of Filth," *The New York Times*, 7 February 1990, p. A24.
10. Steven R. Weisman, "Japan to Propose a Package of Aid Worth $43 Billion," *The New York Times*, 12 July 1989, p. 1.
11. "The New York Times/CBS News Poll," *The New York Times*, 27 May 1990, p. 24.
12. Jane Perlez, "U.S. Forgives Loans to African Countries," *The New York Times*, 10 January 1990.
13. Jack N. Behrman, *The Rise of The Phoenix*. Boulder, Colorado: Westview Press, p. xi.

14. Edward Giradet, "New Wave of Strategists Work to Develop Africa 'from the Bottom up,' " *The Christian Science Monitor,* 27 December 1988.
15. "The Cause of Children," *The Christian Science Monitor,* 18 December 1989.

Chapter 9. The Leadership Challenge

1. Jerry F. Hough, "Gorbachev's Politics," *Foreign Affairs* (Winter 1989), p. 2.
2. Gar Alperovitz, *Atomic Diplomacy.* New York: Penguin Books, 1985.
3. Christopher Simpson, *Blowback.* New York: Weidenfeld & Nicolson, 1988.
4. Editorial, "Take Me to Your Leader," *The New York Times,* 21 May 1989.

Index

Abalkin, Leonid, 71, 105
Abbot Laboratories, 130
Abrams, Elliot, 66, 67
Abuses: crime, 20–22; economic inequality, 22–26; education problems, 32–34; human rights, 13–15; inadequate health care, 26–30; lack of national public service, 34–36; political, 15–20; social ills, 30–32
Adelman, Kenneth L., 148
Advertising, power of, 17
Afghanistan, x, 18, 42, 45, 48, 92, 140, 187; Brzezinski on, 49; casualties in, 172; illegality of invasion, 196; and Salt II, 57; as Soviet ally, 151, 164–165; withdrawal from, 94, 171
African Americans, poverty among, 23
Aga Khan Network, 184
Aganbegyan, Abel G., 105, 110
Agency for international Development, 186
Agriculture: Gorbachev's goals in, 188; problems in, 115
AIDS cases, worldwide, 176
Akhromeyev, Sergei, 97
Alcoholism, 2, 3; in Soviet Union, 31
Algeria, 152
Alienation: of Johnny and Sasha, 3; problem for communism and capitalism, ix-x, 1–11; and the search for meaning, 6; and stress, 3
Allen, Richard V., 61
Allen, V. L., 43–44
Allende, Salvador, 17, 94, 197

Alperovitz, Gar, 89, 196–197
Alterman, Eric, 68
American Enterprise Institute, 59, 62
Andreas, Dwayne, 175
Andropov, Yuri V., 109–110
Angola, x, 53, 92, 125; deaths in, 172; end of war in, 171; Soviet aid to, 151, 152–153, 164–165
Anti-Ballistic Missile Treaty, 95
Anti-communism, 39–42, 193; costs of, ix; and détente, 45; failure of, 198; of technocrats, 77–78; at universities, 72
Anti-Semitism, in Soviet Union, 140–141, 173–174
Aquino, Corazon, 201
Arab–Israeli War, 144–148, 174
Arefieva, Elena, 183
Argentina, 101
Armco, Inc., 134
Armenia, 30, 166, 167
Arms: Gorbachev on reduction of, 188; sales of, 172
Atomic power, 116
AT & T, 206
Austria, 4, 45, 123, 206, 213
Azerbaijan, 30, 121, 166, 167

B-1 bomber, 74, 81, 117
B-2 Stealth bomber. See Stealth bomber
Bahrain, 164
Baker, James III, 97, 119, 174, 190; on Kuwait, 217; and Shevardnadze, 204
Baltic republics, 166–167

Bangladesh, 18
Barbie, Klaus, 47
Barnett, Frank R., 59
Bay of Pigs, 46, 53, 165, 197
Beirut, 42, 156
Ben-Gurion, David, 141
Berlin Wall, 160, 187, 190
Berman, Jay, 53
Blowback (Simpson), 46, 197
Blue-collar workers, treatment of, 3, 4, 5
Boeing, 86
Boesky, Ivan, 22
Boffey, Philip M., 60, 83
Bolivia, 94, 175, 178
Bolschwing, Otto von, 47
Bork, Robert, 96, 98
Bowles, W. Donald, 183
Bradley, Bill, 208
Braun, Wernher von, 47
Brazil, 101, 165; arms sales of, 172; debt of, 181; and rain forest, 179
Brenner, Philip, 153
Bretton Woods agreement, 181–182
Brezhnev, Leonid I., 14, 22, 41, 44, 48, 106; on detente, 45, 187; on emigration of Jews, 139; on foreign policy, 151, 152, 153; Russian aggression under, 92
Brezhnev Doctrine, 156; denounced, 196
Brokaw, Tom, 141
Brown, Harold, 82
Brzezinski, Zbigniew, 46, 49–50, 66, 72, 98; and Carter, 208; and CSIS, 62; on Eastern Europe, 192; on Gorbachev, 68; on Star Wars, 84
Buchanan, Patrick, 63
Buckley, William F., 63
Budapest, 92
Bukharin, Nikolai, 70
Bulgaria, 51, 101, 123; and Israel, 143
Burkina Faso, 176
Burroughs Wellcome, 28, 120
Bush, George, 37; attitude toward Soviet, 187, 190, 199–200; and the CIA, 50; on defense spending, 74; on education, 33; foreign policy opportunities of, 198–205; lack of vision, 205–207; and Latin America, 93; macho diplomacy of, 201; and Malta summit, 97; on

MFN status for Soviet, 148–149, 200; and Middle East, 164, 174; and Panama, 155, 197; problems of, 205; response to invasion of Kuwait, ix, 217, 218; state of union address, 203; on troop reduction, 77; on U.S.-Soviet trade, 138, 195
Bush, Neil, 22, 219
Business schools: goals of students in, 4–5; helpful to Soviets, 132
Byron plant, 90

Califano, Joseph A., Jr., 31
California, University of, 71
Cambodia, x, 165, 171, 172
Canada, 45, 123; health care in, 27, 29
Cancer Ward (Solzhenitsyn), 52
Canosa, Jorge Mas, 54
Capitalism, American, shared problems with communism, ix-xii
Cardinal of the Kremlin, The (Clancy), 86
Carlucci, Frank C., 85, 97
Carnegie-Mellon University, 86
Carter, Hodding III, 33
Carter, Jimmy, 17–18, 45, 49, 205, 207, 208; and the B-1 bomber, 81; on Jewish emigration, 140; and Stealth bomber, 82; on U.S.-Soviet trade, 134, 135, 139
Carthage Foundation, 59
Casey, James E., 11
Casey, William J., 65
Castro, Fidel, 53, 153, 165
Ceausescu, Nicolae, 19, 160
Caterpillar, 134
Center for Security Policy (CSP), 62
Center for Strategic International Studies, 59, 61
Central Committee, Communist Party, 119–120
Central Intelligence Agency (CIA), 17; and military build-up, 68–69; and Nazi war criminals, 46–48, 197; and radio propaganda, 65; on Soviet economics, 108, 111
Chazov, Yevgeny, 26
Cheney, Dick, 76, 77, 200, 219
Chernenko, Konstantin V., xii, 110
Chernobyl, 15, 116, 196
Chile, 94, 101, 197

China, 64, 165; arms sales by, 172; economic reforms, 112, 114, 119; foreign trade of, 129, 130; MFN status, 149; Soviet relations with, 152, 153–154, 163
Chirot, Daniel, 50
Chrysler, 10, 166
Churbanov, Yuri M., 22
Churchill, Winston, xi, 187
Civil War, American, 192–193
Claiming the Heavens (Boffey et al.), 60, 83
Clancy, Tom, 17, 63, 86, 97, 217
Clark, William P., 109
Clemson University, 132
Closest of Enemies, The (Smith), 53
Cochran, Thomas B., 88
Cold War: goals necessary to end, xii–xiii; pundits of, 63
Cold War paranoia: anti-communism in U.S. 39–40; shared problem of communism and capitalism, x, 39–72; Soviet fear of U.S., 40–41
Colombia, 94, 101, 175, 178
Columbia University, 71
Commerce Department, U.S., on technology transfer, 135
Committee on the Present Danger (CPD), 50, 56–58, 67, 126; and Israel, 148; and Solzhenitsyn, 52–53
Communism, Soviet, shared problems with capitalism, ix–xii
Communist Party: Central Committee, 119–120, 121; and the Politburo, 122
Competitiveness: anti-Semitism, 140–141; Arab-Israeli War, 144–148; brain drain, 141–142; double standard, 148-149; high-tech paranoia, 135–138; Jackson–Vanik amendment, 138–139; Jewish emigration issue, 139–140; lack of as common problem, xi, 129–149, 142–144; U.S.-Soviet trade, 129–133; unreliable trading partners, 133–135
Computer-simulation models: in Soviet economics, 106–107, 111
Computers, 5
Congress, U.S.: corruption in, 22; and high-tech military zealots, 92; on invasion of Kuwait, 218; on military programs, 190
Congressional Budget Office, 206
Consultative Coordinating Committee (COCOM), 133, 136, 138, 154; and Japan, 163
Continental Airlines, 25
Cooperatives, Soviet, 124
Corporate executives: ethics of, 5; salaries of, 5
Council for Mutual Economic Assistance (CMEA), 161
Council of Economic Advisers, 206
Crime, 20–22
Crowe, William J., 43, 97
Cuba, 18, 92, 94, 187; and Radio Marti, 64; Soviet aid to, 151, 164–165; troops in South Africa, 153
Cuban American National Foundation (CANF), 54
Cuban Americans, 53–54
Czechoslovakia, 51, 64, 77, 101, 123, 151, 158; invasion condemned, 196; and Israel, 143; pollution in, 179

Daniloff, Nicholas, 142
de Klerk, F. W., 101
Decter, Midge, 148
Defense Intelligence Agency (DIA), 68
Defense Science Board (DSB), 85
Delta Catfish, 131
Democracy, participatory, 209–211
Democratic Party, 207–209
Democratic socialism, 122–125, 189
Democratization, Gorbachev on, 188
Deng Xiaoping, 114, 129; on Soviet relations, 153–154
Denmark, 155
Détente: death of, 208; earlier porribility of, 45; and Jackson–Vanik amendment, 147; trade during, 134, 138
Disease: in Eastern Europe, 179; worldwide, 176
Dornberger, Walter, 47
Dow Chemical, 120, 130
Drexel Burnham Lambert, 22, 25
Drug abuse, 2; in U.S., 31, 101; worldwide, 177–178

Dukakis, Michael S., 208
Dulles, Allen, 47
Dulles, John Foster, 47

Eagleberger, Lawrence, 200
East Germany (German Democratic
   Republic), 75, 101, 122, 151, 158;
   changes in, 160; pollution in, 178–179
"East-West Trade and Joint
   Ventures," conference, 110
Eastern Air Lines, 25
Eastern Europe: aid to, 186;
   ecological disaster, 178–179;
   foreign trade with, 130; and
   Gorbachev, 192; high-tech
   equipment in, 137; Russia in,
   92–93; social democracy in, 123;
   Soviet allies in, 151
Eastern Europeans: and cold war
   paranoia, 48–51; Soviet relations
   in, 158–161
conomic reform, Soviet, 112–114
Economic uncertainty: common
   problems of, 114–119; democratic
   socialism, 122–125; economic conversion, 125–127; power sharing,
   119–122; preview of *perestroika*,
   105–112; shared problem of
   capitalism and communism, xi,
   105–127, 212; Soviet economic
   reform, 112–114
Economists: as critics of *perestroika*,
   69–72; Soviet, 105
Economy, Gorbachev on, 188
Egypt, 139, 144, 152
Eichmann, Adolf, 47
Eisenhower, Dwight D., 55, 83
Ekman, Bo, 8–9
El Salvador, x, 94, 153, 155, 201
Emigration, and Jackson–Vanik
   amendment, 138–139
Emigrés from Soviet, 45–46; from
   Eastern Europe, 48–49; in Radio
   USA, 65
Employee-ownership, 10–11
Empowerment, 212; and *perestroika*, 7
Environmental polution, 178–180
Estonia, 121, 167, 192
Ethiopia, x, 18, 92; and Soviets, 151,
   152, 164
European Community (EC), trade of,
   133

Evans, Rowland, 63
Evil empire, 42–43, 49, 208
Export-Import Bank, on U.S.-Soviet
   trade, 134

Fannie and John Hertz Foundation,
   59
Far East, Gorbachev on, 163
Federal Express, 120
Federal Reserve Board, 206
Fedorenko, Nikolav, 107, 110
Finland, 45, 112, 123, 206, 213; and
   Soviets, 158–159, 167
Finlandization, 158
First Circle, The (Solzhenitsyn), 52
Fitzwater, Marlin, 200
Florida Steel, 10
Ford, Gerald, 21, 205
France, 155
Frankl, Viktor E., on meaning, 6
Friedman, Milton, 5
Freudenheim, Milt, 27

Gaffney, Frank J., 62–63, 66, 97
Game Plan (Brzezinski), 49
Gates, Robert M., 200
Gaza Strip, 144
General Agreement on Tariffs and
   Trade, 181–182
General Electric Co.; on defense, 17;
   and SDI, 86
General Motors, 166, 206
Gervasi, Tom, 55
Gerasimov, General I., 97
Germany, on Persian Gulf, 219. *See
   also* East Germany; West Germany
Ghana, 181
Glasnost, 192; and empowerment, 121;
   and tension reduction, 98–99
Glaspie, April C., 217
Glass Menagerie, The, 11
Global development, 189; as common
   problem, xi, 171–186; development
   strategies, 180–181; drug abuse,
   177–178; environmental polution,
   178–180; host country participation, 183–185; multilateral
   cooperation, 181–183; poverty,
   hunger, and disease, 175–177;
   reduced military aid, 185–186;
   war and terrorism, 171–175
Global warming, 178

Golan Heights, 144
Goldfarb, David, 142
Goldman, Marshall I., 70, 108, 191
Goldstein, Joshua S., 119
Goodwin, Richard, 210
Gorbachev, Mikhail S., 43; on alcoholism, 31; cold war pundits on, 63; on Cuba, 54, 165; and democratic socialism, 122–125; downsizing by, 165–169; in Eastern Europe, 158–161; economic reforms of, 70–71, 109, 112–114, 194–195; on foreign affairs, 151–154; on foreign trade, 129; on global interdependence, 157–169, 213; and goals of *perestroika*, 7; on invasion of Kuwait, ix; on Jewish emigration, 141–144; management policy of, 188–190; on Marxismfigd Leninism, 44; meeting with Schultz, 95–97; on military spending, 75–76; New Year's speech by, xii, 201–202; power- sharing by, 119–122, 193, 213; a public man, 214–215; and Reagan, 98; and SDI, 86–87; Sovietologists on, 68, 191–193; and U.S., 162; in Western Europe, 161–162
Gorbachev, Raisa, 112
Gore, Albert, 208
Gosbank, 117
Gosplan, 107, 108, 136
Grand Failure, The (Brzezinski), 50
Great Britain, 118
Greece, 155
Grenada, x, 42, 94, 155, 156, 197, 201
Grossman, Gregory, 52
Gruson, Sydney, 108
Guatemala, 153
Gulag Archipelago, The (Solzhenitsyn), 43, 52

Hagelstein, Peter, 60
Haig, Alexander, 108
Hammer, Armand, 51, 142
Handguns, 21
Harvard University, 71
Health: as goal to replace Cold War, xiii, 212; inadequate care, 26–30
Health care, 26–30; costs of, 27–28; for the elderly, 28; insurance for,

29; in Soviet Union, 26–27; in U.S., 27
Helms, Jesse, 40, 51, 133, 193
Helsinki, meeting of Bush and Gorbachev at, ix
Helsinki School of Economics, 132
Heritage Foundation, 59, 62, 67, 209; and SDI, 84
Hersh, Seymour, 42
Hertz, John D., 59
Hewett, Ed A,, 70, 111
Hippel, Frank von, 88
Hiroshima, 196
Hispanic Americans, poverty among, 23
Hitler, Adolph, 41, 48, 196
Holtzman, Franklyn D., 69
Homeless, in U.S., 24
Honduras, 94, 153, 155
Honecker, Erich, 123, 160
Hoover, Herbert, 61
Hoover Institution, 59, 61
Hough, Jerry F., 192
Human concerns, fundamental to end of Cold War, xiii
Human-rights abuses, 13–15
Hungary, 51, 64, 75, 77, 101; aid to, 186; changes in, 160; economic reforms of, 110, 112, 123, 151; and Israel, 143; revolution in, 187
Hussein, Saddam, x, 217–220

Inklé, Fred C., 97
India, 152, 165
Indiana University, 71
Indonesia, 152
Infant mortality: in Boston, 28; in Soviet, 26; in U.S., 23
Influence, international: decline a common problem, xi, 151–169; downsizing, 165–169; Eastern Europe, 158–161; Far East, 163; global interdependence, 151–157; international organizations, 157–158; Middle East, 163–164; shattered illusions, 151–157; Third World, 164–165; United States, 162; Western Europe, 161–162
Injustice, shared problem of communism and capitalism, x, 13–37. *See also* Abuses

INSEAD, 132
Institutional obsolescence, 211
Intel, 184
International Business Machines
    (IBM), 10, 86, 120, 166, 184, 206
International Executive Service
    Corps, 184
International Management Center,
    Budapest, 51
International Management Corps
    (IMC), 184–185
International Monetary Fund, 181,
    182
International trade, Soviet, 113
Iran, 95, 140, 152, 205
Iran Air, 43, 198
Iran-Contra affair, 96, 98, 205
Iran–Iraq War, 152, 164, 171–172
Iraq, 143, 152, 174; invasion of
    Kuwait, 217–220; response to
    invasion by, ix
Ishihara, Shintero, 156–157
Israel, 65; and the Arabs, 102, 219;
    and détente, 45; emigration of
    Soviet Jews to, 141–142, 142–144;
    and Gulf crisis, 219, 220; human
    rights in, 18–19; and Jackson–
    Vanik amendment, 138–139,
    147–148; lobby for, 66–67; and the
    PLO, 125; and Soviets, 152, 164;
    support for in U.S., 144, 147; and
    terrorism, 173–174; treatment of
    Palestinians, 149; U.S. relations
    with, 155, 174
Italy, 40
Ivan the Terrible, 13, 14

Jackson, Andrew, 16
Jackson, Henry M., 65, 146–147
Jackson–Vanik amendment, 46, 132,
    134, 138–139, 145, 187; possible
    repeal of, 173
Japan, 40; economic successes of, xi,
    112, 119; foreign aid of, 180, 182;
    foreign trade of, 129; function of
    MITI in, 206; and Persian Gulf,
    219; research in, 117; savings in,
    118; Soviet relations with, 154,
    163; trade deficits with, 76; and
    World War II, 89
Japan That Can Say "No," The (Marita
    and Ishihara), 157, 163

Jefferson, Thomas, 16, 36
Jewish emigration issue, 139–140,
    164
Johnson, Lyndon B., 75, 205
John M. Olin Foundation, 59
Jordan, 144
Journalists, and cold war, 63

Kagarlitsky, Boris, 41, 111
Kaiser Aluminum, 10
Kampelman, Max M., 59, 66, 148
Kantorovich, L. V., 110
Katyn Forest Massacre, 196
Kay, Alan F., 136
Kelso, Louis and Patricia, 26
Kennan, George F., 47, 187
Kennedy, Edward, 27
Kennedy, John F., 21, 86–87
Kennedy, Paul, 74
Kennedy, Robert F., 21
Keyworth, George A. II, 84
Khrushchev, Nikita, 44, 92, 153; and
    Finland, 159
King, Martin Luther, Jr., 21
Kirkland, Lane, 65
Kirkpatrick, Jeane J., 61, 62, 63
Kissinger, Henry, 68
Kohl, Helmut, 99
Korean Air Lines, 42–43, 152, 196
Korean War, 46
Kosygin, Alexei, 70
Krasnoyarsk radar station, 95, 196
Kristol, Irving, 63
Kuril Islands, 154, 163
Kuwait, invasion of, ix, 103, 149,
    217–220

Lafitte's Landing Louisiana Cajun
    Restaurant, 131
Lamar, Lucius Quintus Cincinnatus,
    214
Latin America, 93; and Cuban-
    American lobby, 54; debts of, 181;
    and drug problem, 177–178; U.S.
    relations with, 155, 175. *See also*
    individual countries by name
Latvia, 192
Leadership challenge: common
    problem of communism and
    capitalism, xi, 187–215; Gor-
    bachev's management philosophy,
    188–196; leadership gap in U.S.,

187–188; a kinder America, 198–205; need for public men and women, 214–215; participatory democracy, 209–211; politics, 211–214; real political pluralism, 207–209; U.E. need of *glasnost*, 196–198; vision of the future, 205–207

Lebanon, x, 19, 152, 155–156

Lenin, Vladimir I., 44, 48, 70, 92–93; Soviet criticism of, 196

Lerner, Aleksandr, 142

Libya, x, 42, 143, 152, 155, 156; bombing of, 197, 201

Ligachev, Yegor K., 194

Lipset, Seymour, 61

Lithuania, 99, 149, 166, 192, 203

London Business School, 132

Lorenzo, Frank, 24–25

Macho pride, and cold war paranoia, 41

Malta summit, 68, 97

Management: goals of, 11; Gorbachev's philosophy of, 188–190; inexperience of Soviets, 131; and International Management Corps, 184–185; lack of Soviet training in, 118, 124; training for, 132

Managua, 197

Mandela, Nelson R., 101, 198

Mao Zedong, 44, 92, 153

Marble Hill nuclear plant, 90

Mark, Hans, 78

Marti, José, 64

Martin-Marietta, 86

Marx, Karl, 48

Marxism-Leninism, 44–45; moves away from, 122

McDonald's, 184

McFarlane, Robert, 62

McGovern, George, 197

McNamara, Robert S., 78, 79–80

Meaning, search for, 6, 212

Meese, Edwin, 61

Mercer Meidinger, 2

Mexico, 181 Middle East: Soviet relations with, 163–164; and terrorism, 173. *See also* individual countries by name

Midgetman mobile missile system, 74

Militarization, excessive: and economic performance, 119; reduced military aid, 185–186, 190; shared problem of communism and capitalism, x–xi, 73–103; Soviet threat, 92; and the technocrats, 77–92

Milken, Michael R., 25

Ministry of International Trade and Industry (MIT), Japan, 206, 212

"Misery index," in Sweden, 8

Mitterand, François, 161

Moldavia, 166

Mondale, Walter, 208

Monroe, James, 16

Morita, Akio, 156–157

Morocco, x

Moslems, in Soviet Union, 30

Most Favored Nation (MFN) status: for China, 149; for Soviets, 148, 149

Mozambique, 18, 92, 151, 152; and Soviets, 164

Mozowiecki, Tadevz, 159

Murder in the Air (film), 83

Mussolini, Benito, 48

MX missile, 74, 83

Myth of Soviet Military Supremacy, The (Gervasi), 55

Nagasaki, 196

Namibia, 153, 172

National Academy of Sciences, 135, 137

National Endowment for Democracy, 59

National Public Service Corps (NPSC), 35

National Rifle Association, 21

Native Americans, 16–17; violations of treaties with, 95

Naylor, Thomas: at conference (1985), 110–111; and Russian economists, 106; visit to Russia (1982), 107–109; at White Sands, 78–80

Nazi war criminals, 46–48, 197

Nazis, 144

Nemchinov, V. S., 110

New York Air, 25

Nicaragua, x, 18, 37, 42, 46, 92, 93; Abrams on, 67; casualties in, 172;

Nicaragua *(continued)*
  ending of war in, 171; mining of
  harbors in, 95; Soviet aid to, 151,
  153, 164–165; U.S. relations with,
  155
Nicholas I, 13
Nichols, John Spicer, 54
Nike-X project, 78–81
Nitze, Paul H., 57
Nixon, Richard M., 45, 68, 87, 187,
  205, 207–208; and Ismael, 146; on
  U.S./Soviet trade, 134
Noriega, Manuel Antonio, x, 93, 95,
  155, 197–198, 200, 201, 205
North Atlantic Treaty Organization
  (NATO) 93; future of, 77; military
  supremacy of, 55; summit in
  London, 204; on technology trans-
  fer, 136; and a unified Germany,
  161; U.S. expenditures for, 76
North Carolina, University of, 32–33
North Korea, 92, 164–165
North Star Consortium, 134
North Vietnam, 92, 164
Northrop Corporation, 82–83
Norway, 155
Novak, Michael, 65
Novak, Robert, 63
Nuclear energy, 88–90, 116; projects
  for, 89
Nuclear weapons, 172
Nucor, 10
Nudel, Ida, 142
Nunn, Sam, 208

Occidental Petroleum, 130
Office of Management and Budget,
  206
Office of Technology Assessment
  (OTA), on Star Wars, 85
Oil, increased price of, 217
Oil Producing Economic Community
  (OPEC), 123, 205
Oklahoma City University, 132
*Origins of Backwardness in Eastern
  Europe* (ed. Chirot), 50–51
Orlov, Yuri F., 142
Ortega, Daniel, 101, 200, 205

Pace, Eric, 68
Pacific Basin, Soviet influence in, 163
Packard, David, 61, 81

Palestine Liberation Organization
  (PLO), 143, 149, 152; Israeli
  pressure against, 173
Palestinians, 18–19; in occupied
  territories, 149
Palmer, Mark, 108
Pan Am, 10; flight 103, 102, 173–174
Panama, x, 37, 93, 95, 175; invasion
  of, 155, 197, 201
Participatory management: in Soviet,
  9; in Sweden, 8; in U.S., 10
Peace, as goal, xiii
Peace Corps, 184, 186
Pentagon, 68; on aid to Israel, 147;
  fraud at, 75; on international
  trade, 132; on SDI, 85; on
  technology transfer, 135
Pepsico, 130
Perestroika: and alienation, 7–8;
  foundation of, 111; and lack of
  management training, 131–132;
  and power sharing, 119, 121, 189;
  preview of, 105–112; Sovietolo-
  gists on, 68; U.S. denial of, 190–196
Perle, Richard, 17, 62, 63; on defense,
  81; on Gorbachev, 68; and
  Jackson–Vanik amendment,
  146–147, 148; present role of,
  66–67; on technology transfer, 135
Persian Gulf, 42, 95, 98
Persian Gulf crisis, 143, 217–220
Peru, 94, 101, 175, 178
Peter the Great, 13, 14
Pew Charitable Trusts, 59
Philippines, 76, 155, 201
Pipes, Richard, 46, 49, 50–51, 66, 72;
  on Eastern Europe, 192; on Jewish
  emigration, 148
Podhoretz, Norman, 63, 148
Pluralism, political, 207–209
Poland, 45, 51, 64, 75, 77, 101; brain
  drain in, 141; economic changes
  in, 192; emigres from, 49; and
  Israel, 143; martial law in, 152;
  new government in, 159–160;
  pollution in, 179; socialism in, 123
Politburo, reorganization of, 122
Political injustice, 15–20
Political parties: new, 211–212; old,
  207–209
Population growth, 175–176
Porter, Michael, 138

Poverty: in the U.S., 23; in the world, 175

Prague, 92, 187

Present Danger, The (Podhoretz), 158

Presnyakov, Vassily, 106–107

Press, American, 17; Soviet, 17

Progressive Policy Institute, 209

Public Opinion, 66

Qatar, 164

Quayle, Dan, 193, 200

Rabie, Mohammed, 147

Radio Free Europe, 47, 49, 52, 64, 193, 197

Radio Liberty, 47, 49, 52, 64, 193, 197

Radio Marti, 64

Radio USA, 64–65

Rand Corporation, 59, 61

Raritan River, 10

Ratliffe, Charles E. Jr., 182

Reagan, Ronald, xii, 21, 23, 37, 61, 144; anticommunism of, 39, 40, 41, 152, 187; and Bush, 199; and CPD, 58; on drug problem, 177; on the evil empire, 42–43, 49, 208; foreign policy of, 154; and high priests of Temple of Doom, 65–67; and Israel, 147–148; on labor, 24; and Latin America, 93; and military-industrial complex, 54–46; and military overkill, 73, 117; and military build-up, 17, 208; and narcissism, 198; on *perestroika*, 191; and Pipes, 50; popularity of, 205; on SDI, 83; on U.S.-Soviet trade, 135, 136, 137, 138, 139

Reagan Doctrine, 156

Reaganism, as anti-communism, ix

Reatta Craft Center, 10

Reforming the Soviet Economy (Hewett), 111

Republican Party, 207–209

Right-wing think tanks, 56–63; cold war pundits, 63; Committee on the Present Danger, 56–58; philanthropic foundations, 58–60; policy analysis groups, 60–63

Rise and Fall of the Great Powers, The (P. Kennedy), 74

Robb, Charles S., 208

Rockefeller, John D. IV, 29

Roh Tae Woo, 163

Romania, 51, 101, 123, 139; changes in, 160–161; and Soviet Jews, 19

Roosevelt, Franklin D., xi

Rosenthal, A. M., 63

Rostow, Eugene V., 66, 148

Ruble, the: control of, 117, 130; convertibility of, 131

Rumsfeld, Donald H., 61

Sadik, Nafis, 176

Safire, William, 63

Sakharov, Andrei D., 86, 143

Salaries, of corporate executives, 25

SALT II Treaty, 45, 49, 57, 62; breaking of, 94, 147

Sanford, Terry, 110

Sarah Scaife Foundation, 59, 60

Sary Shagan, 87–88

Saudi Arabia, x, 164, 218

Save the Children, 184

Scaife, Richard M., 59, 61

Schmidt, Alexander, 105–106

Schultz, George P., 108; on human rights, 144; meeting with Gorbachev, 95–97

Security Council, U.N., embargo of Iraq, ix

Sharansky, Natan, 141, 142, 148

Shell Oil, 120

Shevardnadze, Eduard A., 95, 97, 144, 174; and Baker, 204; on Kuwait, 217

Shevchenko, Arkady N., 52

Silverado Savings and Loan Bank, 219

Simes, Dimitri, 52, 68

Simpson, Christopher, 46–47, 197

Sivard, Ruth Leger, 175

Six-Day War, 139, 152

Slavery, in the U.S., 36 Slepak, Vladimir S., 143

Smith, Wayne S. 53

Solzhenitsyn, Aleksandr, 43, 46, 52, 61, 66

Soros, George, 51

Soros Foundation, 184

South Africa, 153; and Soviets, 165

South Carolina, University of, 132

South Korea, 155; Soviet relations with, 163, 165; U.S. military expenses in, 76

South Yemen, 152
Soviet Jews, emigration of, 19, 138–139
Soviet Military Power (Weinberger), 75
Soviet studies, at American universities, 71–72
Soviet threat, 92–103; high-tech spy scandals, 95–97; nonviolence, 99–103; Russian aggression, 92–94; tension reduction, 98–99; treaty violations, 94–95
Soviet Union: aversion to risk, 14–15; crime in, 20; downsizing of, 165–167; economic reforms of, 112–114; foreign policy of, 151–155; foreign trade of, 129, 132–133; health care in, 26–27; on invasion of Kuwait, 217; lack of management training in, 118–119; monetary system in, 117–118; Moslems in, 30; respect for power, 14; shared problems with U.S., ix–xii; technology in, 135–138; unemployment in, 23; use of Swedish example, 8–9. *See also* Gorbachev
Sovietology: death of, 67–72; on *perestroika*, 191, 193
Soviets, as experts on Soviet Union, 51–53
Spain, 155
Sputnik, 86–87, 93
Stalin, Joseph V., xi, 30, 41; and agriculture, 115; and economics, 106; reign of terror by, 43–44; Soviet criticism of, 196; tyranny of, 13, 36, 48
Stalinism: failure of, ix; moves away from, 122–123; possible reversion to, 191, 192
Stanford University, 71
Star Wars, 60, 84, 219
START treaty, 204
State Department, U.S., 108
Stealth bomber, 74, 82–83, 117, 219
Stein, Herbert, 62
Stockholm School of Economics, 132
Strategic Defense Initiative (SDI), 62, 80–81, 83–88, 117, 137, 202
Sudan, 18
Survival Is Not Enough (Pipes), 50
Sweden, 4, 45; as economic role

model, 7–9 22, 112, 123–125, 206; on social welfare, 213
Syria, 139, 143, 144, 152

Tadzhikistan, 166
Takeovers, 25
Target Is Destroyed, The (Hersh), 42
Technocrats, 77–78; and the B-1 bomber, 81; high-tech euphoria, 90–92; Nike-X project, 78–81; on nuclear energy, 88–90; and the Stealth bomber, 82–83; Strategic Defense Initiative, 83–88
Technology: expense of, 117; goal of business school graduates, 5; paranoia over, 135–138; in Soviet Union, 116, 124, 137
Teheran, attack on Soviet embassy, 172
Television: political coverage of, 16; think tank members on, 62
Teller, Edward, 46, 51, 61, 66, 92; and the Hertz Foundation, 60; and SDI, 83–84 87; and the technocrats, 78
Temple of Doom, high priests of, 65–67
Tennessee Valley Authority, nuclear reactors at, 90
Tension reduction, 213
Terrorism, 172–175, 205; by Arab terrorists, 219
Texas Air, 24
Thinking Reed, The (Kagarlitsky), 111
Third parties, U.S., 211–214
Third World: AIDS in, 176; debts of, 180–181 reduced military aid to, 185–186; Soviets in, 153, 164–165; U.S. in, 156
Three Mile Island, 90
Tiananmen Square massacre, 149, 163, 199
Tower, John G., 75; on SDI, 87
Trade, U.S.-Soviet, 129–133
Trade sanctions, 133–134, 195
Treml, Vladimir, 52
Trident II, 90
Truman, Harry, xii, 39; and atomic bombs, 89, 196; and Voice of America, 64
Truman Doctrine, 46

TRW, and SDI, 86
Tuberculosis, increase in, 176
Turkey, 153, 154–155, 166

Uganda, 176
Ukraine, 167
unemployment: in Soviet Union, 114, 126; in U.S., 22–23, 24, 115
Unions, labor: decline in membership, 4; under Reagan, 24–25
United Arab Emirates, x
United Nations, and Soviets, 157
United Nations Children's Fund (UNICEF), 175
United Parcel Service, 10–11
United States: crime in, 20–22; economic conversion in, 125–127; economic inequality in, 22; on foreign aid, 180; foreign policy and Soviets, 154; health care in, 27; lack of participatory management in, 9–10; management training in, 132; monetary problems of, 118; Nazism in, 46–48; need of *glasnost*, 196–198; opposition to *perestroika*, 190–196; political parties in, 207–214; problems of size in, 167–169; shared problems with Soviets, ix–xii; on technology transfer, 135–138; and terrorism, 172; trade deficits of, 129; trade with Soviets, 129–133; use of sanctions, 133 134, 195
U.S. Information Agency (USIA), 64

Van Cleave, William R., 61
Vananu, Mordechai, 19
Vance, Cyrus, 49, 208
Vietnam, 37, 46, 151, 172, 197, 205; and Soviets, 165
Voice of America (VOA), 64
Voter turnout: influence of television, 16; in the U.S., 15–16

Wages, of factory workers, 5
Wallace, George, 16, 21
Warsaw Pact, 93, 161
Washington, George, 16, 36; farewell address, 174
Washington, University of, 71
Washington summit (1990), 148, 204
Watergate, 205
Wattenberg, Ben J., 63, 65, 66
Wealth, in the U.S., 23–24, 25, 26
Webb, James, 97
Webster, William, 69
Weinberger, Caspar, 17, 66, 109; anticommunism of, 39, 68; on defense, 74–75, 81, 105; and Schultz, 96–97
Weirton Steel, 10
West Bank, 144
West Germany, 40, 76; economic successes of, vi, 112, 117, 118; foreign trade of, 129; in new economic order, 182
White, Ralph K., 40
Will, George, 63
William H. Zimmer nuclear facility, 90
Williams, Tennessee, 11
Wood, Lowell L. Jr., 84, 87
World Bank, 181
World Development Fund, 182–183
World War II, 41

Yalta, xi
Yazov, Dmitri T., 97
Yeltsin, Boris, 121, 193
Yom Kippur War, 145

Zaire, 181
Zakharov, Gennadi F., 96, 142
Zhivkov, Todor I., 160

THOMAS H. NAYLOR

Thomas H. Naylor is Professor of Economics at Duke University. As an international management consultant specializing in strategic management, he has consulted with governments and major corporations throughout the world. He lives in Richmond, Virginia, and writes often about the Soviet Union, Eastern Europe, and management philosophy. *The New York Times, International Herald Tribune, Business Week, Christian Science Monitor, Los Angeles Times,* and *Chicago Tribune* have published his articles. He has appeared on ABC's *Nightline,* the Canadian Broadcasting Corporation, National Public Radio, and CNN. Dr. Naylor is the author of twenty-three books, including *The Gorbachev Strategy.*